Artificial Intelligence
in
Finance & Investing

Artificial Intelligence in Finance & Investing

State-of-the-Art Technologies for Securities Selection and Portfolio Management

Robert R. Trippi
Jae K. Lee

IRWIN
Professional Publishing®
Chicago • London • Singapore

This publication is designed to provide accurate and authoritative information in regard to the subject matter covered. It is sold with the understanding that neither the author nor the publisher is engaged in rendering legal, accounting, or other professional service. If legal advice or other expert assistance is required, the services of a competent professional person should be sought.

From a Declaration of Principles jointly adopted by a Committee
of the American Bar Association and a Committee of Publishers.

Irwin Professional Book Team

Publisher: *Wayne McGuirt*
Asociate Publisher: *Michael E. Desposito*
Sponsoring editor: *Kevin Commins*
Marketing manager: *Kelly Sheridan*
Project editor: *Christina Thornton-Villagomez*
Production supervisor: *Dina L. Treadaway/Carol Klein*
Assistant manager, desktop services: *Jon Christopher*
Jacket Designer: *Chip Butzko*
Compositor: *Carol Graphics*
Typeface: *11/13 Times Roman*
Printer: *Buxton Skinner Printing Co.*

◤◤ **Times Mirror**
▶▲ **Higher Education Group**

Library of Congress Cataloging-in-Publication Data

Trippi, Robert R.
    Artificial intelligence in finance and investing : state-of-the-art technologies for securities selection and portfolio management / Robert R. Trippi, Jae K. Lee.
    —Rev. ed.
        p.   cm.
    Includes bibilographical references and indexes.
    ISBN 1-55738-868-7
    1. Portfolio management—Data processing.   2. Investments—
Decision making—Data processing.   3. Expert systems (Computer
science)   4. Neural networks (Computer science)   5. Artificial
intelligence.   I. Lee, Jae K.   II. Title.
HG4529.5.T75   1996
332.1 ' 0285 ' 63—dc20   95–33418

Printed in the United States of America
1 2 3 4 5 6 7 8 9 0   BS   2 1 0 9 8 7 6 5

Dedications

To my wife and best friend, Cecilia.   R. R. T.

To my Lord, my students, and investors.   J.K.L.

Contents at a Glance

1   Introduction   1

2   Nature of the Security Investment Domain   7

3   Modern Approaches to Portfolio Selection   23

4   Artificial Intelligence in Investment Management:
    An Overview   45

5   Portfolio-Selection System Issues   67

6   Knowledge Representation and Inference   81

7   Handling Investment Uncertainties   101

8   Knowledge Acquisition, Integration, and
    Maintenance   119

9   Machine Learning   131

10 Neural Networks   159

11 Integrating Knowledge with Portfolio Optimization   183

12 Integrating Knowledge with Databases   197

13 An Illustrative Session with K-FOLIO   209

14 Concluding Remarks   229

Name Index   233

Subject Index   237

Table of Contents

List of Figures   xv

List of Tables   xix

Preface   xxi

Chapter 1   Introduction   1

1.1   Artificial Intelligence and Investing   1
1.2   The Organization of This Book   3

Chapter 2   Nature of the Security Investment Domain   7

2.1   Characteristics of Investment Assets   8
2.2   Theories of Stock Price Determination   9
    2.2.1   Random, Ordered, and Complex Systems   10
    2.2.2   Value-Based Investing   10
    2.2.3   The Efficient Market Hypothesis   11
    2.2.4   Beyond the EMH   12
2.3   Risk Issues   14
    2.3.1   What Is Risk?   14
    2.3.2   Cognitive Error and Stochastic Risk Modeling   14
2.4   Market Psychology and Noise   15
2.5   Institutional Trading and Market Behavior   15
    2.5.1   Agency and Database Commonality Effects   15
    2.5.2   Trading Dynamics and Instability   16
2.6   The Exploitation of Anomalies   17
    2.6.1   The Cost and Value of Information   17
    2.6.2   Implied Probability Distributions   17

2.6.3	Decision Rules and Black Box Investing	19
2.7	Conclusions	20
Endnotes		20
References		21

Chapter 3	Modern Approaches to Portfolio Selection	23

3.1	Introduction	23
3.2	Goal Programming	25
3.3	Mean-Variance Optimization	27
	3.3.1 The Markowitz Model	27
	3.3.2 The Efficient Frontier	29
	3.3.3 Model Enhancement	30
3.4	Beta and Index Models	31
3.5	Security Risk and Portfolio Risk	35
3.6	The Role of Riskless Assets	36
3.7	Mean Absolute Deviation Optimization	37
3.8	Markowitz and Capital-Asset Pricing Model Limitations	38
3.9	CAPM Extensions and Program Trading	40
Endnotes		41
References		43

Chapter 4	Artificial Intelligence in Investment Management: An Overview	45

4.1	Knowledge-Based Systems, Auto-Learning Systems, and Intelligent Systems	45
4.2	Introduction to Knowledge Representation	46
4.3	Expert Systems and Financial Services	51
4.4	An Early ES for Portfolio Selection	52
4.5	Contemporary Systems	53
4.6	Emerging Artificial Intelligence Technologies	57
4.7	Conclusions	61
Endnotes		62
References		62

Chapter 5	Portfolio-Selection System Issues	67

5.1	Expert System Components	67

5.2   Rule-Based Systems   70
       5.2.1   Representation in Rule-Based Systems   70
       5.2.2   Inference Strategies   71
5.3   Frame-Based Systems   73
5.4   Investment Support Features   75
       5.4.1   Knowledge Representation   75
       5.4.2   Inference and Explanation   77
       5.4.3   Knowledge Acquisition and Maintenance   78
       5.4.4   System Architecture   79
References   79

Chapter 6   Knowledge Representation and Inference   81

6.1   Introduction   82
6.2   The Rule Base   82
       6.2.1   Syntax of Rules   82
       6.2.2   Example Rules   82
6.3   The Database   84
       6.3.1   Relational Database Examples   84
       6.3.2   Inheritance, Average-up, and Sum-up   85
       6.3.3   Working Memory   87
6.4   Security Inference   89
       6.4.1   Conflict-Set Generation   90
       6.4.2   Composite-Grade Generation   90
       6.4.3   Explanation Synthesis   93
6.5   Dialogues   93
       6.5.1   Company-Based Dialogue   95
       6.5.2   Industry-Based Dialogue   96
       6.5.3   Criteria-Based Dialogue   97
       6.5.4   Grade-Based Dialogue   98
6.6   Conclusions   98
References   99

Chapter 7   Handling Investment Uncertainties   101

7.1   Introduction   102
7.2   The Bayesian Approach   102
       7.2.1   Definitions and Formulas   102
       7.2.2   An Illustrative Example   104

	7.2.3	Handling Uncertain Evidence	106
	7.2.4	Handling More Than Two Levels of Hypotheses	108
7.3	Inference Strategy in the Bayesian Approach		108
	7.3.1	The Sequence of Applying Evidence	109
	7.3.2	Stopping Rules	110
	7.3.3	Discussion	111
7.4	The Certainty Factor Approach		111
7.5	The Fuzzy Logic Approach		112
	7.5.1	Possibility Theory	112
	7.5.2	Fuzzy Logic	112
	7.5.3	A Fuzzy Logic-Based Expert System	113
	7.5.4	A Compensatory Fuzzy-Logic Approach	114
	7.5.5	Attenuation by the Credibility of Rules	115
	7.5.6	Discussion	115
7.6	Nonmonotonic Reasoning		116
7.7	Conclusions		116
References			116

Chapter 8   Knowledge Acquisition, Integration, and
             Maintenance   119

8.1	Introduction		119
8.2	The Representation and Integration of Investor Preferences		120
	8.2.1	The Organization of Investor Preference Bases	120
	8.2.2	The Representation of Investor Preferences	120
	8.2.3	The Integration and Interpretation of Preferences	123
8.3	Sources for Knowledge Acquisition		124
8.4	Knowledge Structure and Maintenance		125
	8.4.1	Structuring Knowledge	125
	8.4.2	Maintenance Aids	127
8.5	The Selective Integration of Relevant Knowledge		128
8.6	Conclusions		130
References			130

Chapter 9   Machine Learning   131

9.1	Introduction		131
	9.1.1	Why Machine Learning?	131
	9.1.2	Machine-Learning Systems	132
	9.1.3	Learning Strategies	133

9.2   Implied Distribution Surrogates   133
9.3   Inductive Learning   134
       9.3.1   ID3   135
       9.3.2   The Concept-Learning Algorithm   135
       9.3.3   Application of Inductive Learning to Investment
                Decisions   139
       9.3.4   The Potential of Inductive Learning in Investment   139
9.4   Syntactic Pattern–Based Learning   143
       9.4.1   The SYNPLE Framework   144
       9.4.2   Performance   149
9.5   Genetic Adaptive Algorithms   152
       9.5.1   The Genetic Algorithm Approach to Learning   152
       9.5.2   Problem Representation Issues   153
       9.5.3   A Genetic Algorithm for Trading Rule Generation   154
9.6   Conclusions   156
References   156

Chapter 10   Neural Networks   159

10.1   Introduction   159
10.2   Architecture of Neural Networks   160
10.3   Learning in Neural Networks   162
10.4   Strengths and Weaknesses   164
10.5   Neural Network Applications   166
        10.5.1.   Neural Networks for Stock Price Prediction   167
        10.5.2   Other Neural Network Applications   170
10.6   Example of Integrating Neural Networks and Rules   173
10.7   Conclusions   177
References   178

Chapter 11   Integrating Knowledge with Portfolio Optimization   183

11.1   Introduction   183
11.2   An Unenhanced Markowitz Model Example   184
11.3   The Interpretation of Knowledge   185
11.4   Quadratic Programming with Prioritized Decision Variables   188
11.5   Performance Evaluation   192
11.6   Conclusions   194
References   195

Chapter 12   Integrating Knowledge with Databases   197

12.1   Introduction   198
12.2   Database Evolution   198
       12.2.1   Relational Databases   198
       12.2.2   The Advent of Knowledge Bases   199
       12.2.3   Object-Oriented Databases   200
12.3   The Management of Financial Data   201
       12.3.1   The Organization of Financial Data   201
       12.3.2   The Use of Financial Data   204
12.4   The Management of Price and Trading Volume Data   204
       12.4.1   The Organization of Price and Volume Data   204
       12.4.2   The Uses of Price and Volume Data   205
12.5   Management of the Function Base   205
       12.5.1   Functions   205
       12.5.2   Reserved Words   206
12.6   Conclusions   207
References   207

Chapter 13   An Illustrative Session with K-FOLIO   209

13.1   Introduction   209
13.2   Selecting Investment Characteristics, Environmental
         Assumptions, and Knowledge Sources   210
13.3   Individual Stock Evaluation   212
13.4   Industry Evaluation   212
13.5   Criteria-Based Dialogue   213
13.6   Grade-Based Listing   214
13.7   Portfolio Selection   215
13.8   Conclusions   217
References   227

Chapter 14   Concluding Remarks   229

14.1   System Design Criteria: A Summary   229
14.2   Directions for Future Research   231

Name Index   233

Subject Index   237

List of Figures

3.1   Efficient Risk-Return Frontier   29
3.2   Efficient Frontier and Capital Market Line   36
3.3   Ex Ante and Ex Post Frontiers   39
3.4   Capital Market Surface and CML   41

4.1   Auto-Learning Expert System   47
4.2   Partitioning of ES Output Set (with outputs A, B, C, D)   50
4.3   Interconnected Biological Neurons   58

5.1   Typical Expert System Architecture   68
5.2   Rule Examples   71
5.3   An Illustrative AND/OR Digraph   72
5.4   Structure of Frame-Based Representation   74
5.5   Hierarchical Structure of Frames   75
5.6   Architecture of K-FOLIO   80

6.1   Knowledge Management Subsystem   83
6.2   Overall Syntax of Rules   84
6.3   Example Rules   85
6.4   Company-Based Relational Database   86
6.5   Industry-Based Relational Database   86
6.6   Inheritance, Average-up, and Sum-up   88
6.7   Generated Working Memory in the Matching Process   89
6.8   Rules in Conflict Set of Company ABC   90
6.9   Process of Explanation Synthesis   94
6.10   Example of the WHY Statement   95

6.11   Example of Company-Based Dialogue   96
6.12   Relationships between Questions and Rules   98

7.1   Interpolation Method   107
7.2   An Example of Interpolation   108

8.1   Organization of Expert Knowledge Base and Investor
        Preference Bases   121
8.2   Integrating Expert Knowledge and Investor Preference   123
8.3   Mixed-Knowledge Acquisition Strategy   125
8.4   Hierarchical Knowledge-Structuring by Subject   126
8.5   Extended Syntax of Rules that Include Meta-Knowledge   128

9.1   Machine-Learning Procedure   132
9.2   ID3 Algorithm   136
9.3   Inductive Learning Procedure   137
9.4   Inductively Generated Rules   142
9.5   Illustrative Stock Price Trend Lines   145
9.6   Illustrative Moving-Average Stock Price Curves   145
9.7   Illustrative Moving-Average Trading Volume Curves   146
9.8   Illustrative Price-Volume Correlation Curve   146
9.9   Sensitivity of Duration in Lower Support Line to
        Stock Price Trend Line   149
9.10   Mean Price Change by the Rules Generated from the
        First Data Set   150
9.11   Genetic Adaptive Algorithm   153
9.12   Genetic Crossover Operation   154

10.1   A Neural Processing Element   160
10.2   Typical Neural Network Architecture   161
10.3   Architecture of a Recurrent Neural Network   162
10.4   Four-Layered Network   167
10.5   Candlestick Chart and Triangle Pattern   168
10.6   Performance of the Prediction System   169
10.7   Typical Net2 Decision Map   177
10.8   Typical Neural Network Composite Rule Set Decision Map   178
10.9   S&P 500 Index versus Composite2 System Performance   179
11.1   Integration of Knowledge and Preference Systems
        with the Quadratic-Programming Model   186
11.2   Realized Returns; 12% Target   194

11.3	Realized Returns; 18% Target	195

12.1	Example of Relational Format	199
12.2	Illustrative Facts and Rules in Prolog	200
12.3	Object-Oriented Database	202
12.4	Relational Database	203

13.1	Selection of Investment Characteristics	210
13.2	Selection of Assumptions	211
13.3	Selection of Knowledge Bases	212
13.4	Dialogue Menu	213
13.5	Selection of Individual Stocks	214
13.6	Grade and Reasons for Individual Stock	215
13.7	On-Screen Edit	216
13.8	Modified Screen after Revision	217
13.9	Selection of Industry	218
13.10	Grade and Reason for an Industry	219
13.11	Selection of Criteria	220
13.12	Numeric-Type Criteria Specification	221
13.13	Value-Type Criteria Specification	222
13.14	Output from Criteria-Based Dialogue	223
13.15	Grade-Based List	224
13.16	Input of Investment Amount and Expected Return Target	225
13.17	Selection of Knowledge Application Strategy	225
13.18	Trial Portfolio	226
13.19	Elimination of Unfavorable Stocks	227

List of Tables

5.1 Relationship between Expert Systems and Artificial
    Intelligence   69

6.1 Grades and Corresponding Real Numbers   91

9.1 Potential Cues   140
9.2 Variables Used for Classification   143
9.3 Comparison of Annual Returns in Each Holding Period (%)   144
9.4 Illustrative Elements Specified by Charts, Attributes,
    and Values   148
9.5 Performance of Generated Rules   151

10.1 Performance of Individual Networks   174
10.2 Rules for Combining Outputs of Networks   175
10.3 Performance of Rules 1–7   176

11.1 Monthly Market Returns   192
11.2 Realized Returns of Markowitz Portfolios   193
11.3 Realized Returns of K-FOLIO Portfolios   193

Preface

This book is a revised and expanded edition of the first published book on the application of artificial intelligence (AI), also referred to as knowledge-based systems, to investing. The original edition was published in 1992, under the title *State-of-the-Art Portfolio Selection*. That edition appears to have successfully satisfied a need for direction and perspective in this subject area, as its sales greatly exceeded the authors' most optimistic expectations.

This revised edition, *Artificial Intelligence in Finance and Investing*, continues to cover a broad spectrum of issues associated with the application of computerized knowledge-based systems, also called expert systems (ESs), to investment decision making. The new title reflects the greater attention given to other technologies, such as chaos modeling and neural networks, as well as the addition of new sections to existing chapters and a separate chapter on neural networks and their integration into knowledge-based systems. Because investing is an interesting and important economic activity, and even more powerful and inexpensive computers have become generally accessible in recent years, the application of AI to investing remains an exciting topic.

As researchers and consultants, we became interested in writing a book on AI in investing during the late 1980s, just after writing a series of articles on the subject. At that time, the notion of applying ES, neural network, and related technologies to the financial investment domain was considered quite novel. At around the same time, we were witnessing a shaking-out period that included the rapid acceptance and subsequent abandonment of entire AI theoretical approaches and those commercial products that were based on them. As a result, a much more hardware- and software-independent view of knowledge-based systems now prevails in both industry and academia.

In undertaking this project, we wished to focus on investment activities that could profit most from knowledge-based system deployment. Many of the earliest reported AI implementations, such as credit assessment and market monitoring, merely automated information-intensive or time-consuming tasks. As we gained experience with knowledge-based systems, it became clear that these systems had great potential to provide a significant performance edge in portfolio construction.

The audience for a book such as this appeared minuscule just a few years ago. Since then, reports from both industry and academia of successful deployments of knowledge-based systems for business decision making have exploded from a trickle into a flood. With this observation, and following on the success of the first edition, we are confident that *Artificial Intelligence in Finance and Investing* will continue to find a receptive audience.

The major goals of this book are to (1) inform readers about the potential benefits of knowledge-based systems in investment, (2) examine design issues to enable readers to evaluate the philosophy and features of specific existing or proposed systems, and (3) inspire the development of more advanced systems in the future.

This book is addressed to three audiences. The first is individuals with portfolio decision-making or decision support responsibilities, such as money managers, analysts, traders, and researchers. AI approaches described in this book can be applied to the portfolio operations of brokerage companies, investment management companies, mutual funds, insurance companies, pension funds, foundations, bank trust departments, and other institutions.

Second, this book is addressed to information systems professionals who either work in or are interested in learning about investment management systems. Although some will already be familiar with the basics of AI-based system construction, the unique character of the portfolio selection domain presented here will likely be new to most, as will numerous aspects of implementation, such as designing portfolio optimization models to incorporate both expert and investor inputs.

Finally, we hope to see this book used as a primary or supplemental text in graduate business courses. Most investment texts fail to discuss even rudimentary computer implementations of the economic theories and principles involved in investment management. The approaches to system building and real-life examples presented in this book should give students a clearer idea of what they can expect to encounter upon entering the investment industry.

We wish to thank the School of Business Administration at California State University, Long Beach, and the Department of Economics at the University of California, San Diego, for their support in this endeavor. We also thank Dr. Robert Deans for his encouragement and professors Richard Harriff, Lawrence Sherman, and Hamdi Bilici for their helpful suggestions regarding various portions of the original manuscript. Thanks also to professor Seok Chin Chu at Kyunggi University, professor Hyun Soo Kim of Dong-A University, Dr. Suhn Baum Kwon, Dr. Wooju Kim, and Mr. Ki Young Gwak, who together developed the K-FOLIO system while graduate students at the Intelligent Information Systems Laboratory of the Korea Advanced Institute of Science and Technology; to the Lucky Securities Company, especially its president, N. M. Hur, Dr. Suk-Ryong Lee, and Mr. Chung Chul Shin, who manages the K-FOLIO system known as BRAINS with the help of associates at Lucky and KAIST; and to Ms. Jeong OK Lee, who helped with the editing of the manuscript.

A portion of the royalties from this book will be used to further the study of Mr. Yang Soo Cho, a blind doctoral student who is studying at the University of Pittsburgh.

Robert R. Trippi
Jae K. Lee

CHAPTER 1

Introduction

1.1 Artificial Intelligence and Investing
1.2 The Organization of This Book

1.1 ARTIFICIAL INTELLIGENCE AND INVESTING

We are in the midst of a revolution in investment management. An unprecedented globalization of financial markets, advances in the electronic transmission of data, the accessibility of inexpensive yet extremely powerful computer hardware and software, and the migration during the past decade of so-called quants and computer wizards to Wall Street have all contributed to this revolution. The body of finance theory and empirical evidence related to rational investment decision making has become so large that any future advances are expected to be incremental. Thus, the coming decades will likely bring a consolidation and accelerated application of this knowledge. Today the keyword *apply* is virtually synonymous with *computerize*.

The computerization of investment decision-making activities requires software systems that integrate mathematical models, a source of data, and a user interface. Such systems are generally referred to as *decision support systems*, or *DSSs*. That form of DSS whose database includes relevant theory, facts, and human knowledge and expertise is called a

1

knowledge-based system, also referred to as an *intelligent system* or *expert system (ES)*. Specific techniques such systems employ to achieve their goals are drawn from the field of study known as *artificial intelligence (AI)*. AI techniques are being used in many nonbusiness applications as well, including language analysis, voice and character recognition, and military pattern recognition.

The earliest AI-based systems were used in medicine, engineering, and the sciences. Although originally perceived as a niche area of AI, knowledge-based systems began to receive considerable attention in both the academic and business press in the late 1980s. Despite the sometimes excessive hype and optimism with which knowledge-based systems were first received, their most auspicious applications still lie in the future. AI technology holds great promise for enhancing a multitude of tasks performed in the financial services industries, and particularly in investment portfolio management activities.

The renewed interest in applying knowledge-based systems to business decisions can be attributed mainly to the plummeting costs of hardware and software. In the early 1980s, for example, ES software and a suitable platform on which to run it typically cost $100,000 or more. By the mid-1990s, equivalent or superior hardware–software systems could be had for under $5,000. Financial applications are now viewed as ideal proving grounds for new AI concepts and products, because in the realm of finance, significant, rapid, and easily measurable economic benefits are often possible.

Initially knowledge-based systems were viewed as tools to enable nonexperts to make decisions as effectively as would one or more experts in a particular field, or *domain*. In fact, as will be discussed later in this book, this technology is capable of achieving more *consistent* results, uncovering more knowledge, and reacting more quickly than would a group of humans. (It is not uncommon for systems to respond in real time to a rapidly arriving data stream.)

How would an intelligent system function in the portfolio investment domain? Consider the problem of how to allocate a large sum of money among stocks, bonds, real estate, and precious metals. Early ESs used for this purpose would probably have included in their databases the knowledge of several human experts in each of these investment areas. Such a database is called a *knowledge base*. Today the knowledge base would be likely be built, at least in part, by a machine learning–based subsystem utilizing rule induction, genetic algorithms, or some other paradigm of learning automation. A money manager using such a system could, in theory, manage a portfolio including several asset classes more effectively and at less cost than could any of the individual domain experts. The most obvious advantages of integrating some form of computer intelligence into the portfolio decision-making process over continually consulting with a team of experts include permanence, usually a much lower cost, and a greater consistency of results.

Although not every application of knowledge-based systems to aid investment has been successful, most early failures apparently stemmed from randomly applying some currently popular technology rather than tailoring the system to a particular investment domain. Also, excessive emphasis has sometimes been placed on user friendliness in the form of natural language interfaces and graphic display facilities. The amounts spent on these niceties were amounts not available for improving the economic performance of the system. Fortunately, user friendliness in the form of improved user interfaces can be achieved today at a much lower cost than was possible just a few years ago.

1.2   THE ORGANIZATION OF THIS BOOK

Because it deals with the application of computers to investment management, *Artificial Intelligence in Finance and Investing* can be thought of as a bridge between finance and information science. As such, it covers a broad spectrum of topics, using vocabulary drawn from both disciplines.

Chapter 2 deals in a general way with the investment environment and the characteristics of security markets. Market complexity and efficiency, determination of value, the nature of risk, and other important issues in the investment domain are discussed. Although this book does not focus on the empirical evidence for market anomalies, knowledge-based systems are the most effective means available for recognizing and exploiting in a systematic fashion any anomalies that exist.

Chapter 3 is a brief primer on portfolio theory. It reviews the concepts that are essential to understanding rational portfolio selection, with an emphasis on the Markowitz quadratic programming model. Also discussed are the aggregate market implications of Markowitz portfolio optimization, including the capital asset pricing model. Knowledge-based systems' greatest potential lies in improving investment performance in a portfolio rather than single-asset framework.

Chapter 4 begins with an overview of knowledge-based systems. It also outlines a number of ES applications in the financial services industry.

In each of these applications, the goal is typically to improve risk-return performance in some investment activity. Although this book is concerned mainly with portfolio selection, this chapter also describes systems capable of screening financial information, recognizing patterns in prices, and evaluating credit. Chapter 4 concludes with an introduction to emerging AI technologies such as neural networks, genetic algorithms, and case-based reasoning.

Chapter 5 discusses problem solving in general and outlines the basic elements common to most knowledge-based systems. It also introduces concepts of knowledge representation and inference relevant to the investment domain. (These are examined in greater detail in later chapters.) This chapter also discusses the ways portfolio management systems can be tailored not only to the selection of stocks and industries but also to timing and allocation decisions. In addition, it shows how knowledge-based systems can provide reasons for their decisions in a form that investors can understand (a feat that most traditional quantitative approaches, such as time series models, cannot perform).

Using illustrative examples, Chapter 6 focuses on both the representation of knowledge as rules and the types of rules most pertinent to the investment domain. Issues associated with the construction of synergistic rule bases are discussed, including strategies for resolving conflicts, developing explanations from the rule base, and the types of user dialogue possible with respect to individual securities and industries or sectors.

Chapter 7 deals with handling uncertainty, a topic that is especially germane to the building of knowledge-based portfolio selection systems. Several approaches to making inferences under uncertainty are described, including the Bayesian, certainty factor, and fuzzy-logic approaches.

Chapter 8 covers topics related to knowledge acquisition, integration, and maintenance. These topics include representational adequacy; the collectibility (whether from human experts or from machine-learning systems) and maintainability of relevant knowledge; aids for dynamic knowledge maintenance; and the integration with elicited or synthesized expert knowledge of the knowledge, assumptions, and preferences of investors.

Chapter 9 discusses the role of machine learning in the context of portfolio selection and timing decisions. Acquisition and maintenance of knowledge is a bottleneck of most existing expert systems. Due to the difficulty of acquiring and validating knowledge from humans in a timely manner, extensive application of machine learning is vital for successful systems in the investment domain. Topics covered in this chapter include inductive and pattern-based syntactic learning and the use of genetic algorithms to generate rule sets useful for the prediction of company, security, and index performance.

Chapter 10 focuses on neural networks and how they can be used to predict the performance of companies and securities. The chapter discusses typical neural network architectures, learning processes, and the strengths and weaknesses of neural networks relative to other machine-learning paradigms. It also reports the results of a number of important studies in the financial and investment domains.

Chapter 11 discusses mechanisms for incorporating the Markowitz portfolio optimization model into a knowledge-based system. It shows how the model can be augmented with constraints derived from rules and how the quadratic programming algorithm can be extended to a multistep, sequential algorithm that considers the priority of decision variables. Interpreting up-to-date knowledge in conjunction with optimization represents a crucial technology for portfolio decision making.

Chapter 12 introduces database and knowledge base terminology, outlines the evolution of database technologies of relevance to expert system construction, and discusses methods for interfacing expert systems with conventional investment information systems. This chapter also outlines the major issues associated with managing fundamental and price/volume data and introduces the concept of a function base (one that permits expansion of available data items without adding to the storage burden).

Chapter 13 illustrates the concepts discussed in previous chapters by describing a session that uses the K-FOLIO system. During this session, environmental assumptions are selected, stocks and industries are evaluated, and a portfolio is constructed by applying knowledge and investor preferences to the modified Markowitz model of Chapter 11.

Chapter 14 summarizes conclusions concerning the design of systems for maximum effectiveness in portfolio decision making and suggests several promising areas for further research.

CHAPTER 2

Nature of the
Security Investment
Domain

2.1   Characteristics of Investment Assets
2.2   Theories of Stock Price Determination
      2.2.1   Random, Ordered, and Complex Systems
      2.2.2   Value-Based Investing
      2.2.3   The Efficient Market Hypothesis
      2.2.4   Beyond the EMH
2.3   Risk Issues
      2.3.1   What Is Risk?
      2.3.2   Cognitive Error and Stochastic Risk Modeling
2.4   Market Psychology and Noise
2.5   Institutional Trading and Market Behavior
      2.5.1   Agency and Data Base Commonality Effects
      2.5.2   Trading Dynamics and Instability
2.6   The Exploitation of Anomalies
      2.6.1   The Cost and Value of Information
      2.6.2   Implied Probability Distributions
      2.6.3   Decision Rules and Black Box Investing
2.7   Conclusions

2.1   CHARACTERISTICS OF INVESTMENT ASSETS[1]

Investment assets can be real (physical) or financial. Factories, farmland, and buildings are real assets. Financial assets include contractual commitments of future payment, such as commercial paper and debentures, and claims on assets such as cash, stocks, options, and commodity and currency futures contracts. Securities are formal instruments that represent ownership of financial assets and facilitate their trade; the process of creating securities from assets is called *securitization*. This book deals mainly with investment in financial assets. Buyers of these assets must take into account factors such as *liquidity, size of the trading unit, transaction costs, leverage potential,* and *pattern of returns over time.*

Liquidity is characteristic of assets that can be bought and sold in any quantity without their price changing significantly; liquidity indirectly represents the average trade size as a fraction of total trading volume, and often affects spreads between bid and ask prices. Proposed measures of liquidity include the ratio of dollar volume of trading to the absolute percentage change in the price of completed transactions (e.g., see Cooper, Groth, and Avera, 1985) and the average absolute value of trade-to-trade percentage price change divided by the number of transactions (Marsh and Rock, 1986). Liquidity is important not only because it facilitates trading but also because prices may convey little or no information about an asset's value if the asset does not have at least a minimal level of liquidity. In the hierarchy of asset liquidity, value is most meaningfully represented by prices derived from actively traded organized markets and least meaningfully by prices derived from sparsely traded and unorganized markets.

Financial assets vary considerably in trading unit size. These units may cost a few hundred dollars, as in the case of low-priced exchange-listed stocks and stock options, or tens or hundreds of thousands of dollars, as in the case of certain mortgage-backed debt instruments and futures contracts. Securities such as Treasury bills, notes, and bonds, and common and preferred stock of large corporations are usually tradable in units (shares or lots) that are of moderate size as well as highly liquid.

Commissions for most financial assets, relative to the dollar size of the trade, are generally in the low single digits and decline with the size of the transaction. The structure of transaction costs varies greatly; for example, bid-ask spreads are generally much greater than commissions for commodity futures but smaller than commissions for most options. Transaction costs can effectively constrain the types of investment strategies that can be practically employed. Since total transaction costs are relatively low for futures contracts, investing strategies involving purchase and sale on the same day result in little loss of capital to commissions. In contrast, real estate is almost always a multiyear investment because of the high costs involved in doing any transaction. These costs include not only commissions but also legal and title costs, loan fees, and the managerial attention required to effect a purchase or sale.

Transaction costs may be *symmetrical* or *asymmetrical*. Real estate transaction costs are highly asymmetrical, favoring the purchase. Commissions, figures as a percentage of the gross sale price, are normally paid only by the seller. In contrast, the transaction costs of front-load mutual funds are also asymmetrical but favor the sale. In other words, the purchase of shares involves higher fees than their eventual sale.

Leverage potential refers to the proportion of cash that must be committed at the time of purchase. Most investment assets can be bought using leverage, with loaned funds collateralized by the asset. The leverage potential of securities varies considerably according to *margin requirements* set by exchanges and regulatory agencies. For example, at present the margin requirements for futures contracts are much lower than those for most other securities.

The possibility of receiving returns is the price motivation for owning investment assets. Returns can take the form of price appreciation, periodic monetary payments (for example, rent, interest, and dividends), or both. The precise pattern of returns is significant in investment theory and practice, and statistical parameters such as mathematical expectation, variance, skewness, and distribution of returns over time often figure prominently in the characterization of assets.

2.2   THEORIES OF STOCK PRICE DETERMINATION

Investment theory and practice is an evolving branch of economic science. Since the pioneering work of John Burr Williams (1936) and Graham and Dodd (1934), the valuation of capital stock and other types of securities has been a source of intense interest and constant debate among investors, academicians, and individuals and institutions concerned with wealth. Formidable intellectual resources have been directed toward achieving the goal of buying low and selling high.

2.2.1   Random, Ordered, and Complex Systems

Dynamic systems may be classified according to their degree of orderliness. *Random systems* are totally chaotic, while *ordered systems* operate predictably according to reliable mathematical rules, such as those of physics and chemistry. *Complex systems* possess characteristics of both ordered and random systems. There is much evidence that stock markets behave as complex systems (Jacobs and Levy, 1989).

The stochastic processes that govern nonordered systems may be *stationary* or *nonstationary*. The processes that drive stock markets exhibit a considerable degree of nonstationarity. Forecasting relevant parameters is far more difficult in nonstationary than in stationary systems.

2.2.2   Value-Based Investing

Early theories of stock price determination viewed markets as ordered systems. It seemed logical that the value of an asset should equal the discounted value of its stream of payments or returns, whether in the form of dividends, interest, or earnings. Thus, it was considered desirable to identify factors that affect the return stream, for such knowledge would also confer on its possessor knowledge of whether the asset is currently under- or overpriced in the market relative to its intrinsic value. The *dividend discount model (DDM)*, introduced by Williams (1936), is one of the earliest *value-based investing* approaches. Value-based investing later focused primarily on corporate earnings, accepting Miller and Modigliani's (1961) arguments that the value of the firm should be relatively unaffected by the dividend payout ratio.

One standard approach to security analysis is the methodology known as *fundamental analysis*. In this approach to valuing assets (which received considerable attention in universities in the 1960s and 1970s and is still popular today), the market is viewed as a relatively ordered system and each company is represented by characteristics such as financial ratios and performance measures, which are used to draw inferences about that company.

Accounting ratios that are given substantial emphasis in fundamental analysis include price to earnings (P/E), price to cash flow, market value to book value per share, sales to price and yield, current ratios, debt ratios, and ratios based on leverage factors, sales forecasts, and projected earnings. More recent measures of interest include beta coefficient and variance or standard deviation of earnings (see Chapter 3).

Such measures may be worthy of examination in their own right, but different financial analysts will often reach different conclusions regarding the likely impact of such characteristics on future earnings and/or dividends. As a foundation for value-based investing, fundamental analysis suffers from the fact that, as empirical research has shown, stock prices and discounted dividend streams are generally not very closely correlated (see Jacobs and Levy, 1988). By the 1970s, leading academicians considered fundamental analysis to be a somewhat simplistic approach to value-based investing.

2.2.3   The Efficient Market Hypothesis

In the 1960s, as the field of finance became more scientific, the theory building and testing that followed became based more closely on economic theory, making market efficiency a major issue. The *efficient market hypothesis (EMH)* and the *capital asset pricing model* (see Chapter 3) were consistent with numerous previous studies that found stock price fluctuations to be random (several of the early studies are found in Cootner 1964). According to the EMH, the pattern of past prices provides little or no indication of the direction of future prices.

The essence of the EMH is that at any point in time, prices of securities in an efficient market already reflect the assimilation of all information available to participants in the markets. Several forms of the EMH were proposed, each dealing with a different type of information. The *weak form* considers past price information only, the *semistrong form* considers all publicly available information, and the *strong form* considers all publicly and privately available information. The weak form implies that prices follow a *random walk* in which successive changes in price have zero correlation.

The weak and semistrong forms were fairly well supported with respect to stock and other security markets in a number of research studies. The strong form is difficult to prove or disprove, since profiting from information withheld from the public is an illegal activity in the United States and in most other countries with organized exchanges.

Studies examining publicly disclosed insider trading have generally concluded that insider trades result in higher-than-average returns. Many studies of the strong form of the EMH have focused on the performance of mutual fund managers under the assumption that these individuals may come upon nonpublic information in the course of their business. Generally, these studies have not found fund managers to be superior to other investor types, although there is some evidence that a small group of managers could possess superior knowledge and skills (Lee and Rahman, 1991). Synopses of early empirical studies defending the EMH can be found in Lorie, Dodd, and Kimpton (1985), and a lucid, nontechnical treatment of the subject appears in Malkiel (1990).

By the mid-1970s, most finance theorists conceded that the organized markets for stocks and other securities were for the most part efficient and that proprietary techniques of stock selection would not result in performance consistently superior to those of broad-based market indexes. In fact, choosing portfolios by throwing darts at the newspaper stock market listings was proposed by more than one academician interested in promoting the EMH. Still, while the EMH was not easy to refute, it was difficult to prove beyond a shadow of a doubt. Some research did produce results that, although perhaps inconsistent with parts of the EMH, did not contradict its fundamental assumptions. For example, Fama (1963, 1965) found that the changes in the prices of stocks were distributed more in accordance with the stable Paretian than the more restrictive normal distribution predicted by the random walk theory.

The stock market's equivalent of dart throwing was the passive management of investment funds. Under this strategy, a portfolio representative of the market or a segment of the market is selected and managed using a buy-and-hold strategy, with the only decision making being related to the exclusion of extreme investments. From the late 1970s to the present, index funds have proliferated, which shows investors' faith in the EMH as well as their acceptance of security markets as random systems.

2.2.4   Beyond the EMH

The EMH does not support the *technical analysis* approach to investing, that is, predicting future stock prices by using both historical price and volume data and *indicators*, such as leading indexes and market-derived statistical measures. One popular form of technical analysis is *charting*, in which graphic displays of past price performance, moving-average trends, cycles, and intra- or interday stock price ranges are studied in an attempt to discern cues for profitable trading. Charting, especially when applied to commodity futures trading, makes use of techniques such as moving indexes, trend analysis, turning-point indicators, cyclical spectral analysis, and the recognition of various formations or patterns in prices (with these patterns being assigned names such as "flag," "triangle," and "head-and-shoulders") to forecast subsequent price behavior.

Efficient market theory, which is supported by most academic studies of technical analysis, contradicts the notion that patterns in the price and volume of securities alone can provide any significant advantage in predicting future price movements. In fact, many individuals who have promoted new technical analysis methodologies have earned more by writing books and newsletters based on their creations than they ever did by investing, and services selling technical charts have flourished.

Insights drawn from the EMH framework have been immensely helpful to those who study the behavior of stock market prices and aggregate market behavior. Nevertheless, because security markets are complex, time-variant (nonstationary), and probably nonlinear dynamic systems, noncomplex theories cannot adequately represent their behavior; thus, it is not surprising that naive technical rules are ineffective in exploiting whatever inefficiencies may exist.

The 1980s saw both a resurgence of interest in questions of efficiency and the development of a variety of empirical tests of new and often elaborate theories that sought to explain subtle security-pricing regularities and other anomalies. Although an earlier study by King (1966) did find an economy effect, an industry effect, and a security effect associated with stock price changes, the effects were not consistent for each stock studied; rather, they varied with each company and its unique characteristics.

More recently, attempts have been made to isolate or "purify" individual factors associated with apparent return anomalies, the aim being to expose the factors that are simply proxies for other factors and identify factors that affect returns only when present in tandem. In a regression study in 1988, Jacobs and Levy found that the following pure effects were statistically significant at the 1 percent level: low P/E ratio, small size (capitalization), ratio of sales to stock price, trend in analysts' forecasts of earnings (with one-, two-, and three-month lags), earnings surprise (one-month lag), relative strength, and one- and two-month residual reversals. Although the January seasonal effect was generally strong for the P/E effect, it was insignificant for firm size. *Multidimensional screens* can be used to identify individual stocks exhibiting such convoluted pricing anomalies.

Findings such as the preceding ones suggest that the EMH is not a perfect representation of the realities of markets that behave as complex systems. Moreover, with the growth of large institutional investors, by the 1990s there was widespread suspicion that the behavior of stock markets was becoming more irrational in some respects as small minority interests often mixed with larger sales and could, in some cases, even block and control positions. On the one hand, the evolution of markets dominated by institutional investors using computer-driven program trading systems appeared to be resulting in more anomalies. On the other hand, the level of technological sophistication applied to recognizing and exploiting pockets of market inefficiency, and ultimately eliminating them, was also increasing (Keane, 1991).

2.3   RISK ISSUES

2.3.1   What Is Risk?

Risk means different things to different market participants. For theory-building it is important that risk be defined in terms of rational investors, and it is desirable (though not essential) that a consensus exist among all rational investors as to what constitutes risk. Investors are normally assumed to be averse to risk. In the standard capital asset pricing model, risk is defined in terms of either the deviations of returns from a market index or the standard deviation or variance of returns. This is essentially a behavioral assumption. If behaviorally accurate, models of rational investment that consider probability of loss, mean absolute deviation of returns, or semivariance of returns[2] as the cardinal measure of risk could be just as valid. Moreover, if fundamental measures such as current yield, P/E relationships, trading volume, and cash flow considerations have different meanings to different investor classes, the same would probably be true of any specific measure of risk.

The study of the psychology of investors is still in its infancy. The economic theory on which the capital asset pricing model rests assumes that investors will have a rational response to risk and return known as *utility maximization*. In general, realistic models of rational decision making under this framework must take into account different utility or response functions for different investors or investor classes.

2.3.2   Cognitive Error and Stochastic Risk Modeling

As we will see in Chapter 3, a positive, although sometimes less than perfect, relationship generally exists between investment risk and return. There can also exist substantial error in connection with the assessment of risk. Risk is a function of both company operations, reflected by fundamentals, and the market's interpretation of that information, which is subject to errors of cognition. For this reason, the price of a small firm's stock can fluctuate by 10 percent or more in a single day even if no change has occurred in the firm's profitability, products, or management. To model actual risk accurately, one must take into account the contribution of cognitive error to apparent risk.

2.4   MARKET PSYCHOLOGY AND NOISE

In an attempt to ascribe rationality to market participants, technical analysis often attributes past security price patterns to market psychology. However, it is not past prices but future prices or expectations of future prices that are of concern to most investors (Schmalensee, 1976). In studying the predictive content of prices, industry effects, and market effect, errors are bound to occur because of the uncertain environment and the multiplicity of factors that are subject to different interpretations by market participants. Even insiders sometimes make wrong investment decisions.

The "Black Monday" market crash of October 19, 1987, illustrates that although aggregate mispricing due to faulty perceptions about intrinsic value may persist, eventually adjustments to value considerations take place. Those who attribute aggregate price cycles to investor psychology usually maintain that "bull" markets reflect periods of general optimism and "bear" markets reflect periods of general pessimism.

The loss of principal may have different psychological effects on different investors, resulting in specific securities over- or underreacting to news items (also called *transient over-* and *undershoot*). Strategies that seek to exploit mispricing transients are called *noise-trading* strategies. Successful noise trading requires the rapid detection of short-persistence deviations of prices from intrinsic values.

2.5   INSTITUTIONAL TRADING AND MARKET BEHAVIOR

2.5.1   Agency and Database Commonality Effects

Problems of *agency* make institutional trading somewhat different from other trading. The professional money manager may be punished or fired for poor performance. In such a situation, there is a tendency to gravitate toward investment strategies, such as *portfolio insurance*, that minimize the probability of losses (Perold and Sharpe, 1988). Portfolio insurance is a *convex dynamic* investment strategy requiring almost continuous adjustment of risk-free asset proportions (discontinuous adjustment is discussed in Trippi and Harriff, 1990). Such strategies produce return distributions with shortened or truncated downside tails (positive skewness) and diminished mathematical expectations relative to a buy-and-hold strategy of identical standard deviation risk. Salaried managers may find such strategies appealing because, having one employer, they cannot diversify away their personal income risk. However, at least in the case of public mutual funds, investor clients can diversify away fund-specific risk or at least moderate such risk by allocating a portion of their capital to riskless, interest-paying assets. These clients would thus likely prefer that fund returns have symmetrical distributions with greater expected returns.

In the investment community, few information sources are not available to all participants. Information is often obtained from similar or identical sources and analyzed using similar techniques. Therefore, funds dealing in similar asset classes tend to include similar specific assets. The institutional trader is concerned with short-term fluctuations, but generally has a long-term objective. If the fund's goal is simply to outperform a market index, it follows that a static investment mix with only minor variations from that particular index would be attractive, since it minimizes transaction costs and eliminates the cost of an active portfolio manager.

2.5.2   Trading Dynamics and Instability

If a significant proportion of the trading in a market is driven by convex investment strategies, the market's volatility will increase and returns of buy-and-hold participants in that market will become positively skewed, with longer downside than upside distribution tail. Various authors suggest that this and other types of institutional trading have contributed to an increase in intraday price volatility and that the proliferation of program trading systems may be a cause of instability. When the market is highly stressed, trading may be halted through the use of regulatory *circuit breakers,* which shut down trading when aggregate price movements and/or volumes exceed certain limits, eventually returning the market to a stable condition.

Institutional investors, especially when trading electronically, pay lower commissions than do individual investors. Thus, institutional investors have an incentive to act on minor market imperfections or transient price disequilibria, although less favorable order execution prices resulting from high intraday volatility may easily negate commission savings.

2.6   THE EXPLOITATION OF ANOMALIES

2.6.1   The Cost and Value of Information

One measure of market efficiency is the way the market responds to information that enters it. The phenomenon, mentioned earlier, of over- and underreaction to the arrival of new information has been extensively studied. Ex post evidence of correcting reversals shows up as lagged negative serial correlation in price series (e.g., see DeBondt and Thaler, 1987). Efficiency is a question of degree. If the market exhibits overshoot tendencies, for example, it is important to know in advance whether there is likely to be a net positive gain from acting on such inefficiencies. When transaction costs are substantial, even significant pockets of market inefficiency may be difficult to exploit profitably.

The costs and value of information are important in the context of portfolio construction. As we will discuss in Chapter 3, additional information makes it possible to revise one's assessments of risk and return of various securities, and thus combine those securities in more effective proportions. One measure of the value of information is the increase in expected return obtainable from reoptimizing the portfolio while maintaining the same level of risk. The additional knowledge is worth acquiring only if its cost is less than the difference in expected returns of the original and revised portfolios.

2.6.2   Implied Probability Distributions

Although those who use naive methods of technical analysis, such as charting, rarely succeed in predicting price movements, it is nonetheless possible for price and volume data to have predictive content of a qualitative nature. A form of knowledge that can be partially derived from historical trading data is the implied probability distribution of potential sellers' security costs.

Consider the following observations of trading activity for hypothetical securities A and B, which have identical price histories but different volume histories:

Time Period	−5	−4	−3	−2	−1	Current
A Price	$10	9	9	11	11	$10
A Volume	100	75	75	125	125	
B Price	$10	9	9	11	11	$10
B Volume	100	125	125	75	75	

Let us assume, first, that the 500 shares above represent the total amount of trading done in these securities since they were first offered; second, that none of the traded shares are resales; and third, that the remaining shares are owned by long-term investors who at present are not interested in liquidation. From the above information, we can infer the following table of probabilities associated with potential sellers' share acquisition prices:

Price	9	10	11
Security A	.3	.2	.5
Security B	.5	.2	.3

Suppose that this is the beginning of the last trading day in December and that of the shareholders who have taken losses (i.e., paid more than $10 per share), 40 percent have historically sold their shares on the last tax sale day. If, on the average, 10 percent of other shareholders turn over securities every day, then, from the table of implied probabilities, we can see that the number of shares of security A supplied today at a $10 price will be 500(.5)(.4), or 100, but the number of shares of security B supplied at $10 will be only 500(.3)(.4), or 60. In fact, it is possible to calculate the number of securities offered at every price, in effect constructing supply curves for these two securities before the market has even opened. Even if the securities had identical intrinsic values, in the absence of information about demand it would be reasonable to expect that the market-clearing price of security A today will be less than that of B.

Because securities are accumulated in a more or less continuous fashion over time, some portion of a given period's volume reflects the unwinding of positions already counted in previous periods' volume. Therefore, the implied probability model is incomplete and can never provide exact share-cost probabilities. Nonetheless, if these assumptions about the actively traded pool of shares and the stochastic processes governing share accumulation and liquidation (such as these processes being Poisson) are valid, and if one goes far enough back in time, it should be possible to develop *bounds* on the share-cost probabilities implied by price and volume data for individual stocks. From time to time, there may arise anomalies in such probability bounds (relative to some norm) that are exploitable. This is the theoretical underpinning for certain machine-learning schemes employing price and volume data (see Chapter 9).

2.6.3 Decision Rules and Black Box Investing

Since the turn of the century, investors have developed decision rules for recognizing and acting on promising investment opportunities. Some classes of rules are static; that is, they are parameterized using information from one period. Others are adaptive, or based on knowledge of all past information and evolving over time. Investors may believe in the predictive validity of parsimonious or naive rules either because they have had past success with these rules or because they view the market as essentially noncomplex.

In recent years, theorists have developed numerous clever and complicated systems of decision rules, each of which, it is claimed, can beat the market. Some of these systems are entirely computer automated, while others require human intervention at one or more stages. Proprietary systems that require little or no human judgment are called *black boxes*. Only occasionally has the robustness of the mathematical rules programmed into black boxes been rigorously analyzed by researchers (e.g., see Trippi and Harriff, 1989). The systems most likely to be successful are those that consider the full spectrum of security, industry, market, and exogenous economic factors within the framework of portfolio optimization and that incorporate the knowledge and skills of experts. The theory and architecture of these systems, referred to as *knowledge-based systems,* will be discussed in later chapters of this book.

2.7   CONCLUSIONS

One can argue that the consistently superior performance of some investors and investment experts is *prima facie* evidence that, although organized markets for stocks and other securities are for the most part efficient, pockets of inefficiency that result in irrational pricing arise at least occasionally. The fact that active management and passive management philosophies success-fully coexist reflects the widely divergent views on this subject in the financial community.

Market complexity is manifested in anomalous pricing (i.e., devia-tions of price from some measure of intrinsic or equilibrium value). Anoma-lies may arise from the market's incomplete assimilation of all available information about particular securities, lack of attention by market partici-pants, differences of opinion about the meaning and significance of avail-able data, response inertia, methodological flaws in valuation, or investors' inability to disentangle complex relationships within large data sets. When security markets are complex, the investment approaches most likely to produce exceptional results are those that synergistically combine multidi-mensional, nonlinear, and adaptive value-based decision-making rules. Such rules can be stored, maintained, and updated in a special form of database called a *knowledge base.*

ENDNOTES

1. Thanks to Dr. Lawrence Sherman for his helpful contribution to this chapter.

2. Semivariance is defined as

$$(1/n) \sum_{(i/r_i \leq \bar{r})} (r_i - \bar{r})^2$$

where r_i is the ith return observation and $\bar{r}$ is the mean return. If returns are symmetrically distributed, semivariance is identical to half the variance.

REFERENCES

Cooper, S. K., J. C. Groth, and W. E. Avera. "Liquidity, Exchange Listing, and Common Stock Performance." *Journal of Economics and Business,* February 1985, pp. 21–33.

Cootner, P., ed. *The Random Character of Stock Market Prices.* Cambridge, MA: MIT Press, 1964.

DeBondt, W., and R. Thaler. "Further Evidence on Investor Overreaction and Stock Market Seasonality." *Journal of Finance* 42, no. 3 (July 1987), pp. 557–81.

Fama, E. "Mandelbrot and the Stable Paretian Hypothesis." *Journal of Business* 36, no. 4 (October 1963), p. 420.

Fama, E. "The Behavior of Stock Market Prices." *Journal of Business* 38 (January 1965), pp. 35–105.

Graham, B., and D. Dodd. *Security Analysis.* New York: McGraw-Hill, 1934.

Jacobs, B., and K. Levy. "The Complexity of the Stock Market." *The Journal of Portfolio Management* 16, no. 1 (Fall 1989), pp. 19–27.

Jacobs, B., and K. Levy. "Disentangling Equity Return Irregularities: New Insights and Investment Opportunities." *Financial Analysts Journal* 44, no. 3 (May–June 1988), pp. 18–43.

Jacobs, B., and K. Levy. "On the Value of 'Value.'" *Financial Analysts Journal* 44, no. 4 (July–August 1988), pp. 47–62.

Keane, S. "Paradox in the Current Crisis in Efficient Market Theory." *Journal of Portfolio Management* 17, no. 2 (Winter 1991), pp. 30–34.

King, B. "Market and Industry Factors in Stock Price Behavior." *Journal of Business* 39, no. 1 (January 1966), pp. 139–50.

Lee, C. F., and S. Rahman. "New Evidence on Timing and Security Selection Skill of Mutual Fund Managers." *Journal of Portfolio Management* 17, no. 2 (Winter 1991), pp. 80–83.

Lorie, J., P. Dodd, and M. Kimpton. *The Stock Market: Theories and Evidence.* Homewood, IL: Dow Jones-Irwin, 1985.

Malkiel, B. *A Random Walk Down Wall Street.* New York: W. W. Norton Co., 1990.

Marsh, T., and K. Rock. "Exchange Listing and Liquidity: A Comparison of the American Stock Exchange with the NASDAQ National Market System." American Stock Exchange Transactions Data Research Project Report No. 2, January 1986.

Miller, M., and F. Modigliani. "Dividend Policy, Growth, and the Valuation of Shares." *Journal of Business* 34 (October 1961), pp. 411–33.

Perold, A. F., and W. F. Sharpe. "Dynamic Strategies for Asset Allocation." *Financial Analysts Journal* 44 (January–February 1988), pp. 16–27.

Schmalensee, R. "An Experimental Study of Expectation Formation." *Econometrica* 44, no. 1 (January 1976), pp. 17–41.

Trippi, R. R., and R. B. Harriff. "Performance of Portfolio Insurance with Discrete Rebalance Filter and Serially Correlated Prices." *Advances in Futures and Options Research,* edited by F. Fabozzi. Greenwich, CT: JAI Press, 1990, pp. 177–90.

Trippi, R. R., and R. B. Harriff. "Evaluation of the 'AIM' Dynamic Asset Allocation Strategy." *Southwest Journal of Business and Economics* 6 (Fall 1989), pp. 14–20.

Williams, J. B. *The Theory of Investment Value.* Cambridge, MA: Harvard University Press, 1936.

CHAPTER 3

Modern Approaches to Portfolio Selection

3.1   Introduction
3.2   Goal Programming
3.3   Mean-Variance Optimization
      3.3.1   The Markowitz Model
      3.3.2   The Efficient Frontier
      3.3.3   Model Enhancement
3.4   Beta and Index Models
3.5   Security Risk and Portfolio Risk
3.6   The Role of Riskless Assets
3.7   Mean Absolute Deviation Optimization
3.8   Markowitz and Capital-Asset Pricing Model Limitations
3.9   CAPM Extensions and Program Trading

3.1   INTRODUCTION

To study knowledge-based systems approaches to portfolio selection, it is necessary to know something about the theory underlying the construction of portfolios. As discussed in Chapter 2, investment management strategies involve both *timing* and *selection*. Possessing superior knowledge about individual securities could, in principle, enable an investor to allocate wealth to realize greater returns and/or lower risk over time than other investors. Knowing the future direction of the stock market as a whole could also enable investors in a particular security or collection of securities to time their purchases and sales to reap abnormally high returns.

There are several popular approaches to making decisions regarding portfolio selection or wealth allocation. The simplest, the *conformance* approach, requires that portfolios be constructed with the goal of meeting the specific requirements of the investing institution or entity. Generally, the investor will want to hold fixed proportions of wealth in different broad classes of assets, such as short- and long-term debt, equity, and foreign securities, and, within each class, in securities representing certain industries, geographical locations, or "quality" groupings. Quality assessments may be based on company capitalization, performance history, or other organizations investing in that security. The earliest knowledge-based portfolio selection systems, such as that of Clarkson (described in the next chapter), employed conformance allocation rules.

A strategy in which the asset mix is responsive to the state of the national or global economy (e.g., phases of the business cycle) is referred to as *tactical asset allocation*. Tactical asset allocation is often *contrarian*, shifting wealth into those assets that have suffered recent declines in value. When the proportions of wealth allocated to various asset classes or individual securities are revised in an anticipatory fashion, based on a specific set of forecasts of macroeconomic factors such as real economic growth, real interest rates, inflation rate, oil prices, and defense spending, the strategy is referred to as *scenario allocation*.

In tactical and scenario allocation, it is common to determine the desired asset mix by using regression or other quantitative techniques. If assets are viewed as possessing several relevant attributes and desired mixes are specified in each attribute dimension, it is possible that no feasible combination of assets that satisfies all mix requirements will exist. Although this problem may be resolved heuristically, the final mix is likely to be somewhat subjective.

A more objective portfolio selection paradigm is that of *optimization*, in which wealth is allocated across securities to maximize or minimize some explicit criterion of success, subject to various constraints. Usually two or more success criteria are in contention with one another. Two examples of optimization are *goal programming* and *mean-variance optimization*.

3.2   GOAL PROGRAMMING

In the goal programming approach to asset allocation, the quality of a portfolio is gauged by how close it comes to achieving target values or goals for each of several attributes. A collective measure of the magnitude of positive and negative deviations from attribute goals is used to evaluate the portfolio (e.g., see Ignizio, 1976). Portfolio selection using this approach is represented by the following optimization problem:

$$\underset{X}{\text{Minimize}} \quad D_p = \sum_{j=1}^{m} P_j^+ d_j^+ + \sum_{j=1}^{m} P_j^- d_j^-$$

subject to

$$\sum_{i=1}^{n} x_i C_{ij} + d_j^+ - d_j^- = G_j, \qquad j = 1, \ldots m$$

$$\sum_{i=1}^{n} x_i C_{ij} \geq L_j, \qquad j = 1, \ldots m$$

$$\sum_{i=1}^{n} x_i C_{ij} \leq U_j, \qquad j = 1, \ldots m$$

$$\sum_{i=1}^{n} x_i \leq 1$$

$$d_j^+ \geq 0, \qquad j = 1, \ldots m$$

$$d_j^- \geq 0, \qquad j = 1, \ldots m$$

$$x_i \geq 0, \qquad i = 1, \ldots n,$$

where

n is the available number of assets.

m is the number of different portfolio attributes.

x_i is the fraction of the portfolio held in asset i.

G_j is the target value or goal for portfolio attribute j.

d_j^+ and d_j^- are positive and negative deviations from targets.

P_j^+ and P_j^- are penalties for deviations from target G_j.

D_p is the weighted sum of deviations from the targets.

L_j is the minimum acceptable level of portfolio attribute j.

U_j is the maximum acceptable level of portfolio attribute j.

C_{ij} is a measure of asset i's level of attribute j.

The preceeding *goal program* is a specialized type of *linear program*, since its objective function to be minimized and each of its constraints are linear. The first three sets of constraints define deviations from attribute goals and upper and lower portfolio attribute bounds. The fourth constraint limits the total portfolio investment to no more than 100 percent of the investor's wealth. The remaining constraints ensure that the investment and deviation variables do not take on negative values.

The goal programming approach to portfolio selection is best suited to situations in which investment goals are predetermined or in which it is possible to elicit a clear statement of goals from the investor. Thus, this approach is potentially useful for personal investment advising, in which a relatively small number of assets (such as mutual funds of different types) are being considered (e.g., see Cohen and Lieberman, 1983; Puelz and Puelz, 1989), and for implementing conformance, tactical, and scenario investing in an objective and systematic fashion.

In addition to the factors discussed in the last section, relevant goals might include desired levels of interest and dividend income, expected portfolio appreciation and riskiness, amount of income taxable in the current period, preservation of capital, the probability of experiencing a loss of capital, and desired sector, industry, and country participation levels. The goal programming model is a logical approach to resolving conflicts among such diverse goals. In addition, goal programming can be combined with other optimization approaches, including mean-variance optimization, which is discussed next.

3.3   MEAN-VARIANCE OPTIMIZATION

3.3.1   The Markowitz Model

Probably the most universally accepted approach to portfolio selection today is the mean-variance optimization approach introduced by Harry Markowitz (1952). In the basic Markowitz model, portfolio selection is represented by the following optimization problem:

$$\text{Minimize} \atop X \qquad V_p = \sum_{i=1}^{n} \sum_{j=1}^{n} \sigma_{ij} x_i x_j \qquad (3.1)$$

or, equivalently,

$$V_p = \sum_{i=1}^{n} \sigma_i^2 x_i^2 + \sum_{i=1}^{n} \sum_{\substack{j=1 \\ j \neq i}}^{n} \sigma_{ij} x_i x_j \, ,$$

subject to

$$\sum_{i=1}^{n} R_i x_i = R_p \qquad (3.2)$$

$$\sum_{i=1}^{n} x_i = 1 \qquad (3.3)$$

$$x_i \geq 0, \quad i = 1, \ldots n, \qquad (3.4)$$

where

n is the number of available securities.

x_i is the fraction of the portfolio held in security i.

$R_i \equiv E(r_i)$ is the expected value of return on security i.

$R_p \equiv E(r_p)$ is a target level of expected return on the portfolio.

σ_t^2 is the variance of returns of security i.

σ_{ij} is the covariance of returns of securities i and j.

V_p is the variance of the portfolio's return.

In this problem, which is called a *quadratic program* or *QP*, the goal is to minimize the riskiness or variance, V_p, of the entire portfolio while achieving the minimally acceptable expected return, R_p, imposed by constraint (3.2). Constraint (3.3) ensures that available wealth is fully allocated, and the n nonnegativity constraints (3.4) ensure that only a positive or zero investment is made in each security. If short selling was permissible for some subset of securities, the nonnegativity constraint for those securities would be omitted. The objective function (3.1) is quadratic and the constraints are linear. Several highly efficient algorithms are available for solving this problem.[1] Portfolio risk is also commonly represented by the standard deviation σ_p, which, as the square root of variance, is a monotonically increasing function of V_p.

When R_p is varied parametrically, solutions of the QP model result in a set of efficient points representing portfolios with the property of minimal V_p and thus minimal σ_p for a given expected return or, equivalently, maximum return for a given level of σ_p. These are called *efficient portfolios*. An alternative formulation of the risk-return optimization problem is

$$\text{Minimize}_{X} \qquad V_p' = \theta \sum_{i=1}^{n} \sum_{j=1}^{n} \sigma_{ij} x_i x_j - (1 - \theta) \sum_{i=1}^{n} R_i x_i$$

subject to

$$\sum_{i=1}^{n} x_i = 1$$

$$x_i \geq 0, \quad i = 1, \ldots n.$$

In this formulation, θ is a weighting parameter. When this QP is solved for every value of θ between 0 and 1, the entire set of feasible efficient points is generated.

3.3.2   The Efficient Frontier

Collectively, the set of efficient points defines a line referred to as the *efficient frontier* (Figure 3.1). Enlarging the universe of assets from which the portfolio selection is made never results in a lower efficient frontier, since new securities can always be included at a level of zero. By including in a portfolio new assets whose returns are not highly positively correlated with those of other assets, investors may develop significantly improved risk-return combinations. This explains the current trend toward global investing and the inclusion of real estate and other nontraditional assets in the portfolios of major institutional investors.

Which portfolio is chosen from among those on the efficient frontier will depend on the investor's *utility function*, which represents preferences with respect to risk and return. As discussed in Chapter 2, different investors

Figure 3.1
Efficient Risk-Return Frontier

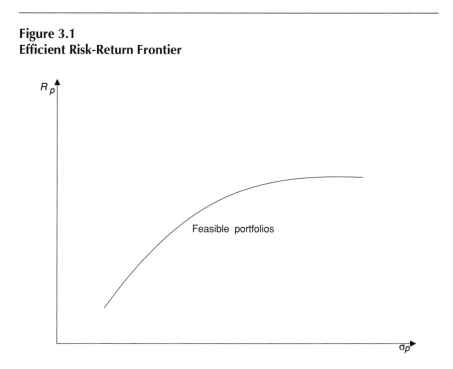

facing an identical efficient frontier are likely to choose efficient portfolios having at least somewhat differing levels of risk and expected return.

Viewing R_p as a function of σ_p, the efficient frontier $R(\sigma)$ will be *concave* over its range. This is because if any of the points $R(x'),\sigma(x')$ were to lie on a locally convex portion of the efficient frontier, they would be dominated with respect to risk and return by a portfolio comprising a linear combination of two portfolios, x^a and x^b, just on either side of that point. That is,

$$\left[R(\theta\, x^a + (1-\theta)x^b), -\sigma(\theta x^a + (1-\theta)x^b)\right] \geq \left[R(x'), -\sigma(x')\right]$$

for at least some value of θ such that $0 \leq \theta \leq 1$. If portfolio risk were measured by variance V_p rather than by standard deviation σ_p, the efficient frontier given by $R_p(V_p)$ would be *strictly concave* because $\sigma = \sqrt{V}$ is a strictly concave function, and a strictly concave function of a concave function is also strictly concave.

3.3.3   Model Enhancement

The basic Markowitz model can be embellished with additional constraints. For example, if it is determined that no more than fraction F_K of the portfolio should be invested in securities k of one or more industries K, additional constraints can be added of the form

$$\sum_{k \in K} x_k \leq F_K, \quad K = 1, \ldots$$

The basic Markowitz model can produce solutions with hundreds of securities included in the portfolio, some at levels approaching or even exceeding the total number of shares available and others at levels so low that their inclusion is uneconomical due to the high transaction costs of placing small orders. Therefore, it may be desirable to limit the degree of diversification in some way. To restrict the portfolio to no more than N different securities, the Markowitz model could, for example, be augmented with the following $2n + 1$ constraints:

$$x_i - y_i \leq 0, \quad i = 1, \ldots n$$

$$\sum_{i=1}^{n} y_i \leq N$$

$$y_i = 0,1 \quad i = 1, \ldots n.$$

Here the y_i variables are restricted to the values of 0 or 1, and the problem becomes a *mixed zero-one integer program*, whose solution requires specialized optimization algorithms. (For other limited diversification models, see Faaland [1974].)

It is fairly easy to incorporate linear transaction costs into the Markowitz model; in this case, the transaction cost associated with security i is assumed to diminish its expected return, R_i, by δ_i percent. For security i already held in amount W_i, the amount to be purchased or sold can be represented by the nonnegative variables x_i^+ and x_i^-. For each security a constraint is added of the form

$$x_i - W_i - x_i^+ + x_i^- = 0,$$

and the expression for net expected return,

$$R_i x_i - \delta_i (x_i^+ + x_i^-),$$

is substituted in place of each of the $R_i x_i's$ in constraint (3.2) of the basic model.

3.4   BETA AND INDEX MODELS

If the Markowitz model is used to select from a universe of thousands of securities, there will be difficulties associated with data acquisition. Nevertheless, investors have successfully used simple but effective computerized mean-variance optimization systems that limit investment allocation decisions to a few broad classes of asset types, such as domestic and foreign stocks, bonds, and bills, or to economic sectors, such as capital goods, consumer, and business cycle sensitive (e.g., see Franks, 1990).

Sharpe (1963) developed a practical answer to the problem of computering numerous stock return covariances. His method requires knowing both the covariance of each security i, with an index, I, representing the market, and the *beta coefficient* for each security. Beta measures the responsiveness of the security's return to the return r_I of the index and can be viewed as the slope of the linear equation

$$r_i = \alpha_i + \beta_i r_I \, ,$$

which is called the security's *characteristic line*.

The value of beta in this equation can, in principle, be estimated by regressing historical security returns against returns on the index, using the estimating equation

$$r_{it} = \alpha_i + \beta_i r_{It} + \varepsilon_{it} \, ,$$

where ε_{it} is the residual for each observation t, representing the variation in security return not explained by variations in the market. Beta is said to measure the *systematic* or *market risk* of an asset. This source of risk cannot be reduced or eliminated through diversification without a diminishment of expected return, so it is also called *nondiversifiable risk*.

The portion of a security's risk that is represented statistically by the residuals, specifically the magnitude of the sum of their squares in relation to the security return variance, is called *unsystematic, company-specific,* or *diversifiable* risk. This source of risk *can* be reduced by diversification, since the residuals of a collection of securities, when summed together, will tend to cancel one another out.

Another way to look at this is to examine the variance of the return of a collection of securities that is not explained by variations in the return of the index. This unexplained variance, represented by σ_u^2, will decrease as the number of securities increases. The covariances of the residuals of securities i and j can be represented by $\sigma_{\varepsilon_i \varepsilon_j}$. It is reasonable to expect the values of $\sigma_{\varepsilon_i \varepsilon_j}$ for $i \neq j$ to be randomly distributed and about half to be of positive and half of negative sign. If each of n securities is held in equal fractional amounts $1/n$, the unexplained collective return variance is

$$\sigma_u^2 = \sum_{i=1}^{n} \sum_{j=1}^{n} (1/n)^2 \, \sigma_{\varepsilon_i \varepsilon_j}$$

or, equivalently,

$$\sigma_u^2 = (1/n)^2 \sum_{i=1}^{n} \sigma_{\varepsilon_i}^2 + (1/n)^2 \sum_{i=1}^{n} \sum_{\substack{j=1 \\ j \neq i}}^{n} \sigma_{\varepsilon_i \varepsilon_j},$$

where $\sigma_{\varepsilon_i}^2$ is the residual variance for security i.

To see how unsystematic risk can be diversified away, we need only impose the relatively weak assumption that the *average* of the $\sigma_{\varepsilon_i \varepsilon_j}$'s, $i \neq j$, is zero. Under this assumption, $\sigma_u^2 \to 0$ as $n \to \infty$. This occurs because the second term of the above expression approaches zero through the cancellation of positive and negative covariances, and the first term approaches zero because the factor $(1/n)^2$ decreases at a rate faster than the linear rate at which new elements are added to the summation. Empirical studies of small portfolios of both human-selected and randomly selected stocks have shown that nearly all of the unsystematic risk has been eliminated when $n \geq 30$.

A logical source of data for estimating beta via regression would be observed pairs of daily, weekly, or monthly security and index prices from the recent past. Since it is future beta that matters for portfolio decisions, more sophisticated methodologies have been proposed for developing accurate forecasts of betas (e.g., see Rosenberg and Guy, 1976; Elton, Gruber, and Urich, 1978). Beta estimates computed using different methodologies and with a variety of adjustments are available from commercial services for stocks listed on major exchanges; note that betas can be computed for portfolios as well as for securities.

For securities highly correlated with some index having return variance σ_I^2, the product $\beta_i \, \beta_j \, \sigma_I^2$ provides a good estimate of covariance σ_{ij}. The computational burden of generating objective function parameters for the Markowitz model can be greatly reduced by using this relationship, as only n betas plus the index variance need to be computed, instead of n security variances and $n(n-1)/2$ covariances of every security against every other. (Division is by 2 because $\sigma_{ij} \equiv \sigma_{ji}$.)

If the only common source of variation in individual security returns is the market return, the covariance of the residuals of every security with those of every other security will be zero ($\sigma_{\varepsilon_i \varepsilon_j} = 0$, $i \neq j$), and the quadratic optimization problem can be greatly simplified at the expense of adding just one new variable and constraint. Under this assumption, the Markowitz objective function can be rewritten as

$$V_p = \sigma_I^2 \left(\sum_{i=1}^{n} \beta_i x_i \right)^2 + \sum_{i=1}^{n} \sigma_{\varepsilon_i}^2 x_i^2 \; ;$$

or, equivalently, by substituting z for the weighted average β, as

$$V_p = \sigma_I^2 z^2 + \sum_{i=1}^{n} \sigma_{\varepsilon_i}^2 x_i^2 \; ,$$

where the linear constraint

$$\sum_{i=1}^{n} \beta_i x_i - z = 0$$

is added to the basic model. Rather than comprising a dense $n \times n$ matrix, the objective function now consists of only n diagonal matrix elements plus the term associated with index return variance.

The index model approach can readily be extended to multiple indexes. Analogous to the characteristic line would be a plane or hyperplane that best fits security returns to the returns of two or more indexes. A multiple regression of security returns against several indexes (also called *factors*) results in a beta for each security with respect to each index ($\beta(1)_i$, $\beta(2)_i$, $\beta(3)_i$, etc.) plus residuals representing, as before, the unsystematic risk that is not explainable by movements in these indexes. In addition to the market return index, indexes of inflation rate, money supply, or other economic variables may be employed. It is important that the indexes themselves not be highly correlated, or little improvement will result over the single-market index model. If indexes are carefully chosen, the resulting portfolios should not be greatly suboptimal in risk and expected return to those that would be chosen using Markowitz's original model.

3.5   SECURITY RISK AND PORTFOLIO RISK

Total portfolio risk is given by σ_p, which includes both systematic and unsystematic risk components. The more diversified the portfolio, the smaller its unsystematic risk, which approaches zero for highly diversified portfolios. The risk of a security i whose returns are totally uncorrelated with other assets in a portfolio could be adequately represented by σ_i. Such securities are rare, however. Most securities have returns that are correlated with others, if for no other reason than that they are jointly dependent on the market; thus, the riskiness of a particular security must be viewed in relation to that of all the other securities in the portfolio.

Since diversifying a portfolio by combining securities is possible, at least in principle, for all investors, the *relevant risk* of the addition of a security to a portfolio is related to the security's impact on the systematic risk of the portfolio. This is represented collectively by security i's covariances with the other securities in the portfolio or, in a shorthand way, by the effect of its inclusion on the portfolio's beta.

Portfolios have many of the same characteristics individual securities do; that is, expected returns, standard deviations, and betas. The beta of portfolio P plus security A is given by the weighted average of their betas (i.e., $\beta_{P+A} = x_P \beta_P + x_A \beta_A$, where $x_P + x_A = 1$); depending on the security's beta relative to that of the portfolio, its addition may increase or decrease the portfolio's systematic risk.

Therefore, both securities and portfolios should be priced such that those with progressively greater systematic risk or beta offer greater expected return. At the same time, expected returns should be independent of unsystematic risk, since this risk can be virtually eliminated by further diversification. A great deal of empirical evidence supports this proposition. The functional relationship between expected return and beta is represented by a line called the *security market line*, which is precisely defined in the next section.

3.6   THE ROLE OF RISKLESS ASSETS

Most conventional treatments of portfolio theory introduce a riskless asset into the risk-return space (see Figure 3.2). This asset is represented by a point on the vertical axis. In the finance literature, one-month Treasury bills are often assumed to be riskless assets because they are guaranteed by the federal government, have such short maturities that they pose negligible maturity risk, and have a highly liquid secondary market. Since a portfolio can consist of a combination of riskless and risky assets, every point on the straight line beginning at R_f and tangent to the Markowitz efficient frontier represents some feasible portfolio. The point of tangency, M, is that of a portfolio called the *market portfolio*. Its expected return is R_m and its risk is σ_m. The market portfolio's beta is 1, and the beta of a portfolio or index that approximates the market portfolio ought to be close to 1.[2] Points to the right of the market portfolio are efficient risk-return combinations achievable only if one can borrow at the risk-free rate.[3]

Figure 3.2
Efficient Frontier and Capital Market Line

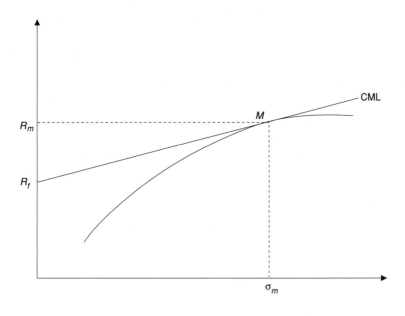

Thus, the riskless asset serves to linearize the risk-return combinations available to the investor. The resultant line is called the *capital market line (CML)*. The equation for the CML is

$$R(\sigma) = R_f + (R_m - R_f)\, \sigma/\sigma_m .$$

Since market risk can be eliminated through diversification, the only relevant risk of *individual securities* is beta, and it follows that in market equilibrium the expected return of an individual security i ought to be a function of only its beta risk, the risk-free rate, R_f, and the market risk premium, $R_m - R_f$. The relationship is given by the *security market line (SML)*:

$$R_i = R_f + \beta_i (R_m - R_f).$$

These relationships between expected return and risk are the basis for the *capital-asset pricing model (CAPM)*, developed independently by Sharpe (1964), Mossin (1966), and Lintner (1965). The CAPM can be used in a normative fashion to determine the required risk-return characteristics of assets in a variety of settings, both internal and external to a firm.[4]

3.7   MEAN ABSOLUTE DEVIATION OPTIMIZATION

The assumption of variance or standard deviation as the primary portfolio risk measure may be rejected completely, as in models that define portfolio risk as the *mean absolute deviation (MAD)* of returns from their expected values, or

$$E(|r_p - R_p|).$$

Konno and Yamazaki (1991) have shown that minimizing a portfolio's mean absolute deviation is equivalent to minimizing its standard deviation when portfolio returns are generated by a multivariate normal process.

In addition to having a superior correlation with subjective assessments of risk, the MAD model has several advantages over the Markowitz or index model QPs. It can be formulated as a linear program that permits portfolio optimization over a much larger asset universe for a given level of computational effort; it generally produces a smaller number of securities at positive levels in optimal portfolios; and it does not require the prior computation of large covariance matrices.

A capital asset price model analogous to the conventional CAPM can be constructed using the mean absolute deviation risk measure, in which equilibrium prices of individual securities are given by

$$R_i = R_f + \mu_i (R_m - R_f),$$

and the derived parameter μ has an interpretation similar to that of beta. With securities selected from those included in the Nikkei 225 index, Konno and Yamazaki found that the dense-matrix Markowitz model's efficient frontier and security mixes were closer to those of the MAD model than to those of a single-index Sharpe-type model.

3.8   MARKOWITZ AND CAPITAL-ASSET PRICING MODEL LIMITATIONS

There is evidence that the CAPM, in both its standard form and with distribution parameter extensions, is an incomplete model of asset pricing. That is, not all of the expected return of efficient portfolios can be explained by their standard deviation, variance, or higher distribution moments, and not all of the expected returns of individual securities are explainable by their betas.

The *arbitrage pricing theory (APT)* model (Ross 1976) attempts to address some of these shortcomings by postulating that expected returns of assets are a function of several *factors*; and that an arbitrage process will drive the prices of assets up or down so that if assets have a similar response to movements in these factors, they will offer similar returns. In other words, there may be several sources of systematic risk common to most securities. Although the price movement of the market as a whole is a significant (and probably dominant) factor in the expected returns of individual securities, the APT model does not say specifically which other factors ought to be considered; however, it does relax some of the CAPM's assumptions about investor preferences, while imposing the requirement that the return-generating function be linearly separable with respect to its components. Considerable empirical research has been directed to verifying the APT model; a more comprehensive treatment of both the CAPM and the APT models may be found in standard texts such as Elton and Gruber (1987), Haugen (1986), Sharpe (1985), and Reilly (1985).

From a practical standpoint, a more serious problem with using the Markowitz model or the CAPM for portfolio selection is that neither provides a mechanism for incorporating superior knowledge of industries, companies, products, corporate management, or market anomalies into portfolio-mix decisions. These decisions can have a profound effect on ex post portfolio returns. Many assets possess negligible risk yet have returns slightly superior to those of Treasury bills. These assets are near-substitutes at the low-risk end of the spectrum.

At greater levels of risk, near-substitutes are assets that have covariances similar to those of other assets in the market portfolio. Given that there are thousands of securities to choose from, one would expect to find many near-substitutes among risky assets, or a certain amount of redundancy in efficient portfolios. Small departures from the theoretically optimal mix of

---

Figure 3.3
Ex Ante and Ex Post Frontiers

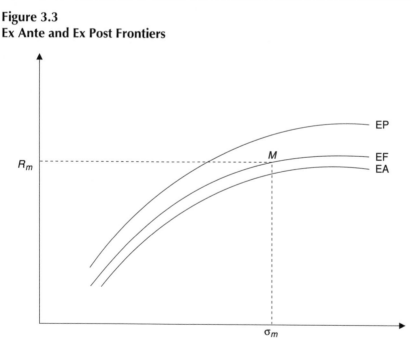

many securities, or large departures in the case of a smaller number of near-substitutes, will have little impact on the ex ante level of portfolio risk for a given expected return. This is depicted by line EA in Figure 3.3, which reverses the amounts invested in some near-substitute pairs in each of the portfolios on the efficient frontier EF. Knowledge that results in superior estimates of future returns of individual securities (or future returns of the market as a whole) could easily outweigh the small loss of expected return from following an investment policy that is technically suboptimal in the CAPM framework, with the end result being an ex post frontier such as line EP. Later chapters of this book will discuss how such knowledge is represented and incorporated into the portfolio selection process.

3.9   CAPM EXTENSIONS AND PROGRAM TRADING

The CAPM can be extended to consider other measures of portfolio performance. In addition to expected return and risk, many investors have preferences with respect to median, mode, skewness, and other higher-return distribution moments and to the probability of returns below zero or below that of a riskless asset (Rubinstein, 1973; Kraus and Litzenberger, 1973). For example, a small body of literature has developed that attempts to explain the popularity of portfolio insurance–type program trading rules even though they generate returns, in both theory and practice, below the CML (see Trennepohl, Booth, and Tehranian, 1988). Thus, it appears that skewness, at least, is priced in some way by portfolio insurers.

Static portfolios on the CML have symmetrical, unimodal return distributions. Asymmetrical (and even multimodal) portfolio return distributions can be generated through the use of decision rules that continuously rebalance between the risky and riskless components of the portfolio. Some rules result in return distributions that are positively skewed (characteristic of *convex* investment strategies), while other rules result in return distributions that are negatively skewed (characteristic of *concave* investment strategies). Program trading rules can be either *efficient* or *inefficient* in the sense of achieving either an optimal or a suboptimal level of a particular performance measure—say, probability of loss—for fixed levels of other measures, such as mathematical expectation and standard deviation of returns (e.g., see Trippi, 1994). Investors with preferences that go beyond expectation and standard deviation of returns must then select not only an efficient risky portfolio component but also an *efficient dynamic allocation*

Figure 3.4
Capital Market Surface and CML

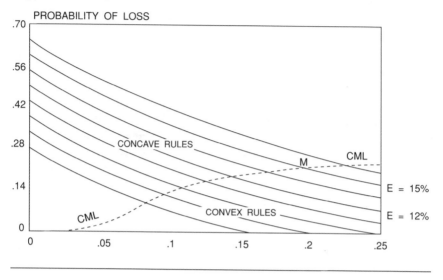

strategy from among those that lie on a *capital market surface* (see Figure 3.4).

Rebalancing rules for reshaping the return distribution of a portfolio to the tastes of the investor can be quite complex. In practice, the optimization of such rules with respect to both the distance from the capital market surface and the desired return distribution shape can become a difficult task when rebalancing discontinuities and transaction costs are fully taken into account (Trippi and Harriff, 1991). The machine-learning methodologies to be discussed in Chapter 9 can be applied to synthesize optimal program trading rule sets for dynamically managed portfolios.

ENDNOTES

1. The objective function is convex if the matrix $\|\sigma_{ij}\|$ is positive semidefinite. One of the earliest algorithms to solve this problem was the modified simplex method of Wolfe (1959), which is still in use. Those familiar with mathematical optimization will note

that the Kuhn-Tucker optimality conditions for the Markowitz QP comprise a set of linear equalities, plus a set of pairs of dual and slack variables whose products must equal zero (complementary slackness). These conditions can be achieved by solving a linear program (LP) that drives "artificial" variables to zero while maintaining complementary slackness. The essence of Wolfe's method is to solve the Kuhn-Tucker equations by using the ordinary LP simplex algorithm augmented with additional checks to determine whether each prescribed pivot operation will maintain the required complementary slackness condition. Whenever a normal pivot would result in a violation of complementary slackness, the next-best variable is brought into the basis instead. Programs for solving QP problems are widely available, including inexpensive student versions of the most popular software packages that are capable of solving problems with several dozen variables and constraints.

2. If all investors are rational in the Markowitz sense, then they should invest in risky assets only in the mix given by the market portfolio. Market clearing of risky assets would require that the market portfolio include each risky asset in exact proportion to its value, or price times number of shares outstanding. Under these assumptions, the market portfolio would represent a value-weighted security index.

3. If borrowing is possible only at an interest rate greater than R_f, the portion of the CML to the right of point M will be a straight line through that borrowing rate on the vertical axis and tangent to the Markowitz efficient frontier. This results in a downward bend in the CML beyond point M. If the risk-free asset is not included in the market portfolio, the return on a zero-beta portfolio is sometimes used in place of R_f in the capital asset pricing model.

4. For individual securities, one would expect to find empirically that

$$r_{it} = R_f + \beta_i (R_m - R_f) + \varepsilon_{it},$$

where $E(\varepsilon_i) = 0$. If $E(\varepsilon_i) > 0$, the security exhibits *excess returns to beta*, a disequilibrium condition that is considered an anomaly within the CAPM framework.

REFERENCES

Elton, E. J., and M. J. Gruber. *Modern Portfolio Theory and Investment Analysis*. New York: John Wiley & Sons, 1987.

Elton, E., M. Gruber, and T. Urich. "Are Betas Best?" *Journal of Finance* 13, no. 5 (December 1978), pp. 1375–84.

Faaland, B. "An Integer Programming Algorithm for Portfolio Selection." *Management Science* 20, no. 10 (June 1974), pp. 1376–88.

Franks, E. "A Decision Support System for Revision of Portfolios to Achieve Pre-Specified Real Returns with Reliability and Efficiency." in *Investment Management: Decision Support and Expert Systems,* edited by R. Trippi and E.Turban. New York: Van Nostrand Reinhold, 1990.

Haugen, R. A. *Modern Investment Theory*. Englewood Cliffs, NJ: Prentice Hall, 1986.

Ignizio, J. P. *Goal Programming and Extensions*. Lexington, MA: Lexington Books, 1976.

Konno, H., and H. Yamazaki. "Mean-Absolute Deviation Portfolio Optimization Model and Its Applications to the Tokyo Stock Market." *Management Science* 37, no. 5 (May 1991), pp. 519–31.

Kraus, A., and R. Litzenberger. "Skewness Preference and the Valuation of Risky Assets." *Journal of Finance* 31 (September 1976), pp. 1085–1100.

Lintner, J. "Security Prices, Risk, and Maximal Gains from Diversification." *Journal of Finance* (December 1965), pp. 587–615.

Markowitz, H. "Portfolio Selection." *Journal of Finance* 7 (March 1952), pp. 77–91.

Mossin, J. "Equilibrium in a Capital Market." *Econometrica* 34 (October 1966), pp. 768–83.

Puelz, A., and R. Puelz. "Personal Financial Planning: An Interactive Goal Programming Model Using U-Shaped Penalty Functions." *Proceedings, 1989 Annual Meeting*, Decision Sciences Institute, New Orleans, 1989, pp. 327–29.

Reilly, F. K. *Investment Analysis and Portfolio Management.* Hinsdale, IL: Dryden Press, 1985.

Rosenberg, B., and J. Guy. "Prediction of Beta from Investment Fundamentals—Part I." *Financial Analysts Journal* 32, no. 4 (May–June 1976), pp. 60–72.

Rosenberg, B., and J. Guy. "Prediction of Beta from Investment Fundamentals—Part 2." *Financial Analysts Journal* 32, no. 4 (July–August 1976), pp. 62–70.

Ross, S. A. "The Arbitrage Theory of Capital Asset Pricing." *Journal of Economic Theory* (December 1976).

Rubinstein, M. "The Fundamental Theorem of Parameter-Preference Security Valuation." *Journal of Financial and Quantitative Analysis* 8 (January 1973), pp. 61–69.

Sharpe, W. F. "A Simplified Model for Portfolio Analysis." *Management Science* 9, no. 2 (January 1963), pp. 277–93.

Sharpe, W. F. "Capital Asset Prices: A Theory of Market Equilibrium Under Conditions of Risk." *Journal of Finance* 19 (September 1964), pp. 425–42.

Sharpe, W. F. *Investments.* Englewood Cliffs, NJ: Prentice Hall, 1985.

Trennepohl, G. L., J. R. Booth, and H. Tehranian. "An Empirical Analysis of Insured Portfolio Strategies Using Listed Options." *Journal of Financial Research* 11 (Spring 1988), pp. 1–12.

Trippi, R., and R. Harriff. "Dynamic Asset Allocation Rules: Survey and Synthesis." *Journal of Portfolio Management* 17, no. 4 (Summer 1991).

Trippi, R. R. "A Note on Dynamic Investment Strategies and Mean-Variance Dominance of the Constant-Mix Rule." *Advances in Futures and Options Research*, Vol. 7. Greenwich, CT: JAI Press, 1994, pp. 323–27.

Wolfe, P. "The Simplex Method for Quadratic Programming." *Econometrica* 27 (1959), pp. 382–98.

CHAPTER 4

◆

Artificial Intelligence in Investment Management: An Overview[1]

4.1 Knowledge-Based Systems, Auto-Learning Systems, and Intelligent Systems
4.2 Introduction to Knowledge Representation
4.3 Expert Systems and Financial Services
4.4 An Early ES for Portfolio Selection
4.5 Contemporary Systems
4.6 Emerging Artificial Intelligence Technologies
4.7 Conclusions

4.1 KNOWLEDGE-BASED SYSTEMS, AUTO-LEARNING SYSTEMS, AND INTELLIGENT SYSTEMS

This chapter provides a survey of expert system applications in investing and an overview of emerging AI technologies. The term *expert system* is not perfectly synonymous with *knowledge-based system*. In practice, however, the two terms are often used interchangeably because the knowledge base is such a crucial technology in a successful expert system.

Knowledge-based systems may be divided into two categories: those with and those without *auto-learning* (or *machine learning*) capability. Some knowledge-based systems require the explicit input of decision rules to acquire the knowledge from which to make inferences; most conventionally implemented expert systems fall into this category. Auto-learning systems, on the other hand, create the knowledge base themselves through exposure to attribute-outcome examples and may be "trained" with either test data or a subset of actual (i.e., historical) data. A common method of validating the performance of an auto-learning system prior to implementation is to measure the proportion of correct decisions that are made on the remaining subset of actual data.

Figure 4.1 illustrates the adjustment of decision rules and/or system parameters in response to the ex-post performance of an auto-learning system. One way conventionally implemented expert systems can operate in an auto-learning mode is through *rule induction* or *learning-from-example (LFE)*. The specific mechanisms of learning in auto-learning systems are more generally referred to as *machine-learning* processes. Several machine-learning methodologies useful in financial decision making, including inductive learning, syntactic pattern-based learning, and genetic algorithms, are described in more detail in Chapter 9. In recent years, the learning-based technology referred to as *artificial neural networks* or *artificial neural systems* has been very successfully used to develop *intelligent systems*. *Intelligent systems* is a catch-all term that includes all software implementations of AI-based decision support systems, that is, decision support systems that include at least one knowledge-based subsystem. In addition to proven technologies, emerging technologies with potential for incorporation into knowledge-based systems, such as fuzzy logic, case-based reasoning, and chaos theory, are also briefly discussed in this chapter.

4.2   INTRODUCTION TO KNOWLEDGE REPRESENTATION

Knowledge representation, goals, and methodology are the major components of problem representation. Talluru and Ackgiray (1990) describe the solution process as involving the three steps of (1) *abstraction*, (2) *structuring*, and (3) *model selection*. In this process, the *size* of the problem space (Newell and Simon, 1972), its *character*, and the *solution methodology* all place economic limits on the scope of the problem that can be solved. In a

Figure 4.1
Auto-Learning Expert System

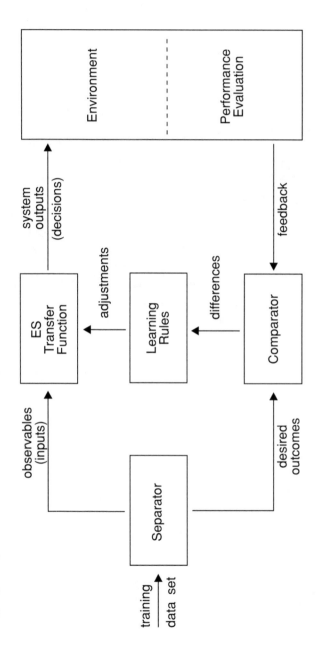

Source: Trippi (1990).

knowledge-based system, the character of the solution space is defined primarily by the way that knowledge is represented.

Knowledge representation is a formalism for the systematic computer storage of facts and rules about a subject or specialty. In knowledge-based systems, knowledge may come from human experts. A person who encodes the knowledge into the knowledge base is called, in ES jargon, a *knowledge engineer.* The process of knowledge acquisition often requires that the knowledge engineer interview, observe, and interact with domain experts. This process, known as *knowledge engineering,* can be difficult and time consuming. In auto-learning systems, in contrast, knowledge acquisition may take place through the system's analyzing examples by itself, without the presence of a domain expert.

In conventional ESs, knowledge may be represented in a number of ways. The most common representations are known as *production rules, semantic networks,* and *frames.* Production (condition-action) rule representation is the most frequently encountered approach in commercial ESs and the one on which this book will be focused. Rules may be implemented either through logic-based computer languages such as PROLOG or through the use of an ES *inference engine* or *shell,* an application software package that frees the user from doing detailed computer programming tasks. By using an ES shell, one may explicitly enter knowledge and inference rules into the knowledge base in a form close to that of natural language. Some rules may relate to the handling of knowledge or manipulation of rules; these are referred to as *meta-rules.* Following are examples of rules that might be included in a hypothetical portfolio management knowledge base:

IF   the price of gold is less than the four-year average
AND   the inflation rate exceeds the T-bill rate
THEN   include 15 percent gold in the portfolio;
            (knowledge rule)

or

IF   index has moved more than 12 points from last rebalance
THEN   rebalance cash to stocks using formula 1;
            (knowledge rule)

or

IF   dollar-yen exchange rate is not in the system
THEN request it from the user
            (meta-rule).

In a rule-based ES, the subset and sequence of knowledge rules that "fire," or have their antecedents fulfilled, will depend on the user's answers to a series of critical questions asked by the ES. Rule-based ESs may have hundreds or even thousands of questions and rules available in the knowledge base. The final action recommendation of such a "consultant" ES is called its *goal*. We will discuss more complex types of rules in later chapters.

In an auto-learning rule-based system, rules are developed through the use of algorithms that best match problem attributes and goals or that select the most effective rule subset from a larger set of potential rules. Through data-driven induction, a rule structure is developed to satisfy a given set of instances. Conflicts may be resolved by nesting mediating rules within earlier derived rules or by using heuristic procedures that reform the tentative rule set. In model-driven induction, rejection of rules in an a priori set would be guided by the tolerance for misclassification of test examples. In using this type of induction, a human expert must often be called on to review the remaining rules for consistency and bias. In certain domains, the rule induction procedure can be formalized. For example, Holsapple, Whinston, and Tam (1987) have developed a methodology for updating rule sets for security trading that generates new rules by simply running the procedures on new examples as they arrive. In a conventional ES, the successive invocation of rules partitions the output, or goal set, into complex, though usually linearly separable regions (see Figure 4.2b).

In contrast, neural network-based expert systems do not employ explicit rules. The mechanism by which relevant attributes result in outputs, such as action recommendations, is more subtle. The final input-output mapping will depend on the topology of the network, node transfer functions, and network interconnect weights that result from training. Knowledge is diffused throughout the network and is represented by the interconnect weights only in a collective sense. There may be thousands or even millions of such weights. Therefore, unlike conventionally implemented expert systems, neural networks do not easily provide explanatory insights. Nevertheless, there do exist specialized software products that derive explanations from networks with varying degrees of success. Learning and other aspects of neural network-based systems are discussed later in this chapter and also in Chapters 9 and 10.

Figure 4.2
Partitioning of ES Output Set (with outputs *A, B, C, D*)

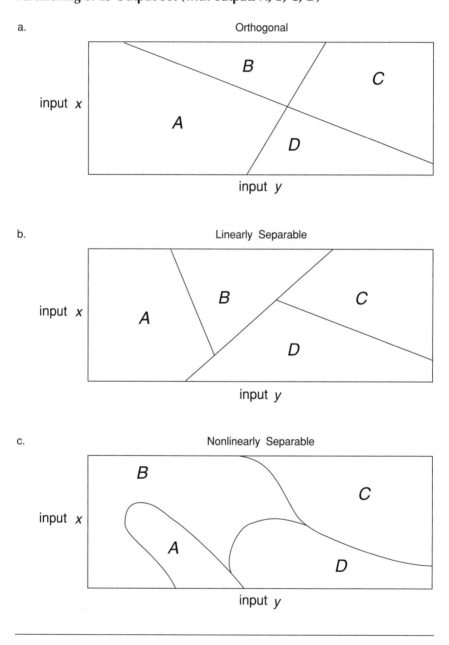

a.   Orthogonal

input *x*

B

C

A

D

input *y*

b.   Linearly Separable

input *x*

A

B

C

D

input *y*

c.   Nonlinearly Separable

input *x*

B

C

A

D

input *y*

4.3   EXPERT SYSTEMS AND FINANCIAL SERVICES

Considerable success has been reported in applying conventional ESs to routine financial decision-making operations such as approval of credit lines, mortgage underwriting, financial planning, and the underwriting of complex insurance policies (e.g., see Bestor, 1987; Shannon, 1985; Sviokla, 1988; and the survey by Friedland, 1988). These activities involve risk assessment, which is a generalization problem. Active portfolio management, on the other hand, includes elements of recognition (seizing opportunities) as well as generalization. To be successful, an ES for such an application must have a considerably greater degree of sophistication than a pure generalization system.

The portfolio management process involves a number of stages amenable to ES. These include the following (adapted from Talluru and Akgiray, 1988).

- Identification of goals and constraints

- Generation of a set of feasible investments

- Formulation of alternative strategies

- Selection of an appropriate strategy

- Implementation of the selected strategy

- Explanation of results and consultation.

Not all portfolio management ESs need to perform all of these functions. Goals, constraints, and even the strategy may be predetermined exogenously to the ES (e.g., by using the philosophy or charter of the investing entity or sponsor). In many applications, the ES's primary functions are limited to implementation and explanation.

Areas of portfolio management for which ES technology holds the greatest promise include:

- Static asset diversification (or asset allocation) decisions

- Market-timing decisions

- Implementation of dynamic diversification and hedging strategies (e.g., portfolio insurance)

- The systematic application of inclusion/exclusion criteria to specific asset classes.

Static diversification involves selecting a portfolio that is likely to meet specific investment goals. When the investments are of a long-term nature, the portfolio may need to be revised only infrequently. Therefore, the primary use of an ES for this purpose might be to elicit investment goals and make long-term investment commitments.

Buy-sell timing decisions for individual assets (or asset classes) are especially amenable to the ES approach, since the goal (but not necessarily the set of rules) lacks complexity. Typically, investment experts use various cues or factors to make timing decisions, and these cues or factors can often be elicited through interviews or inferred from examples.

Dynamic strategies similar to those discussed in Section 3.9 involve making incremental rather than wholesale changes to the portfolio. These strategies may be directed through interaction with an ES; for example, an ES could rebalance a portfolio between cash and stock index futures in a constant-proportion insurance strategy. The purchase and sale of options as a hedging mechanism could also be categorized as a dynamic strategy because of the relatively short-term nature of such hedges. Yet another example of a dynamic strategy is to continually revise optimally diversified portfolios in response to an incoming stream of relevant data.

For prescreening, ESs can also be constructed that will systematically and consistently apply inclusion criteria (in addition to risk and return) to specific asset classes; for example, a manager of commercial real estate investments could select projects from a short list generated with the assistance of an ES that employs expert-derived criteria related to location, type, size, age, projected financial performance, and so on. The next system to be discussed implements such screening operations quite effectively.

4.4   AN EARLY ES FOR PORTFOLIO SELECTION

Clarkson (1963) made one of the earliest attempts to apply artificial intelligence to investment decision making, using a system that allowed a computer to imitate a manager's selection of common stocks for bank trust fund portfolios. The human who was managing these funds used criteria such as the stocks' quality (e.g., whether or not they were held by another leading trust institution) and historical performance record to make selections. With the system developed by Clarkson, more than two-thirds of the stocks chosen by the computer for four test accounts, ranging from income to high growth, were identical to those selected by the human. The remainder were in the same industry group and of similar risk. Since the stocks were chosen for long-term investment, this was essentially a static diversification problem.

The system operated in several stages. First, an "A" list of stocks was created, based on the current value of each stock as well as its average value over 10 years and the rate of change of that value. Expectations relating to the economy, industry, and 10 company attributes were also factored in. Next, a relative value list, based on a three-year forecast of earnings per share, was created; from this list, a set of "B" stocks was drawn up for potential inclusion in each common and individual account. Which stocks were selected for this B list depended on the account's specific goals.

From a historical perspective, the success of Clarkson's system is remarkable considering that ES programming languages and shells were not available at the time. By the mid-1980s, the widespread availability of such tools had caused both investors and academicians to take renewed interest in ES applications for investment management as well as for other applications.

4.5   CONTEMPORARY SYSTEMS

Because security analysis is a time-consuming and error-prone process, it can be improved considerably by automation. In 1988, Kandt and Yuenger developed an ES workstation that could help an operator perform technical and fundamental analyses for stock selection. Kandt and Yuenger's system analyzes the signals generated by various indicators, oscillators, and indexes, determines the appropriateness of these signals in light of current economic conditions, and then makes acquisition and diversification decisions. Their system also incorporates interday heuristic rules related to statistical evidence, such as

IF   the first five trading days are up by 1 percent
THEN   the year will be too, by about 20 percent
WITH   93 percent certainty;

intraday rules such as

IF   the opening has been strong
THEN   a sell-off may occur between 10:30 and 11:00;

and rules related to recurring patterns in stock movements. Most of the data the system needs are acquired electronically, which drastically reduces the tedium and errors associated with human input. Rules are validated by replaying past history against the knowledge base, with wide latitude given for experimenting to see how new algorithms and heuristics perform on actual data.

One ES developed exclusively as an aid in recognizing investment opportunities is the Washington Square Advisors WATCHDOG Investment Monitoring System (Gerkey and Landerholm, 1988). WATCHDOG screens commercially available financial data on over 7,000 companies using about 15 financial ratios and analyzes trends and changes in risk measures. Its knowledge base incorporates the experience and skills of two expert financial analysts who concentrate on corporate bond investments. A junior analyst using WATCHDOG was reportedly able to accomplish in an hour what had previously taken experts weeks to do. An interesting financial analysis application in a related domain is the LBOCON ES, which assesses the soundness of potential takeover candidates (Mostert, Chandra, and Rao, 1989). Using rules based on publicly available financial ratios, this system identifies prospective candidates for leveraged buyouts.

Through electronic means, a large amount of economic and financial information can now be accessed rapidly and accurately. Rau (1988) describes a knowledge-based system for text retrieval, developed at GE's Corporate Research and Development Center, that signals potential takeover targets and other nonrecurring investment opportunities. The system, called SCISOR (System for Conceptual Information Summarization, Organization and Retrieval), was developed using the AI language LISP. Its function is to develop natural language synopses of the history of news releases in a particular domain from diverse sources through the use of an array of novel mapping, pattern selection, and restriction operations. SCISOR produces summaries of activities such as stock price movements, purchase offers, and status of transactions.

Having real-time data available is necessary to do most forms of program trading, including index arbitrage. Liang and Chen (1987) describe a prototype system used for this purpose, called PROTRADER. In this system, rules are developed for monitoring both trading and position-unwinding signals from the market. The spot-future premium level is continuously compared with statistical limits computed from an analysis of recent premium means and standard deviations. The rules generate a sophisticated variance-based dynamic strategy that is highly responsive to changes in the volatility of the market.

In contrast to the relatively focused domains of opportunity-seizing systems, the knowledge bases of ES that assist in diversification usually do not require real-time, or even daily, maintenance. The purpose of these systems is to develop portfolios that not only meet certain industry or other diversification constraints, but are also risk-return efficient and capable of achieving other investment goals.

One such ES, called FOLIO, is an expert assistant for professional money managers (Cohen and Lieberman, 1988). FOLIO is used to allocate account assets across funds rather than select individual securities. It employs nine asset classes, including high-growth stocks; dividend-oriented, low-growth stocks; tax-free bonds; and government and highly rated bonds. The average degree of risk and return in each fund is a known quantity.

The ES portion of FOLIO selects client goals and measures the importance of these goals to each account. There are 14 types of goals, ranging from hedges to goals associated with balancing risk and income from different sources. FOLIO has three major components: a set of interview functions, a formal chaining production rule system for inferring clients' goals, and a goal programming algorithm that minimizes the deviation of the portfolio from the goals that FOLIO is to satisfy. In this application, the ES only selects goals and their weights; the goal programming algorithm allocates assets to various funds.

Another example of a successful contemporary commercial portfolio management ES is the LA-COURTIER security advisory system, developed by Cognitive Systems. In contrast to FOLIO, which was developed to assist the professional manager, LA-COURTIER is designed to assist wealthy individual investors who are customers of its sponsor, a Belgian bank. This ES performs many of the same functions a portfolio advisory consultant would, thus saving the bank the expense of assigning a trained investment counselor to each branch.

After interviewing customers to collect information about their financial situation, LA-COURTIER makes specific recommendations as to which stock and other investment purchases would be appropriate for each customer. Users can interrupt the system to ask questions or express likes or dislikes. If a customer rejects a specific security recommendation, the system will revise the suggested portfolio to exclude that security or its industry group. In addition, users can query the database for specific information about individual securities, such as price or earnings.

Similar in function to the LA-COURTIER system is an ES called INVEST, which was developed for a large German bank (Heuer, Koch, and Cryer, 1988). INVEST is a frame-based system that dialogues with bank officials when they make investment recommendations to their clients. Frames, which avoid the predicate redundancies sometimes seen in production rules, are an efficient means of representing knowledge. Frame-based systems employ the principle of inheritance, which makes it possible to define general facts only once. During a consultation with INVEST, information is first built up about the customer; this customer profile then determines any subsequent questions to be asked. The developers assert that all investment possibilities in the German securities market can be represented by about 50 basic hypotheses, which the system seeks to validate or invalidate. The inference engine on which INVEST was developed employs a matching mechanism across frames that returns a number between $-1,000$ (exact opposite) and $+1,000$ (identical). The matching process is ideal for comparing a particular customer's profile with a prototype for which the appropriate advice has already been developed. Problems of effectively interfacing such consultant systems with the user are discussed in detail by King (1988). With the rapid growth of public and private corporate-sponsored personal financial planning in the 1990s, a huge market has developed for systems, such as Applied Expert Systems' popular Plan Power product, that "advise the adviser."

The potential of rule induction for improving investment timing decisions was shown in a study done by Braun and Chandler in 1987. This study, which used an ES software package designed for this purpose, used past examples of a market analyst's behavior to formulate decision rules. These rules were developed to predict the expert's in- and out-of-market calls as well as actual market movement. This approach freed the knowledge engineer from having to explicitly elicit the decision model from the decision maker through a lengthy interview process.

The performance of the expert, who relied more on technical than on fundamental analysis to make predictions, was very good over the period examined, with average annual returns in excess of 40 percent. Potential cues included economic, financial, and subjective indexes and their direction of change. The rules induced from 60 examples accurately predicted the analyst's timing calls about 50 percent of the time and accurately predicted market movements an average of 64.4 percent of the time. The latter predictive performance was approximately as good as that of the expert.

Other ESs developed for portfolio selection include NYU's PMIDSS (Portfolio Management Intelligent Decision Support System) and The Athena Group's Portfolio Management Advisor (see Lee and Stohr [1985] and The Athena Group [1987]). The former approaches the problems of timing and selection simultaneously, but was somewhat experimental; the latter evolved into a commercial product supporting several portfolio management methodologies. Another early experimental system, ISPMS (Intelligent Stock Portfolio Management System), the precursor to the K-FO-LIO ES described later in this book, integrated the Markowitz quadratic programming optimization model with representation and inference of an expert's personal preferences as well as knowledge (Lee, Trippi, Chu, and Kim, 1990).

4.6   EMERGING ARTIFICIAL INTELLIGENCE TECHNOLOGIES

Several promising AI-related technologies had emerged by the early 1990s. These include neural networks, inductive learning, syntactic pattern recognition, genetic algorithms, fuzzy logic, case-based reasoning, and chaos theory.

Neural network theory has its origins in the study of the brain. The average human brain is composed of 10^{11} neurons with 10^{15} connections, as depicted in Figure 4.3. An important biological insight is that although its neuron-processing time is only at the millisecond level, the human brain can perform pattern classification tasks much faster than today's nanosecond-speed Von Neumann computers. This suggests that a drastic architectural revolution is needed to effectuate the requisite pattern recognition for image processing, voice recognition, and natural language processing.

The neural network paradigm is referred to as *connectionism*, because the concept of memory in the artificial neural network is based on the collection of connecting weights between neuronlike processing elements. Although both hardware and software designed to simulate aspects of the human brain have come a long way in terms of capabilities and usability,

Figure 4.3
Interconnected Biological Neurons

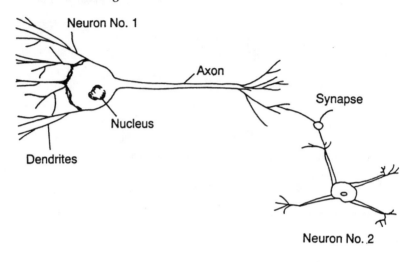

the intention of such products is not to create humanlike creatures but to devise tools with which to solve particular problems more effectively than with traditional methods.

Investors' interest in artificial neural networks centers on whether or not this technology can consistently outperform existing classification techniques such as regression analysis, multiple discriminant analysis, and inductive-learning schemes. Because of their multiple-layered architectures, these neural networks are able to capture implicit nonlinear relationships between input and output variable sets better than competing methods. Thus, expenditures on neural networks in the investment community have become substantial. Several large mutual funds routinely use neural networks for either portfolio selection or timing decisions. Chapter 10 focuses in greater detail on the use of neural networks in investing.

Among the other popular machine-learning schemes, the one with the most widely available commercial software is based on decision tree *induction* from past instances. This approach selects paired attribute values that can contribute most to reducing uncertainty in the discrimination of events into classes. This process is repeated incrementally, branching deeper and deeper into a treelike structure until the current attribute value set is sufficiently reliable for the intended use. In this way, any decision tree can be transformed into rules, and the resulting rules can be automatically fed into the rule base. In addition, since the events can be represented both qualitatively and quantitatively, this method offers some advantages over statistical regression analysis, which can handle qualitative factors only in a limited way through the use of dummy variables.

An important feature of both neural networks and tree-based inductive learning is that neither approach is dependent on data following a particular empirical distribution, such as the normal distribution. However, a trade-off occurs in terms of the testing capabilities that normal distribution–based statistical analyses can provide. In general, the only usable measures of performance for these techniques are those related to the number or magnitude of errors in the testing cycle, which may or may not be sufficient for investment applications. For more on this issue, refer to Section 9.3.

Another fairly new approach, *syntactic pattern recognition,* attempts to evolve elementary patterns into higher-level composite patterns along the lines of the syntactic grammar of composition. Typically beginning with multiple sets of chart and numerical data, this method focuses on the precedence and concurrence relationships among primitive patterns. As the primitives are composed of increasingly salient composite patterns, the predictive power becomes more effective. This approach has not yet been widely adopted in the financial domain, but experimental results have been quite promising (e.g., see Lee, Kim, and Trippi, 1992). Syntactic pattern recognition is discussed in more detail in Section 9.4.

Genetic algorithms (GAs) are another type of learning scheme. GAs can be used for rule optimization in knowledge-based systems through a process in which an initially randomly selected rule set is evolved toward more effective rule sets. At each iteration, genetic operators such as crossover, inversion, and mutation are applied to generate new potential rules. The new rules are evaluated using an evaluation function (sometimes called a *fitness value*), and the best rules survive into the next generation. Since GA is a method for sampling a subset of the solution space, it is best suited to those problems in which the solution space is too large to be enumerated, typically due to a high order of dimensionality. Although a number of researchers are applying GAs to investment selection and timing problems, the method has yet to prove its utility in the investment world. GA is discussed in more detail in Section 9.5.

Fuzzy logic and *fuzzy set theory* are other buzzwords to which investment professionals are becoming increasingly exposed. From the expert systems standpoint, a fuzzy expert system provides a way to handle uncertainty in knowledge and its inference, referred to as *approximate reasoning*. An easy-to-understand and quite usable type of fuzzy logic system component is described in Section 7.5. Although frameworks for applying fairly sophisticated fuzzy logic "possibility" distributions have been demonstrated in some research papers (e.g., see part 3 of Deboeck, 1994), their usefulness has yet to be proven.

Case-based reasoning (CBR) is another important knowledge representation and inferencing method. The idea behind CBR is to reuse past actual cases wherever possible. The first step, then, is to store past cases in a usable format. The next step is to find those cases that are most similar to the current case to be resolved. For this purpose, the cases are indexed and a measure of similarity is defined for use in retrieving the "closest" old case to a new case. The retrieved case is adjusted after identifying discrepancies between the new case and the retrieved case. At this adjustment stage, domain knowledge must be available. CBR may be combined with case-based learning (not the same thing as inductive learning if the structures of cases are identical). Integrated architectures of cases and rules are common in the use of CBR (Rissland and Skalak, 1989).

Applications of CBR in investment decision making can be found in Buta and Barletta (1991), Chi, Chen, and Kiang (1993), Berg-Cross and Claudio (1991), and Slade (1991). Although their demonstrations of specific CBR frameworks are interesting, an important issue in applying CBR to investment problems is CBR's lack of generalization capability. As mentioned earlier, CBR looks for the closest single historical case that is believed to be consistent with the present case. Since much white noise occurs in the investment domain, it is not always true that the best-fitting case will provide the best solution. Moreover, the adjustment process is often difficult. Neural networks, on the other hand, are not subject to these problems. Therefore, it may be advantageous to combine CBR with a neural network configured to override the CBR in those investment decisions in which the most relevant factors are numeric. However, CBR may be still be used to provide insights and serve an explanatory purpose by showing the analyst similar past cases.

The last issue to be addressed in this section is *chaos theory*, which originated in the physical sciences. Chaos theory deals with behavior arising in nonlinear systems that seems random but actually has some hidden order. Many analysts believe the weather and stock and bond prices exhibit such properties. A "chaotic" process is one that, although deterministic, generates time paths of variables of interest that give the appearance of being generated by some random process. Obviously, the notion of the existence of at least some deterministic component in the dynamics of prices has great appeal to those interested in incorporating forecasts of the time paths of market prices into their investment decisions.

In recent years, a considerable body of research has accumulated that attempts to view stock, commodity, and other financial markets as chaotic, nonlinear systems (e.g., Larrain, 1991; Scheinkman and LeBaron, 1989; Hsieh, 1991; Willey, 1992; Chen, 1988; Mayfield and Mizrach, 1992; Peters, 1991; part 4 of Deboeck, 1994). Powerful statistical tests specifically designed to detect chaos in seemingly random time series have been developed, and neural networks have been applied to the detection of such chaotic components (Deco, Schuermann, and Trippi, 1995). For a comprehensive survey of chaos theory applied to the financial markets, see Trippi (1995).

4.7   CONCLUSIONS

The application of knowledge-based systems to portfolio selection and related investment management activities is still at a relatively early stage, with much of the current work still taking place at the research level. As we have seen, auto-learning systems have certain advantages for knowledge acquisition. Although generally more difficult to implement initially, machine learning can offer significant benefits when reliable expert knowledge is difficult or impossible to come by and when pattern recognition capability is important.

To date, the most successful commercial deployments have been consultant systems for assisting professionals in one or more specific aspects of their work, such as formulation of goals and preferences or implementation of a particular investment strategy. Preprogrammed personal computer "black box" ESs for security selection have become popular for personal investing (e.g., AIQ Systems' STOCKEXPERT), and investment recommendations based on such systems' assessments are offered through subscriber services accessible via computer modem. Many ready-made neural network software products that address various investment markets and are at different levels of sophistication are available to both institutional and individual investors. New techniques are continually emerging, some of which may prove viable enough to eventually become generally accepted tools for investment decision making.

ENDNOTES

1. Much of the material in this chapter originally appeared in Trippi (1990).

2. The references preceded by asterisks are reprinted in Trippi and Turban (1990).

REFERENCES[2]

The Athena Group. "Portfolio Management Advisor." *Expert Systems*, February 1987, pp. 54–65.

Berg-Cross, G., and L. Claudio. "Master: A Case-Based Design to Augment Corporate Mergers and Acquisitions Decisions." *Proceedings of the First International Conference on Artificial Intelligence Applications on Wall Street*, 1991, pp. 188–93.

Bestor, J. "Using Expert Systems to Improve Lenders' Performance During Mergers and Acquisitions." *Journal of Commercial Bank Lending,* March 1987, pp. 10–16.

* Braun, H., and J. Chandler. "Predicting Stock Market Behavior Through Rule Induction: An Application of the Learning-From-Example Approach." *Decision Sciences* 18 (1987), pp. 415–29.

Buta, P., and R. Barletta. "Case-Based Reasoning for Market Surveillance." *Proceedings of the First International Conference on Artificial Intelligence Applications on Wall Street,* 1991, pp. 116–21.

Chen, P. "Empirical and Theoretical Evidence of Economic Chaos." *Systems Dynamics Review* 4, no. 2 (1988), pp. 81–108.

Chi, R., M. Chen, and M. Y. Kiang. "Generalized Case-Based Reasoning System for Portfolio Management." *Expert Systems with Applications* 6 (1993), pp. 67–76.

* Clarkson, G. P. "A Model of the Trust Investment Process." *Computers and Thought,* edited by E. Feigenbaum and J. Feldman. New York: McGraw-Hill, 1963.

* Cohen, P., and M. Lieberman. "A Report on Folio: An Expert Assistant for Portfolio Managers." *Proceedings of the International Joint Conference on Artificial Intelligence,* 1988, pp. 212–14.

Deboeck, G. J. *Trading on the Edge: Neural, Genetic, and Fuzzy Systems for Chaotic Financial Markets.* New York: John Wiley & Sons, Inc., 1994.

Deco, G., B. Schuermann, and R. Trippi. "Neural Learning of Chaotic Time Series Invariants." In *Chaos and Nonlinear Dynamics in the Financial Markets: Theory, Evidence, and Applications,* edited by R. Trippi. Burr Ridge, IL: Irwin Professional Publishing, 1995, pp. 467–88.

* Friedland, J. "The Expert Systems Revolution." *Institutional Investor,* July 1988, pp. 77–90.

* Gerkey, P., and K. Landerholm. "Watchdog Investment Monitoring System." *PC AI,* July–August 1988, pp. 14–17.

* Heuer, S., U. Koch, and C. Cryer. "INVEST: An Expert System for Financial Investments." *IEEE Expert,* Summer 1988, pp. 60–68.

Holsapple, C., A. Whinston, and K. Tam. "Inductive Approaches to Acquire Trading Rules." *ES in Business '87 Proceedings,* 1987, pp. 103–19.

Hsieh, D. A. "Chaos and Nonlinear Dynamics: Application to Financial Markets." *Journal of Finance* 46, no. 5 (1991), pp. 1839–77.

* Kandt, K., and Yuenger, P. "A Trader's Workstation." *Proceedings, 1988 Annual Meeting, Decision Sciences Institute,* 1988, pp. 298–301.

King, D. "Building Computerized Financial Advisors: The User Model and Human Interface." Working paper, Execucom Systems Corporation, 1988.

Larrain, M. "Testing Chaos and Nonlinearities in T-Bill Rates." *Financial Analysts Journal,* September–October 1991, pp. 51–62.

* Lee, J. K., S. Chu, and H. Kim. "Intelligent Stock Portfolio Management System." *Expert Systems* 6, no. 2 (April 1989), pp. 74–87.

Lee, J. K., H. S. Kim, and R. R. Trippi. "Security Trading Rule Synthesis: A Syntactic Pattern-Based Learning Approach." *Heuristics: The Journal of Knowledge Engineering* 5, no. 4 (Winter 1992), pp. 47–61.

* Lee, J. B., and E. Stohr. "Representing Knowledge for Portfolio Management Decision Making." *Proceedings of the Second Conference on Artificial Intelligence,* 1985.

Lee, J. K., R. R. Trippi, S. Chu, and H. Kim. "K-FOLIO: Integrating the Markowitz Model with a Knowledge-Based System." *Journal of Portfolio Management* 16, no. 5 (Fall 1990), pp. 89–93.

* Liang, T., and K. Chen. "Issues in Developing Expert Systems for Program Trading." *ES in Business '87 Proceedings,* 1987, pp. 145–59.

Mayfield, E. S., and B. Mizrach. "On Determining the Dimension of Real-Time Stock-Price Data." *Journal of Business and Economic Statistics* 40, no. 3 (1992), pp. 367–74.

Mostert, J., M. Chandra, and S. Rao. "LBOCON Leveraged Buy Out Consultant: An Application of Expert Systems in Finance." *Proceedings, 1989 Annual Meeting, Decision Sciences Institute,* New Orleans, 1989.

Newell, A., and H. A. Simon. *Human Problem Solving.* Englewood Cliffs, NJ: Prentice Hall, 1972.

Peters, E. E. "A Chaotic Attractor for the S&P 500." *Financial Analysts Journal,* March–April 1991, pp. 55–62.

Peters, E. E. *Chaos and Order in the Capital Markets.* New York: John Wiley & Sons, 1991.

Rau, L. "Conceptual Information Extraction from Financial News." *Proceedings of the Hawaii International Conference on Systems Science,* 1988, pp. 501–9.

Rissland, E. L., and D. B. Skalak. "Combining Case-Based and Rule-Based Reasoning: A Heuristic Approach." *Proceeding of the International Joint Conference on Artificial Intelligence,* 1989, pp. 524–30.

Scheinkman, J. A., and B. LeBaron. "Nonlinear Dynamics and Stock Returns." *Journal of Business* 62, no. 3 (1989), pp. 311–37.

Shannon, S. "The 'Expert' That Thinks Like an Underwriter." *Management Technology,* February 1985.

Slade, S. "Case-based Reasoning for Financial Decision Making." *Proceedings of the First International Conference on Artificial Intelligence Applications on Wall Street,* 1991, pp. 232–37.

Sviokla, J. "Expert Systems and Their Impact on the Firm: The Effects of Planpower Use on the Information-Processing Capacity of the Financial Collaborative." *Proceedings of the Hawaii International Conference on Systems Science,* 1988, pp. 791–802.

* Talluru, L. R., and V. Akgiray. "Knowledge Representation for Investment Strategy Selection." *Proceedings of the Hawaii International Conference on Systems Science,* 1988.

Talluru, L. R., and V. Akgiray. "Problem Representation in Decision Support Systems: An Illustration from Financial Investments." *Proceedings, 1990 Annual Meeting, Decision Sciences Institute,* San Diego, 1990, pp. 481–83.

Trippi, R. "Intelligent Systems for Investment Decision Making." In *Managing Institutional Assets,* edited by F. Fabozzi. New York: Harper & Row, 1990.

Trippi, R. *Chaos and Nonlinear Dynamics in the Financial Markets: Theory, Evidence, and Applications.* Burr Ridge, IL: Irwin Professional Publishing, 1995.

Trippi, R., and E. Turban. *Investment Management: Decision Support and Expert Systems.* Boston: Boyd & Fraser Div., Southwestern Publishing Company, 1990; New York: Van Nostrand Reinhold, 1991.

Willey, T. "Testing for Nonlinear Dependence in Daily Stock Indexes." *Journal of Economics and Business* 44, no. 1 (February 1992), pp. 63–76.

CHAPTER 5

Portfolio-Selection System Issues

5.1 Expert System Components
5.2 Rule-Based Systems
    5.2.1 Representation in Rule-Based Systems
    5.2.2 Inference Strategies
5.3 Frame-Based Systems
5.4 Investment Support Features
    5.4.1 Knowledge Representation
    5.4.2 Inference and Explanation
    5.4.3 Knowledge Acquisition and Maintenance
    5.4.4 System Architecture

5.1 EXPERT SYSTEM COMPONENTS

As discussed earlier, artificial intelligence is the branch of information science concerned with enabling computers to imitate human intelligence. The question is: To what degree can a computer be made to imitate the intellectual activities that make a human expert in an area such as security analysis? To design a knowledge-based system, it is necessary to understand exactly what the required type and level of intelligence are.

As Figure 5.1 shows (Forsyth, 1984; Waterman, 1986), the key elements of a traditional expert system are a knowledge base, an inference

Figure 5.1
Typical Expert System Architecture

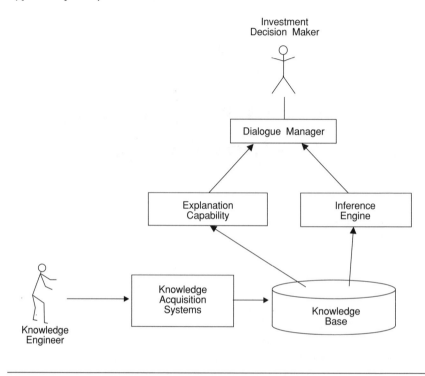

engine, explanation capability, and a knowledge acquisition system. The goals of the system are achieved through the effective management of knowledge. If the fields of AI are mapped with the architecture of expert systems, they will have the correspondence summarized in Table 5.1.

1. The knowledge representation chosen—for example, *rules*—provides the syntax of the specific knowledge base. By knowledge, most ES developers mean a set of certain types of symbolic expressions in contrast to numeric ones.

2. Reasoning, logical inference, and problem-solving capabilities are normally built into the ES's inference engine. In the AI literature, the term *problem solving* refers to a methodology for *finding paths from initial status to goal status*. Problem-solving

Table 5.1
Relationship between Expert Systems and Artificial Intelligence

Expert System Components	Artificial Intelligence Fields
Knowledge base	Knowledge representation
Inference engine	Reasoning, logic, problem solving
Explanation capability	Reasoning, logic, problem solving
Knowledge acquisition system	Machine learning
Dialogue manager	Natural language processing
	Voice recognition

techniques include general problem solver and search algorithms, some of which have been given names (e.g., the A^* algorithm).

3. Explanation synthesis is a type of inference used to justify a certain conclusion and organize the justification information in a form suitable for interpretation by the decision maker.

4. Intelligent editing capability is a virtual necessity for a knowledge acquisition system. Machine learning is one mechanism for automating knowledge acquisition. Vision may also be used to recognize iconic or visual information during the knowledge acquisition process.

5. Natural language processing and voice recognition may be beneficially employed to provide a user-friendly dialogue.

Many expert system researchers agree that AI is a major source for enriching ES; however, AI is not the only source. Investment decision experts also use mathematical programming models for optimization and statistical models for estimation. (Without these decision aids, the ES would imitate a handicapped expert and produce unsatisfactory results.) To choose the appropriate tools, it is necessary to expand the notion of a knowledge base and inference engine. Numerical models may be seen as another type of knowledge representation and algorithms, such as a simplex algorithm to solve linear programming problems, as a means of numerical inference for problem solving. To expand and unify the notion of representation and inference, it will be helpful to reinterpret mathematical models from the ES's point of view.

In addition, machine learning and statistical inference are closely related. One major goal of statistics is to extract parameters from a large data set; thus, statistical methods such as discriminant and regression analysis could be used as a means of inductive learning.

For these reasons, the architecture of integrating knowledge and mathematical models is an important topic. Chapter 11 focuses on the integration of an optimization problem derived from the Markowitz model with a knowledge base. Before studying the characteristics of ES for investment decisions, however, it will be beneficial to review the terminology and basic concepts of knowledge representation and inference strategies for rule- and frame-based systems.

5.2   RULE-BASED SYSTEMS

Some typical knowledge representation schemes used in commercial expert system building tools are rules and frames. The term *frame* can be used interchangeably with the term *object*.

5.2.1   Representation in Rule-Based Systems

A rule-based system contains two types of knowledge: rules and facts. A rule is composed of a pair of conditions and actions. Figure 5.2 shows a part of the rule base that can be used as an investment decision aid.

Facts are a collection of assertions and derivations from the rules. A fact base is sometimes called a *database*. For example, assume the following facts are known about a certain stock:

Industry	= Electronics
Debt Ratio	= 80%
Growth Rate	= 40%

Using the above facts, which could have been retrieved from a simple database, the following facts may be derived according to Rule 21 and Rule 31:

Growth	= High
Debt	= Low

Figure 5.2
Rule Examples

RULE	Rule 10	
IF	Industry	= Electronics
AND	Debt	= Low
AND	Growth	= High
THEN	Grade	= AA or AAA
RULE	Rule 21	
IF	Growth Rate	≥ 30%
THEN	Growth	= High
RULE	Rule 22	
IF	Growth Rate	< 30%
AND	Growth Rate	≥ 10%
THEN	Growth	= Medium
RULE	Rule 23	
IF	Growth Rate	< 10%
THEN	Growth	= Low
RULE	Rule 31	
IF	Debt Ratio	≤ 100%
THEN	Debt	= Low

It is also possible to derive the following fact according to Rule 10:

$$Grade = AA \text{ or } AAA$$

This sort of fact base may be generated for each consulting session and for each stock.

5.2.2   Inference Strategies

There are two general types of inference strategies: forward chaining and backward chaining. To explain these strategies, the rule base is converted to an acyclic AND/OR digraph (see Figure 5.3). *Digraph* means *directed graph,* while the arc in the figure indicates the AND relationship.

Figure 5.3
An Illustrative AND/OR Digraph

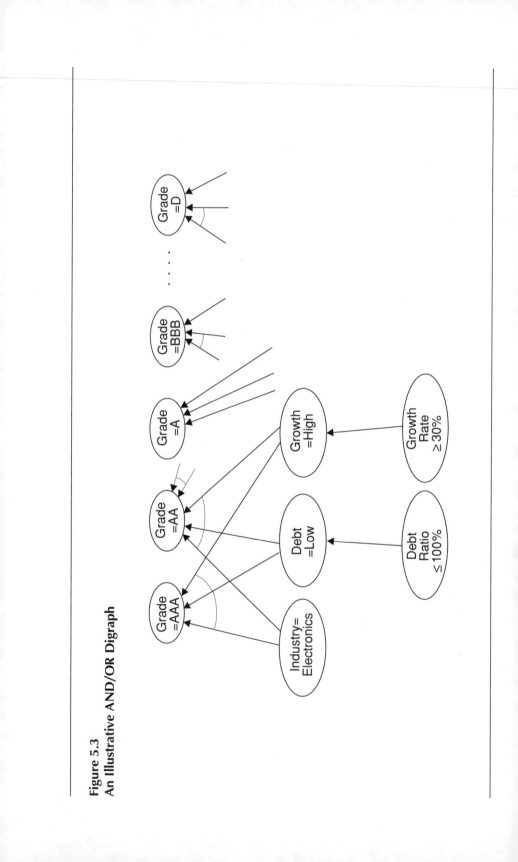

Forward-Chaining Strategy

From the graph, forward chaining begins the reasoning process by asking about the facts at the leaf nodes, such as industry, debt ratio, and growth rate. Once the facts are given, the debt and growth status are derived by tracing the directed nodes. The iteration is continued until a certain conclusion is reached, at which time the inference is ended. The forward chaining strategy is sometimes called a *bottom-up strategy* or *data-driven inference.*

Backward-Chaining Strategy

A backward chaining strategy starts with a conclusion node such as *Grade = AAA.* To confirm whether or not an indicated stock satisfies the conclusion, the system traces down the directing nodes, eventually reading leaf nodes such as industry, debt ratio, and growth rate, at which point questions are asked. The first question might be

What is the industry?

If the answer is *Electronics,* more questions will follow concerning debt ratio and growth rate; these, in turn, will be followed by additional questions. If the answers to these questions satisfy the conditions for the current conclusion, the satisfaction of current goal has been confirmed, and the inference process may be stopped. However, if the goal *AAA* is not satisfied, the procedure of searching for satisfaction of next-level goals must be continued in an iterative fashion. Simply showing the rules that are related to the conclusion *Grade = AAA* is often a good source of explanation.

5.3   FRAME-BASED SYSTEMS

Frames are an effective medium for representing the concept of objects, class-instance relationships, and demons (procedures attached to slots, as will be explained later). In a frame, the attributes of an object are represented in *slots* (see Figure 5.4). For instance, in the example frame IBM, there are slots for sales, growth rate, and debt ratio. The value of a slot may be a single value or multiple values in the form of a list. As illustrated by the sales slot, multiple values may be further specified in the lower-level frame or *facet* attached to the slot.

Frames can be arranged in a hierarchical structure (see Figure 5.5). Hierarchical relationships are an effective means of representing the way

Figure 5.4
Structure of Frame-Based Representation

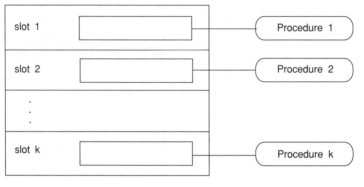

the linked lower-level frames inherit values from the higher-level frames. Bottom-up summation and averaging can also be managed using the hierarchy. The procedures attached to slots are called *demons*. The typical roles of demons fall into three categories:

IF-ADDED	: Execute the procedure when a value is added to the slot.
IF-REMOVED	: Execute the procedure when a value is removed from the slot.
IF-NEEDED	: Execute the procedure when the value of the slot is requested.

Figure 5.5
Hierarchical Structure of Frames

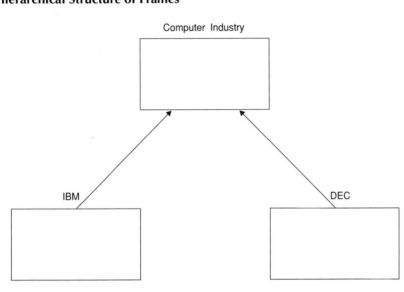

Since frames are just another way of organizing data, the frame base is also called an *object-oriented database*. Therefore, the fact base of a rule-based system may adopt the frame-based representation. Currently the trend is to integrate frames and rules together in this manner. Most advanced tools in the expert system building tool market belong to this category. Well-known software tools include Prokappa, ART-IM, NEXPERT Object, Level-5 Object, G2, EXSYS, VP-EXPERT, and UNIK.

5.4   INVESTMENT SUPPORT FEATURES

The following are some distinctive characteristics of the expert systems that support security investment decisions. Each of them will be examined in more detail in later chapters.

5.4.1   Knowledge Representation

Knowledge representation for investment must satisfy the following requirements.

Industry versus Company Classification

Since information must be kept at both the industry level and the individual company level, it is necessary to distinguish between the class (e.g., industry) and individuals within the class (e.g., particular companies). Classifying criteria such as countries or sectors may also be used as higher-level classes. Frame-based representation makes it possible to handle these features in an efficient manner. The inheritance of industry data by individual companies, as well as the averaging up and summing up of individual companies' data into the class, is facilitated by the frame representation. The *exception* representation is also necessary to express a situation such as

Good industry except for bad companies in the industry
or
Bad industry except for good companies in the industry

Uncertainty Handling

In the illustrative rules given in Figure 5.2, no uncertainties exist. In practice, however, it is rare to come to a conclusion with 100 percent confidence. Therefore, it is desirable that each rule contain information about the *level of confidence*. The same holds true for facts. For example, a company may sell both electronic products and machinery. In this case, the industry classification is not deterministic. Again, estimated values about sales amount and growth rate cannot normally be predicted with 100% confidence. Therefore, facts also need to contain confidence-level information. (Uncertainty issues are dealt with further in Chapters 6 and 7.)

Multiple Sources of Knowledge

Knowledge may be acquired from several sources. At the minimum, a commonly shared expert's knowledge must be distinguished from each individual investor's knowledge and preferences. To accommodate diverse sources of knowledge, the syntax of the knowledge should be uniform and conflicting knowledge from different sources should be systematically resolvable. (See Chapter 8.)

Integration with Optimization

Since an optimization model such as the Markowitz model can be used as a tool in portfolio decision making, integration of knowledge with the appropriate optimization model should be attempted. (See Chapter 11.)

Integration with a Database

Since historical data about stock prices, trading volumes, and financial statements can be effectively maintained in a traditional database such as a flat-file or relational database, integration of the ES with such a database is essential. (See Chapters 8 and 12.)

5.4.2   Inference and Explanation

To identify the ES inference and explanation capabilities required, it is necessary to define the dialogue capability appropriate to investment. Typical dialogues might be the following.

Individual Stock Evaluation

Each individual stock may be evaluated and classified into one of the following 10 grades: AAA, AA, A, BBB, BB, B, CCC, CC, C, or D. Grading stocks is essentially a classification problem involving the concepts of value discussed in Chapters 2 and 3. Either a forward- or backward-chaining inference strategy may be adopted; however, since some numeric factors are compensatory in grading, these factors may have to be combined through a weighted linear combination scheme. Thus, the inference method described in this book is not exactly the same as the typical forward- and backward-chaining strategies. (See Chapter 8.)

Industry-Level Evaluation

Stocks in an industry may be evaluated with the same grading scheme that is used for individual stock evaluation.

Criteria-Based Evaluation

The grade of a group of stocks that satisfy certain criteria may be requested by the user. If the questioned criterion is exactly the same as that in a rule already available, the grade can be directly retrieved from the conclusion part of the rule. If the criterion is not exactly the same, however, a conclusion should be synthesized through a case-based reasoning process.

Ordering Stocks by Grade

This is a simple sorting of stocks that have already been evaluated.

Explanation Generation

The rules associated with a certain conclusion should be organized to explain the reasons a stock has been evaluated in a certain way. After examining the reasons, the decision maker may wish to change the weights of some reasons interactively. Therefore, there is a need to support interactive sensitivity analysis from the explanation screen.

Dynamic Decision Making

A sequence of dynamic selling/buying decisions for a stock may be necessary for some investment strategies.

5.4.3   Knowledge Acquisition and Maintenance

To accommodate the changing security market environment, a user-friendly knowledge-editing and machine-learning process should be supported.

Knowledge-Editing Aids

Classifying knowledge categories is useful for deciding the relative locations of frames to be added, updated, or deleted.

Meta-Knowledge Guide

To determine how frequently a particular type of knowledge needs to be updated, the expected life span of each knowledge component should be maintained. The bits of knowledge that exhaust their life spans each day can be displayed so that their authors can review the knowledge to decide whether to delete, modify, or extend its life span. The names of these authors should also be kept so that the knowledge of each individual author can be accessed while maintaining an appropriate level of security protection.

Machine Learning

Inductive learning schemes, such as ID3 and neural networks, can be used to generate rules from instances of historical investment data. For example, when charts are used to search for buy or sell cues, a facility for automatic recognition of patterns and synthesis of rules from those patterns is necessary. (See Chapter 9.)

5.4.4   System Architecture

The expert system known as K-FOLIO effectively handles many of the issues raised in this chapter. Its overall architecture is shown in Figure 5.6. The K-FOLIO system will be used to illustrate many of the concepts discussed in subsequent chapters.

REFERENCES

Forsyth, R., ed. *Expert Systems: Principles and Case Studies.* New York: Chapman Hall Computing, 1984.

Waterman, D. A. *A Guide to Expert Systems.* Reading, MA: Addison-Wesley, 1986.

Figure 5.6
Architecture of K-FOLIO

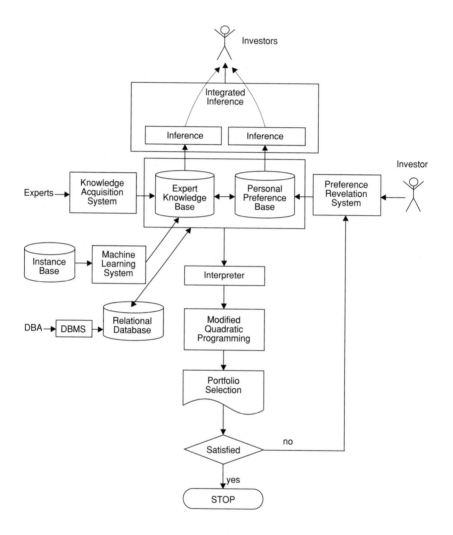

CHAPTER 6

Knowledge Representation and Inference

6.1   Introduction
6.2   The Rule Base
    6.2.1   Syntax of Rules
    6.2.2   Example Rules
6.3   The Database
    6.3.1   Relational Database Examples
    6.3.2   Inheritance, Average-up, and Sum-up
    6.3.3   Working Memory
6.4   Security Inference
    6.4.1   Conflict-Set Generation
    6.4.2   Composite-Grade Generation
    6.4.3   Explanation Synthesis
6.5   Dialogues
    6.5.1   Company-Based Dialogue
    6.5.2   Industry-Based Dialogue
    6.5.3   Criteria-Based Dialogue
    6.5.4   Grade-Based Dialogue
6.6   Conclusions

6.1   INTRODUCTION

This chapter describes how a typical investment ES represents knowledge, evaluates individual stocks, and explains the reasons for its actions. The structure of the knowledge base and inference procedure of K-FOLIO are shown in Figure 6.1 (Lee, Chu, and Kim, 1989). Three key components of K-FOLIO's knowledge system are the rule base, the database, and an inference procedure.

There are three rule bases; these contain company-based, industry-based, and attribute-based rules. Rules incorporate knowledge into the system using a consistent representational format. There are also three databases: a company-based relational database, an industry-based relational database, and a working memory base. The working memory base stores list-type data and derived statements from rules in an unstructured fashion.

The inference procedure begins by matching each rule base with its own relevant databases, which generates a rule set for each individual company and industry. The rule set is called a *conflict set* because each rule may support a different conclusion. The conflict set is used to evaluate stocks and synthesize explanations.

6.2   THE RULE BASE

6.2.1   Syntax of Rules

Figure 6.2 shows the syntax of rules. A rule has the reserved words RULE, CREDIBILITY (CR), IF, AND, OR, GRADE, EXCEPT, THEN, and BE-CAUSE, plus arithmetic operators. CR stands for the credibility of the rule as a percentage between 0 and 100.

6.2.2   Example Rules

Examples of rules appear in Figure 6.3. Note the following:

1. RULE is followed by the rule name.

2. CR stands for the credibility of a rule, expressed as a percentage.

Figure 6.1
Knowledge Management Subsystem

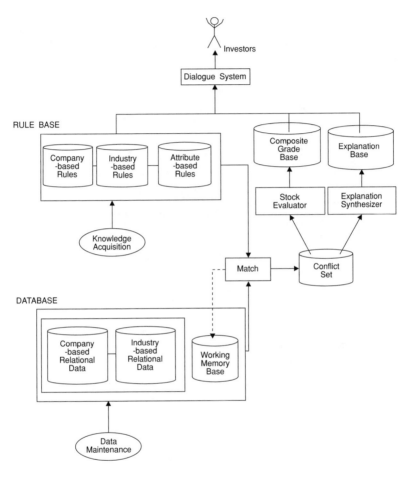

3. The conditional statements are organized in AND and OR relationships.

4. THEN statements conclude with a GRADE such as the ones in rules 40, 42, and 43 or a statement such as the one in Rule 41.

5. An EXCEPT statement, such as the one in Rule 42, excludes a company even if the company satisfies the conditions.

Figure 6.2
Overall Syntax of Rules

RULE   rulename
CREDIBILITY = percentage
IF   statement a
(AND   statement b)
(OR   statement c)

. . .

THEN   statement zz
                GRADE = a grade
                (BECAUSE statement)
                (EXCEPT statement)
Legend
Capital letters : reserved words
( ) : optional statement

6. A BECAUSE statement, such as the one in Rule 40, explains why a stock is given a certain grade.

Rule 40 is a company-based rule; Rule 42 is an industry- and attribute-based rule; and Rules 41 and 43 are attribute-based rules.

6.3   THE DATABASE

6.3.1   Relational Database Examples

Examples of relational databases appear in Figures 6.4 and 6.5. The company-based relational database in Figure 6.4 lists the company name, industry, major market, price-earnings ratio, annual sales growth rate, debt ratio, fixed ratio, sales and amount of exports, and so on. The industry-based relational database includes industry-level information such as preferential tax advantages and stage of life cycle.

Figure 6.3
Example Rules

RULE	Rule 40
CR =	0.7
IF	Company = ABC
THEN	GRADE = A
	BECAUSE The company ABC has developed a new compact disc player.

RULE	Rule 41
CR =	0.6
IF	Major Market = Overseas
AND	Annual Sales Growth Rate $\geq 50\%$
AND	The ratio of indirect and direct financing cost ≥ 1.2
THEN	Issuing convertible bond in the foreign financial market is expected

RULE	Rule 42
CR =	0.6
IF	Industry = Electronics
AND	Issuing convertible bond in the foreign financial market is expected
THEN	GRADE = AA
	EXCEPT Company = KK

RULE	Rule 43
CR =	0.6
IF	P/E Ratio ≥ 10
AND	Debt Ratio $\geq 200\%$
THEN	GRADE = C

6.3.2   Inheritance, Average-up, and Sum-up

Between the industry database and company database, the principles of inheritance, average-up, and sum-up will apply. The attributes of an industry can be inherited by default to the companies that belong to that industry,

Figure 6.4
Company-Based Relational Database

Company	Industry	Major Market	P/E Ratio	Annual Sales Growth Rate	Debt Ratio	Fixed Ratio	Sales	Amount of Exports
ABC	Electronics	Overseas	15.0	90%	500%	450%	60 million	40 million
XYZ	Electronics	Domestic	8.0	60%	400%	300%	120 million	50 million

Figure 6.5
Industry-Based Relational Database

Industry	Tax Benefits	Stage of Life Cycle
Electronics	Preferable	Growth
Shipbuilding	Not Preferable	Decline

and the attributes of companies can be averaged and summed up for the industry. (See Figure 6.6.)

As shown in Figure 6.6, the attributes of the electronics industry, Tax Benefit and Stage of Life Cycle, are inherited by all companies in the industry, except those that have a prespecified value (such as "no preferences" in the Tax Benefit column of company ABC). On the other hand, some average values of attributes of companies, such as the average annual sales growth rate, can be used for the industry. In the same way, the total amount of exports can also be used for the industry.

These derivations can be invoked by the following declarations in the data definition section:

TITLE	INDUSTRY
FATHER	NONE
CHILD	COMPANY
INHERIT	Tax Benefit, Stage of Life Cycle

TITLE	COMPANY
FATHER	INDUSTRY
CHILD	NONE
AVERAGE-UP	Annual Sales Growth Rate
SUM-UP	Amount of Exports

6.3.3   Working Memory

Working memory may be inserted directly into the working memory base, but most working memory will be generated as intermediate outcomes of the matching process (see Figure 6.7).

Figure 6.7 gives four facts about company ABC:

Industry = Electronics
Major Market = Overseas
Annual Sales Growth Rate = 60%
Ratio of Indirect and Direct Financing Cost = 1.3.

Since the currently known facts satisfy the conditions of Rule 11, the conclusion is derived and added to the working memory of company ABC. Other companies, such as company DEF, will also include the derived statement.

Figure 6.6
Inheritance, Average-up, and Sum-up

Industry-Based Database

Industry	Tax Benefit	Stage of Life Cycle	Average Annual Sales Growth Rate	Total Amount of Exports
Electronics	Preferable	Growth	75%	90 million
Shipbuilding	Not Preferable	Decline		

Company-Based Database

Company	Industry	Major Market	P/E Ratio	Annual Sales Growth Rate
ABC	Electronics	Overseas	15.0	90%
XYZ	Electronics	Domestic	8.0	60%

Amount of Exports	Sales	Fixed Ratio	Debt Ratio	Tax Benefits	Stage of Life Cycle
40 million	60 million	450%	500%	Not Preferable	Growth
50 million	120 million	300%	400%	Preferable	Growth

INHERITANCE

AVERAGE-UP

SUM-UP

Figure 6.7
Generated Working Memory in the Matching Process
A Matched Rule

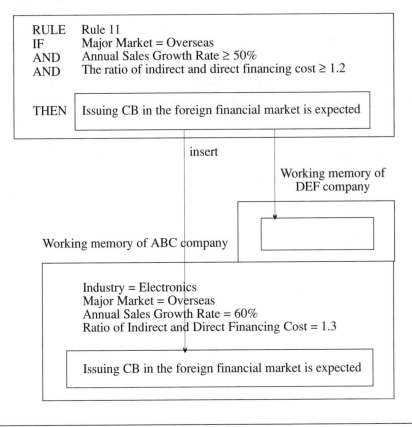

If the conclusion of the matched rule is a GRADE statement, however, the conclusion will not be included in the working memory; rules with GRADE statements are goal rules, which do not have any succeeding rules. The matching process will stop if all the matched rules have GRADE statements.

6.4   SECURITY INFERENCE

The security inference procedure comprises three steps: (1) conflict-set generation, (2) composite-grade generation, and (3) explanation synthesis.

6.4.1   Conflict-Set Generation

The conflict set consists of multiple GRADE-type rules matched for a company or industry. As Figure 6.8 shows, different rules support different grades.

6.4.2   Composite-Grade Generation

To resolve the conflicts in the conflict set, it is necessary to use the grades and CR in the rules to compute a composite grade. To permit numeric computation, the grades are transformed into numbers between −1 and +1. (The mapping values are shown in Table 6.1.)

The rules in the conflict set are then categorized into two groups, one composed of rules that support positive evidence, and the other of rules that support negative evidence. If the evidence conflicts, the positive and nega-

---

Figure 6.8
Rules in Conflict Set of Company ABC

RULE	Rule 40
CR =	0.7
IF	Company = ABC
THEN	Grade = A
	BECAUSE The company ABC has developed a new compact disc player.

RULE	Rule 42
CR =	0.6
IF	Industry = Electronics
AND	Issuing CB in the foreign financial market is expected
THEN	GRADE = AA

RULE	Rule 43
CR =	0.6
IF	P/E Ratio ≥ 10
AND	Debt Ratio ≥ 200%
THEN	GRADE = C

---

tive evidence should be compensatory to each other. To operationalize this idea, one may adopt a composition scheme in which credibility levels are used as weighting factors to generate composite subgrades; the subgrades are then combined by the formula shown in Table 6.1.

Table 6.1
Grades and Corresponding Real Numbers

Grade	Real Number	Median	Description
AAA	$0.8 < n \le 1.0$	0.9	Highly recommended
AA	$0.6 < n \le 0.8$	0.7	
A	$0.4 < n \le 0.6$	0.5	
BBB	$0.2 < n \le 0.4$	0.3	
BB	$0.0 < n \le 0.2$	0.1	Unknown
B	$-0.2 < n \le 0.0$	-0.1	
CCC	$-0.4 < n \le -0.2$	-0.3	
CC	$-0.6 < n \le -0.4$	-0.5	
C	$-0.8 < n \le -0.6$	-0.7	
D	$-1.0 \le n \le -0.8$	-0.9	Highly prohibited

The composite stock-grading model employs the following notation:

G_i = composite grade of stock i based on all rules.

G_i^+ = composite grade of stock i based on rules with positive grades.

G_i^- = composite grade of stock i based on rules with negative grades.

g_r^+ = positive grade of stock i by rule r.

g_r^- = negative grade of stock i by rule r.

C_r = credibility of rule r.

P = rule set with positive grade for stock i.

N = rule set with negative grade for stock i.

p = number of rules in set P.

n = number of rules in set N.

Positive and negative subgrades are given by

$$G_i^+ = \sum_{r \in P} C_r g_r^+ - \sum_{\substack{s < t \\ s,t \in P}} (C_s g_s^+)(C_t g_t^+) + \ldots$$

$$+ (-1)^{p+1} \prod_{r \in P} C_r g_r^+$$

and

$$G_i^- = \sum_{r \in N} C_r g_r^- + \sum_{\substack{s < t \\ s,t \in N}} (C_s g_s^-)(C_t g_t^-) + \ldots$$

$$+ \prod_{r \in N} C_r g_r^- .$$

These are combined into the composite grade of stock i by

$$G_i = \frac{G_i^+ + G_i^-}{1 - \min\{|G_i^+|, |G_i^-|\}} . \tag{6.1}$$

For example, consider the rules associated with company ABC in Figure 6.8:

$$G_{ABC}^+ = (0.6 \times 0.7 + 0.7 \times 0.5) - (0.6 \times 0.7 \times 0.7 \times 0.5) = 0.623$$

$$G_{ABC}^- = 0.6 \times (-0.7) = -0.42$$

and

$$G_{ABC} = \frac{0.623 - 0.42}{1 - 0.42} = 0.35.$$

ABC stock is evaluated as 0.35, which can also be converted into the grade BBB. The composite grade is stored in the composite-grade base.

Two special types of preemptive grades are GRADE = *** and GRADE = ZZZ. If a GRADE = *** exists in the conflict set, the stock will be evaluated as AAA regardless of which grades may exist in other rules. In the same way, the grade ZZZ will set the stock to the D grade preemptively.

Formula (6.1) has the following desirable properties:

1. $0 \leq G_i^+ \leq 1$.

2. $-1 \leq G_i^- \leq 0$.

3. $-1 \leq G_i \leq 1.4$.

4. Positive grades and negative grades are mutually compensatory.

5. The mutual compensation is symmetric.

6.4.3   Explanation Synthesis

The conflict set can also be used to generate explanations of why stocks are evaluated in a certain way (see Figure 6.9). An explanation is synthesized using the IF and BECAUSE statements in the conflict set. This explanation may be grouped into positive reasons and negative reasons, and the reasons in each group are ordered by the level of GRADE. The reasons are stored in the explanation base.

   If users want to see the reasons for statements made in the explanation, they may select a statement and ask why. For example, the reasoning behind the statement "Issuing Convertible Bond in the foreign financial market is expected" can be determined by using the associated rules shown in Figure 6.10.

6.5   DIALOGUES

By using the composite-grade base, the explanation base, the rule bases, and the databases, K-FOLIO can support four types of dialogue. The first of these is an individual company-based dialogue, which helps users to obtain recommendation levels for specific stocks, as well as the reasons the stocks are recommended. The second dialogue is an industry-based one that is similar to the dialogue described for an individual company. The third dialogue is a criteria-based one whose questions are a combination of various attributes. The fourth dialogue is a grade-based one that is performed by using the composite-grade base. Users may select each type of dialogue from a menu; they may also gain supplementary access to the database for a company and an industry at any given moment.

Figure 6.9
Process of Explanation Synthesis

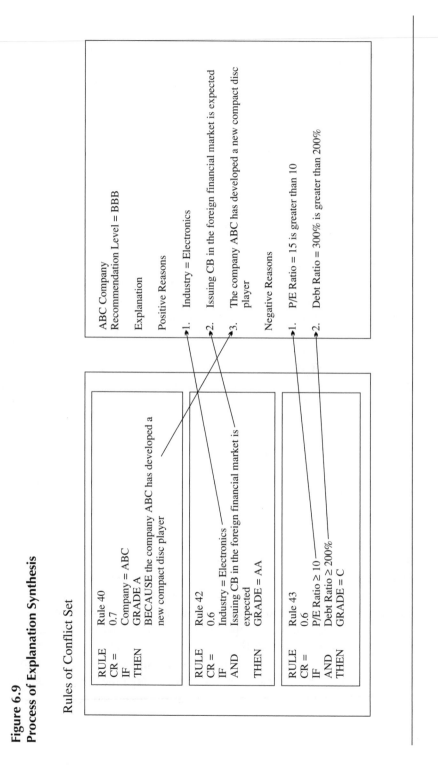

Rules of Conflict Set

RULE	Rule 40
CR =	0.7
IF	Company = ABC
THEN	GRADE A
	BECAUSE the company ABC has developed a new compact disc player

RULE	Rule 42
CR =	0.6
IF	Industry = Electronics
AND	Issuing CB in the foreign financial market is expected
THEN	GRADE = AA

RULE	Rule 43
CR =	0.6
IF	P/E Ratio ≥ 10
AND	Debt Ratio ≥ 200%
THEN	GRADE = C

ABC Company
Recommendation Level = BBB

Explanation

Positive Reasons

1. Industry = Electronics
2. Issuing CB in the foreign financial market is expected
3. The company ABC has developed a new compact disc player

Negative Reasons

1. P/E Ratio = 15 is greater than 10
2. Debt Ratio = 300% is greater than 200%

Figure 6.10
Example of the WHY Statement

Issuing convertible bond (CB) in the foreign financial market is expected

WHY

According to the rule

RULE   Rule 41

IF   Major Market = Overseas

AND   Annual Sales Growth Rate ≥ 50%
AND   The ratio of indirect and direct financing cost ≥ 1.2
THEN   Issuing CB in the foreign financial market is expected

WHY

According to the rule

RULE   Rule 8
IF   Amount of Exports > Domestic Sales
THEN   Major Market = Overseas

6.5.1   Company-Based Dialogue

A typical dialogue with user responses underlined is shown in Figure 6.11. The dialogue is generated from the composite-grade base and explanation base for HHH Motors. (Note that the reason inherited from the automobile industry is also included.) If decision makers do not agree with the expla-

---

Figure 6.11
Example of Company-Based Dialogue

Type the company name

HHH Motors

Grade of HHH Motors = A

Explanation

    Positive Reasons

        (1) GRADE = AA with CR = 0.9
              BECAUSE: New model of HHH motors company was
                        recorded as one of the most favorable cars
                        in the U.S. market.

        (2) GRADE = A with CR = 0.7 for Automobile Industry

    Negative Reasons

        (1) GRADE = D with CR = 0.6 for P/E Ratio = 20 is greater
                 than 15

---

nations, they may modify the GRADE and CR as they think appropriate. The system will then interactively recompute the composite grade in accordance with the changes. Personal modifications are local and do not change the values in the common conflict set.

6.5.2   Industry-Based Dialogue

The dialogue for an industry is similar to that for an individual stock. In industry-level inference, the average-up and sum-up features are utilized. A special property of industry-based dialogue is the fact that a threshold for exceptionally recommended companies and exceptionally prohibited companies can be denoted by using EXCEPT statements.

6.5.3   Criteria-Based Dialogue

Consider the following question, asked by criteria:

IF   Annual Sales Growth Rate $\geq 40\%$
AND   Debt Ratio $\leq 200\%$

The criteria are matched with the conditional parts of the rules in the rule base. If a matching rule exists, that rule will be displayed. For instance,

CR =   0.9
IF   Annual Sales Growth Rate $\geq 35\%$
AND   Debt Ratio $\leq 200\%$
THEN   GRADE = A

Note that the questioned annual sales growth rate (40 percent) is larger than the one in the matched rule (35 percent). We can therefore conclude that the questioned criteria can "at least" satisfy GRADE = A. In general, questions by criteria belong to one of four cases (See Figure 6.12):

a   The questioned criteria are stricter than the condition of the matched rule.

b.   The questioned criteria are looser than the condition of the matched rule.

c.   Only a portion of the questioned criteria can be matched with rules.

d.   There is no directly matching rule.

For case (a), the rule "at least" or "surely" satisfies the question. For cases (b) and (c), however, it is necessary to conclude with the qualification "maybe" or "possibly." Case-based reasoning techniques may be applied if multiple similar rules exist. In this case, a scheme similar to the composite grade computation formula discussed in Section 6.4.2 may be applied. If no corresponding rule exists, as in case (d), the questioned grade cannot be answered directly.

Another indirect approach for criteria-based questions is to retrieve the companies that satisfy the criteria and compute the average grade of those companies, which may take an enormous amount of effort. For cases (b), (c), and (d), however, the indirect method may be used as a supplement.

Figure 6.12
Relationships between Questions and Rules

(a)

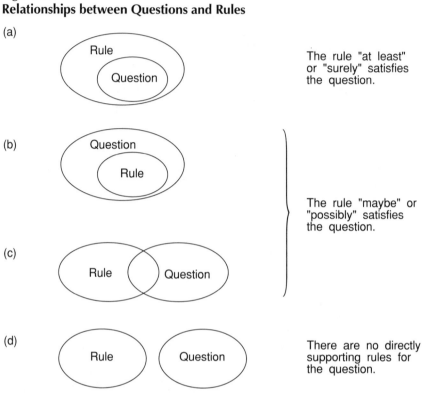

The rule "at least"
or "surely" satisfies
the question.

(b)

The rule "maybe" or
"possibly" satisfies
the question.

(c)

(d)

There are no directly
supporting rules for
the question.

6.5.4   Grade-Based Dialogue

When the user simply asks about stocks with a certain grade—AAA, for example—the system displays all stocks with that grade. The composite-grade base can support this kind of dialogue.

6.6   CONCLUSIONS

A number of steps are involved in constructing, manipulating, and evaluating rules to arrive at a set of reliable, consistent, and mutually supporting rules. This process is referred to as *rule synergy.*

REFERENCES

Lee, J. K., S. Chu, and H. Kim. "Intelligent Stock Portfolio Management System." *Expert Systems* 6 (April 1989), pp. 74–87.

CHAPTER 7

Handling Investment Uncertainties

7.1   Introduction
7.2   The Bayesian Approach
    7.2.1   Definitions and Formulas
    7.2.2   An Illustrative Example
    7.2.3   Handling Uncertain Evidence
    7.2.4   Handling More than Two Levels of Hypotheses
7.3   Inference Strategy in the Bayesian Approach
    7.3.1   The Sequence of Applying Evidence
    7.3.2   Stopping Rules
    7.3.3   Discussion
7.4   The Certainty Factor Approach
7.5   The Fuzzy Logic Approach
    7.5.1   Possibility Theory
    7.5.2   Fuzzy Logic
    7.5.3   A Fuzzy Logic–Based Expert System
    7.5.4   A Compensatory Fuzzy Logic Approach
    7.5.5   Attenuation by the Credibility of Rules
    7.5.6   Discussion
7.6   Nonmonotonic Reasoning
7.7   Conclusions

7.1   INTRODUCTION

Within the AI literature are several methods for handling uncertainty, all of which can be classified as either *numeric* or *nonnumeric*. Numeric methods include *probability theory, possibility theory,* and *evidence theory.* Nonnumeric methods include *nonmonotonic reasoning* and those based on the *theory of endorsement* (Kanal and Lemmer, 1986). The methods most applicable to investment decision making are *Bayesian theory* and *certainty factors* in probability theory, *fuzzy logic* in possibility theory, and nonmonotonic reasoning. This chapter will explain each of these approaches through the use of simple investment examples.

7.2   THE BAYESIAN APPROACH

7.2.1   Definitions and Formulas

To demonstrate how Bayesian theory can be applied to investment decision making, it will be helpful to review *Bayes' theorem* by using the following notation (Naylor, 1984):

H : Hypothesis H

H' : Hypothesis "Not H"

E : Evidence E

E' : Evidence "Not E "

$P(H)$: Prior probability to conclude the hypothesis H

$P(H/E)$: Posterior probability to conclude the hypothesis H with the evidence E

$P(H \cap E)$: Joint probability of occurrence of hypothesis H and evidence E

By definition of conditional probability,

$$P(H|E) = P(H \cap E) / P(E) \tag{7.1}$$

$$P(E \cap H) = P(E|H)\, P(H). \tag{7.2}$$

By substituting (7.2) into (7.1), we obtain

$$P(H|E) = P(E|H)\, P(H) \,/\, P(E). \tag{7.3}$$

Since

$$P(E) = P(E|H)\, P(H) + P(E|H')\, P(H')$$

and

$$P(H') = 1 - P(H),$$

equation (7.3) can be transformed into

$$P(H|E) = P(E|H)\, P(H) \,/\, [P(E|H)P(H) + P(E|H')\, (1 - P(H))]. \tag{7.4}$$

By using equation (7.4), it is possible to compute the posterior probability of satisfying the hypothesis H with the given evidence from the available probabilistic data $P(E/H)$, $P(E/H')$, and $P(H)$.

The computation of (7.4) can be operationalized by utilizing the notions of *odds* and *likelihood ratio*. By definition, the odds $O(H)$ and $O(H/E)$ can be expressed as follows:

$$O(H) \quad = P(H) \,/\, [1 - P(H)] \tag{7.5}$$

$$O(H|E) = P(H|E) \,/\, [1 - P(H|E)]. \tag{7.6}$$

Equation (7.6) can be rewritten as

$$O(H|E) = [P(E|H) \,/\, P(E|H')]O(H). \tag{7.7}$$

If the likelihood ratio $LR(H/E)$ is defined as

$$LR(H|E) = P(E|H) \,/\, P(E|H'), \tag{7.8}$$

(7.7) becomes

$$O(H|E) = LR(H|E)\, O(H). \tag{7.9}$$

According to equation (7.9), posterior odds can be computed as the product of $O(H)$ and $LR(H/E)$. Thus, (7.9) can be utilized to compute the effect of evidence.

7.2.2   An Illustrative Example

The precding formulas can now be used in making an investment decision. Consider the following data:

Example 7.1

Industry	Yield		Total
	High ($\geq 30\%$)	Low ($< 30\%$)	
Electronics	40	10	50
Other	50	100	150
Total	90	110	200

This two-dimensional frequency table is created from information about 200 stocks.

Hypothesis H = *High in yield*
Hypothesis H' = Low in yield
Evidence E = *Electronics industry*
Evidence E' = Not electronics industry

If there is no information about a stock, yield can be estimated from the prior probability by

$P(\text{High}) = 90/200 = 0.45$
$P(\text{Low}) = 1 - P(\text{High}) = 0.55.$

If the industry to which a stock belongs is known, formula (7.9) may be used. A prior odds $O(\text{High})$ is computed as

$$O(\text{High}) = P(\text{High}) / [1 - P(\text{High})]$$
$$= (90/200) / [1 - 90/200]$$
$$= 0.8181.$$

The likelihood ratio is

$$LR(\text{High} \mid \text{Electronics}) = P(\text{Electronics} \mid \text{High}) / P(\text{Electronics} \mid \text{Low})$$
$$= (40/90) / (10/110)$$
$$= 4.888.$$

Therefore, from formula (7.9),

$$O(\text{High}) \mid \text{Electronics}) = LR(\text{High} \mid \text{Electronics}) \, O(\text{High})$$
$$= (0.8181)(4.888)$$
$$= 3.996.$$

Converting to the posterior probability from yields

$$P(\text{High} \mid \text{Electronics}) = 3.996 / (1 + 3.996)$$
$$= 0.8006.$$

Thus, from the evidence that the stock belongs to the electronics industry, the probability of obtaining a yield greater than 30 percent increases from 0.45 to 0.80.

Assuming additional evidence exists about whether the company has either an export-oriented or a domestic-oriented market, the frequency table for the market might look like this:

Market	Yield		Total
	High ($\geq$ 30%)	Low (< 30%)	
Export	50	30	80
Domestic	40	80	120
Total	90	110	200

In the same way, the posterior probability can be computed as

$$LR(\text{High} \mid \text{Export}) = P(\text{Export} \mid \text{High}) / P(\text{Export} \mid \text{Low})$$
$$= (50/90) / (30/110)$$
$$= 2.037.$$

Thus,

O(High | Electronics, Export)

$= LR$ (High | Export) LR(High | Electronics) O(High)

$= LR$ (High | Export) O(High | Electronics)

$= (2.037) (3.996)$

$= 8.14,$

and

P(High | Electronics, Export) = 0.8907.

With the possession of two pieces of evidence, the industry and the major market, the probability of receiving a higher yield has increased from 0.45 to 0.8907.

7.2.3   Handling Uncertain Evidence

Thus far, we have assumed the evidence is known with certainty, but this may not be true in many cases. For instance, in Example 7.1 we assumed companies can be dichotomized according to industry or market criteria; in reality, such characterizations are often a question of degree. A company may produce 60 percent of its products for the electronics industry and sell 50 percent of the total amount to foreign markets.

One way to accommodate uncertain evidence is to apply an interpolation method. As Figure 7.1 shows, the probabilities $[P(H \mid E), P(H),$ $P(H \mid E')]$ may be mapped to $[-1, 0, 1]$. If the position of the evidence on the $[-1, 0, 1]$ scale is known, its corresponding probability can be linearly interpolated.

Example 7.2

If a company produces 100 percent of its products for the electronics industry, $Ev = 1$; if the company sells no electronics products, $Ev = -1$. If a company sells electronics products at the average proportion of all electronics products relative to the GDP (e.g., 30 percent, the best guess in the absence of industry-specific information), the normalized value of Ev is

Figure 7.1
Interpolation Method

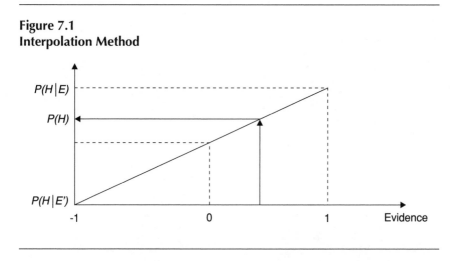

zero. Assuming the company produces 60 percent of its products for the electronics industry, the evidence can be normalized as

$$Ev(\text{Electronics}) = (60 - 30) / (100 - 30) = 0.43;$$

therefore,

$$P(\text{High} \mid Ev(\text{Electronics}) = 0.43)$$
$$= P(\text{High}) + [P(\text{High} \mid \text{Electronics}) - P(\text{High})] \; Ev(\text{Electronics})$$
$$= 0.45 + (0.80 - 0.45)(0.43)$$
$$= 0.60.$$

Note that the posterior probability is attenuated from 0.80 to 0.60 because of the uncertainty of the evidence (see Figure 7.2).

Again, assuming the normalized evidence of export is

$$Ev(\text{Export}) = 0.5,$$

the attenuated posterior probability with both pieces of evidence is

$$P(\text{High} \mid Ev(\text{Electronics}) = 0.43, \; Ev(\text{Export}) = 0.5)$$
$$= P(\text{High}) + [P(\text{High} \mid \text{Electronics}) - P(\text{High})] \; Ev(\text{Electronics})$$
$$+ [P(\text{High} \mid \text{Electronics, Export}) - P(\text{High} \mid \text{Electronics})] \; Ev(\text{Export})$$

Figure 7.2
An Example of Interpolation

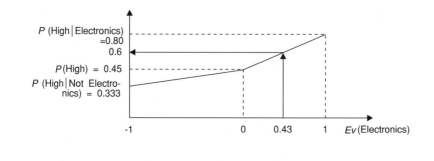

$$= 0.45 + (0.80 - 0.45)\ (0.43) + (0.89 - 0.80)\ (0.5)$$
$$= 0.645.$$

7.2.4   Handling More Than Two Levels of Hypotheses

Thus far, we have categorized stocks into two classes. Stocks may be categorized into more than two classes (e.g., class A, B, C, and D) by straightforwardly extending equations (7.1) through (7.4) into equation (7.10) below, in which $P(H_i \mid E)$ denotes the probability of satisfying hypothesis H_i:

$$P(H_i \mid E) = [P(E \mid H_i)\ P(H_i)] / [\sum_i P\ (E \mid H_i)\ P(H_i)]. \tag{7.10}$$

7.3   INFERENCE STRATEGY IN THE BAYESIAN APPROACH

The simplest strategy involving multiple evidence is to use all of the evidence without considering the sequence of application. However, this strategy is inefficient because some evidence will, in retrospect, be deemed to have made no contribution at all. Thus, it is desirable to order as efficiently as possible the sequence of applying evidence. It is also necessary to set inference-stopping conditions.

7.3.1   The Sequence of Applying Evidence

The sequence in which evidence is applied becomes particularly important when the expert system is being used interactively. Three useful sequencing strategies are random ordering, ordering by importance, and the rule-value approach.

Random Ordering

The chief advantage of random ordering is that it is simple. On the other hand, this method may force the decision maker to deal with trivial evidence.

Ordering by Importance

Because of their previous experience, investors or investment experts may have a good idea of the relative importance of various bits of evidence. They may then order the evidence accordingly.

Rule-Value Approach

When time is short and abundant computing resources are available, it may be prudent to apply the rule-value approach, which orders according to the value of evidence by using

$$RV_j = \sum_i |P(H_i|E_j) - P(H_i|E_j')| \tag{7.11}$$

for evidence E_j. Formula (7.11) represents the sum of posterior probability changes that may occur as a result of knowing whether the evidence E_j is true or false. The system can find evidence such that

$$RV_k = \min_j [RV_j, j = 1, \ldots, n].$$

Formula (7.11) may be modified to sum of squares instead of absolute differences. Weights may also be applied to hypotheses. The major disadvantage of the rule-value approach is its computational burden.

7.3.2   Stopping Rules

The following factors may be applied to set a stopping rule:

M_U : An upper threshold of satisfactory probability

M_L : A lower threshold of unsatisfactory probability

P(MAX) : Maximum probability with all remaining evidence Positive

P(MIN)   : Maximum probability with all remaining evidence negative

It is reasonable to stop when any of the following conditions are satisfied:

1. If there is no more evidence left,
    compare the $P(H_i | E_j, j = 1, \ldots, n)$, and
    choose H_i with $\max_i \ P(H_i | E_j, j = 1, \ldots, n)$.

2. If P(MIN) of $H_k > P$(MAX) of all H_i, $i \neq k$,
    the hypothesis H_k is the best alternative.

3. If P(MIN) of $H_k > M_U$, the hypothesis H_k is satisfied.

It is reasonable to eliminate or prune hypotheses that satisfy the following conditions:

4. If P(MAX) of $H_k < P$(MIN) of all H_i, $i \neq k$,
    the hypothesis H_k is hopeless.

5. If P(MAX) of $H_k < M_L$,
    the hypothesis H_k is too hopeless to continue.

If none of the conditions 1 to 5 are satisfied, it is necessary to continue the inference; that is, continue if

$$P(\text{MAX}) > M_L \text{ and}$$
$$P(\text{MIN}) < M_U.$$

7.3.3   Discussion

The Bayesian approach is an attractive way to handle uncertainty. Nevertheless, one must be careful not to use highly correlated evidence, because applying additional correlated evidence may result in meaningless changes in probabilities.

7.4   THE CERTAINTY FACTOR APPROACH

The certainty factor (CF) was introduced in MYCIN, an early ES developed for medical diagnosis. A variation on probability theory, CF is composed of a *measure of belief* (MB) and a *measure of disbelief* (MD).

   MB is a measure of a user's increased belief in hypothesis H, based on evidence E; MD is a measure of the user's increased disbelief in hypothesis H, based on the same evidence. Formally, MB and MD are defined as

$$MB(H,E) = \begin{cases} 1 & \text{if } P(H) = 1 \\ \dfrac{\max[P(H|E), P(H)] - P(H)}{1 - P(H)} & \text{if } 0 \leq P(H) < 1 \end{cases} \qquad (7.12)$$

and

$$MB(H,E) = \begin{cases} 0 & \text{if } P(H) = 0 \\ \dfrac{P(H) - \min[P(H|E), P(H)]}{P(H)} & \text{if } 0 < P(H) \leq 1 \end{cases} \qquad (7.13)$$

Using the above definitions, CF is defined as

$$CF(H,E) = MB(H,E) - MD(H,E). \qquad (7.14)$$

Some important properties of these measures are as follows:

   i. $0 \leq MB \leq 1$

   ii. $0 \leq MD \leq 1$

   iii. $-1 \leq CF \leq 1$

Although *CF* ranges between –1 and 1, the basic concept is similar to that of the Bayesian approach.

Example 7.3

From Example 7.1, *CF* can be computed as follows:

$$MB \text{ (High, Electronics)} = (0.8 - 0.45) / (1 - 0.45) = 0.6364$$
$$MD \text{ (High, Electronics)} = (0.45 - 0.45) / (0.45) = 0$$
$$CF \text{ (High, Electronics)} = 0.6364$$

The scheme used to compute a composite security grade in K-FOLIO is a variation on *CF* (see Section 6.4.2).

7.5   THE FUZZY LOGIC APPROACH

7.5.1   Possibility Theory

The notion of *possibility* was proposed by Zadeh (1985) as an alternative to *probability*. Since possibility measures the degree of each event's occurrence on a [0,1] scale, it is easily understood by most decision makers. Suppose there is a stock whose possibility of achieving each of the grades is as follows:

Grade	A	B	C	D
Possibility	1	0.8	0.3	0

Note that the sum of the possibilities is not equal to 1. When uncertainty is represented by possibility, fuzzy logic can be applied.

7.5.2   Fuzzy Logic

Stock x's possibility of earning a high yield can be denoted as P_S (High(x)). The function $P_S (\bullet)$ is called a *membership function*, where

$$0 \le P_S (\bullet) \le 1.$$

Suppose P_S (High(Electronics)) = 0.8. To integrate fuzzy evidence, the following basic AND, OR, and NOT operators are used:

$$P_1(\bullet) \text{ AND } P_2(\bullet) = \text{MIN } (P_1(\bullet), P_2(\bullet))$$
$$P_1(\bullet) \text{ OR } P_2(\bullet) = \text{MAX } (P_1(\bullet), P_2(\bullet))$$
$$\text{NOT } P_1(\bullet) = 1 - P_1(\bullet).$$

7.5.3   A Fuzzy Logic-Based Expert System

The fuzzy logic approach can be applied to an expert system. Suppose there are two rules with fuzziness as follows.

Example 7.4

Rule 1

IF	\<X\> exports well	(1.0)
AND	\<X\> belongs to electronics industry	(0.6)
THEN	\<X\> provides high yield	

Rule 2

IF	\<X\> belongs to a large conglomerate	(0.5)
AND	\<X\> has high R&D activity	(0.25)
THEN	\<X\> provides high yield	

where the variable \<X\> stands for the names of companies.

Any stock that satisfies rule 1 and/or 2 can be concluded to provide high yield with a given possibility. Since each rule has evidence in the AND relationship,

Rule 1: MIN(1.0, 0.6) = 0.6;
Rule 2: MIN(0.5, 0.25) = 0.25.

Next, the two rules are integrated by the OR relationship:

Rule 1 or 2:   MAX(0.6, 0.25) = 0.6.

According to the system of fuzzy logic, we may conclude that a stock <X> that satisfies either rule 1 or 2 provides high yield with the possibility 0.6.

7.5.4   A Compensatory Fuzzy Logic Approach

One limitation of the pure fuzzy logic approach is that much information can be lost during the evidence integration process. In Example 7.4, the information

<X>	exports well	(1.0)
<X>	belongs to a large conglomerate	(0.5)

was not used at all. To compensate for this deficiency, the following updating formula (Shortliffe, 1976) may be used:

$$P_S (H: \text{Rule } i, \text{Rule } j)$$
$$= P_S (H: \text{Rule } i) + P_S (H: \text{Rule } j) (1 - P_S (H: \text{Rule } i)). \qquad (7.15)$$

Shortliffe originally called formula (7.15) the "measure of belief." But since his terminology may be confused with MB as defined in (7.12), it is best to refer to (7.15) as *compensatory fuzzy logic.*

Example 7.5

For Example 7.4, equation (7.15) is applied:

$$P_S (\text{High: Rule } 1, \text{Rule } 2)$$
$$= P_S (\text{High: Rule } 1) + P_S(\text{High: Rule } 2) (1 - P_S (\text{High: Rule } 1))$$
$$= 0.6 + 0.25 (1 - 0.6)$$
$$= 0.75.$$

The concluded possibility of 0.75 differs from the value of 0.6 obtained by the noncompensatory fuzzy logic approach. Although we cannot be sure which value is correct, the result obtained by using compensatory fuzzy logic seems more reasonable.

7.5.5   Attenuation by the Credibility of Rules

Thus far, we have assumed that rules themselves are not uncertain, only the facts. In practice, this may not be the case. To attenuate the possibility of conclusion due to uncertainties in rules, the notion of the *credibility* of Rule i, or CR_i, may be introduced. In this case,

$$P_S (H: \text{Rule } i, \text{Rule } j)$$
$$= CR_i\, P_S (H: \text{Rule } i) + CR_j\, P_S (H: \text{Rule } j)\, (1 - P_S (H: \text{Rule } i)). \quad (7.16)$$

Example 7.6

In Example 7.4, suppose

$$CR \text{ of Rule } 1 = 0.9$$
$$CR \text{ of Rule } 2 = 0.8.$$

The possibility that <X> provides high yield can be computed as

$$P_S (\text{High: Rule } 1, \text{Rule } 2)$$
$$= CR_1\, P_S (\text{High: Rule } 1)$$
$$\quad + CR_2\, P_S (\text{High: Rule } 2)\, (1 - P_S (\text{High: Rule } 1)) \quad (7.17)$$
$$= (0.9)\,(0.6) + (0.8)\,(0.25)\,(1 - 0.6)$$
$$= 0.62.$$

Note that the possibility of obtaining a high yield has decreased from 0.75 to 0.62 because of attenuation.

7.5.6   Discussion

The fuzzy logic approach has the advantages of representational compatibility with rules and a small computational burden. Nevertheless, to measure uncertainty about rules and facts, fuzzy logic requires as much data as the Bayesian approach.

7.6   NONMONOTONIC REASONING

One important feature of investment decisions is *nonmonotonic reasoning,* in which the accumulation of additional knowledge does not necessarily increase the number of derived facts (also called *theorems*). This phenomenon occurs when certain facts are implicitly assumed. If a newly acquired fact disproves previous assumptions, the facts derived from these assumptions should be modified. This process is called *truth maintenance* (Doyle, 1979).

In securities investment, there are many things to be assumed. For example, some investors might have assumed the 1991 Persian Gulf Crisis would continue longer than six months. In that case, the rules pertaining to that assumption should have been invoked and the rules of the contrary assumption suppressed. Other implicit assumptions might relate to the political stability of former Soviet-dominated nations, the progress of government regulations, the outcome of domestic elections, and so forth.

To invoke rules relevant to investor assumptions, one might begin with dialogue about assumptions for controversial issues. Then the system would invoke only those rules that are congruent with these assumptions.

7.7   CONCLUSIONS

Uncertainty-handling methods include the Bayesian, certainty factor, fuzzy logic, and nonmonotonic reasoning approaches, which help decision makers represent uncertain information and render approximate reasoning. In the K-FOLIO system, a variant of the certainty factor approach and assumption-based reasoning (to overcome nonmonotonicity problems) are used. To fill the gap between the knowledge-providing expert's view and the system user's view, a sensitivity analysis capability is also provided.

REFERENCES

Doyle, J. "A Truth Maintenance System." *Artificial Intelligence* 12 (1979), pp. 231–72.

Kanal, L. N., and J. F. Lemmer, eds. *Uncertainty in Artificial Intelligence.* Amsterdam: North-Holland, 1986.

Naylor, C. "How to Build an Inferencing Engine." In *Expert Systems: Principles and Case Studies*, edited by R. Forsyth. New York: Chapman and Hall Computing, 1984.

Shortliffe, E. *Computer-Based Medical Consultations: MYCIN*. New York: Elsevier, 1976.

Zadeh, C. V. *Expert Systems and Fuzzy Systems*. New York: Benjamin/Cummings, 1985.

CHAPTER 8

Knowledge Acquisition, Integration, and Maintenance

8.1 Introduction
8.2 The Representation and Integration of Investor Preferences
    8.2.1 The Organization of Investor Preference Bases
    8.2.2 The Representation of Investor Preferences
    8.2.3 The Integration and Interpretation of Preferences
8.3 Sources for Knowledge Acquisition
8.4 Knowledge Structure and Maintenance
    8.4.1 Structuring Knowledge
    8.4.2 Maintenance Aids
8.5 The Selective Integration of Relevant Knowledge
8.6 Conclusions

8.1 INTRODUCTION

Chapters 5, 6, and 7 showed how knowledge relevant to investment decisions can be represented and how stocks and other securities can be inferentially evaluated by using knowledge. Questions still remain concerning where to obtain the required knowledge, how to design an efficient

119

knowledge entry and maintenance process, and how to integrate multiple relevant knowledge bases (Gaines and Boose, 1988). Hence, this chapter discusses the representation of investor preferences and their integration with expert knowledge, sources for knowledge acquisition (human experts and machine-learning systems), the use of knowledge structuring and meta-knowledge to aid in the knowledge entry and maintenance process, and the selective integration of relevant knowledge in a way that does not compromise inference efficiency.

8.2   THE REPRESENTATION AND INTEGRATION OF INVESTOR PREFERENCES

Investors who make investment decisions generally rely not only on experts' knowledge but also on their own knowledge, constraints, and preferences. Thus, it is necessary to develop a representation for these factors, referred to collectively as *preference*, and a methodology for timing and integrating preference with experts' knowledge.

8.2.1   The Organization of Investor Preference Bases

Two factors to consider in representing investor preference are syntactic compatibility with experts' knowledge and the unique features of personal preference. Commonly shared expert knowledge may be used to evaluate stocks, but the decision about how much to invest must be made by the investor according to the investment model he or she uses. Because of this, the investor preference base should be distinguished from the expert knowledge base (see Figure 5.6). In the K-FOLIO system, the expert knowledge base and investor preference bases are organized as shown in Figure 8.1 (Lee, Chu, and Kim, 1989). Theoretically, every investor will have a unique preference base.

8.2.2   The Representation of Investor Preferences

The syntax of rules for expert knowledge representation was shown in Figure 6.2. Investor preference may be represented using a similar syntax, but if information about investment amounts is to be included, additional

Figure 8.1
Organization of Expert Knowledge Base and Investor Preference Bases

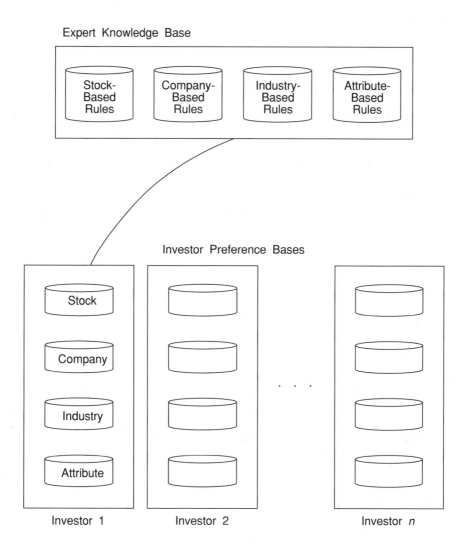

Expert Knowledge Base

| Stock-
Based
Rules | Company-
Based
Rules | Industry-
Based
Rules | Attribute-
Based
Rules |

Investor Preference Bases

Stock

Company

Industry

Attribute

. . .

Investor 1   Investor 2   Investor *n*

facilities will be needed. In K-FOLIO, the two reserved words AMOUNT and PERCENTAGE can be supported in the THEN part of the rules, as in the following examples.

Example 8.1

> RULE   Rule 81
> CR = 0.7
> IF   Stock = C_1
> OR   Stock = C_2
> THEN GRADE = AA
>   AMOUNT ≤ 100,000
> AND   PERCENTAGE = 10%

According to Rule 81, the amount invested in stocks C_1 and/or C_2 should not exceed $100,000, and the two stocks represent 10 percent of the portfolio.

Example 8.2

> RULE   Rule 82
> CR = 0.8
> IF   Industry = I1
> THEN AMOUNT ≤ 500,000
> OR   PERCENTAGE ≤ 20%
>   EXCEPT C_3, C_4

Rule 82 limits the amount and percentage of total investment in industry I1 (excluding stocks C_3 and C_4).

Example 8.3

> RULE   Rule 83
> CR = 0.9
> IF   P/E Ratio ≤ 7
> AND   Annual Sales Growth Rate ≥ 30%
> THEN AMOUNT = 400,000

Rule 83 indicates that the investor wishes to invest $400,000 in stocks whose price-earnings ratios are less than 7 and whose annual sales growth rates are greater than or equal to 30 percent.

8.2.3   The Integration and Interpretation of Preferences

Integration of the preferences of a specific investor (e.g., investor 1 in Figure 8.1) with expert knowledge can be achieved simply by merging corresponding rules (see Figure 8.2). Note, however, that this merge should occur only during the conflict-set generation process (Section 6.4.1). The original knowledge base and preference base should be kept intact.

To resolve potential conflicts in grades and credibilities between expert knowledge and investor preferences, priority may be declared at the global or rule level. For global declaration, either the statement

   PRIORITY   =   EXPERT

or

   PRIORITY   =   INVESTOR

may be used. To declare priority of preference at the rule level, the PRIORITY statement may appear within a rule, as in

---

Figure 8.2
Integrating Expert Knowledge and Investor Preference

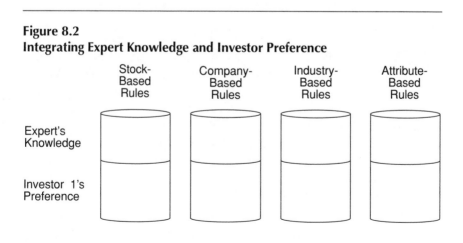

```
RULE          Rule 10
PRIORITY =    OVERRIDE
CR = 0.8
IF            Company = XYZ
THEN          GRADE = A
              BECAUSE . . .
```

OVERRIDE implies that the preference in Rule 10 takes precedence over any potentially conflicting expert knowledge. A YIELD statement implies the opposite.

In computing the composite grade encompassing expert knowledge and investor preferences, the grades in individual rules in the preference base may be treated in the same way as the ones in the expert knowledge base (see Section 6.2).

Preferences could be revealed during interactive dialogue with the screen (see Figure 6.11). The user of the system may add new reasons, delete existing ones, and change grades and credibilities, but these modifications should not be stored in the preference base permanently. (The process of modification is illustrated in Figures 13.6 through 13.8.) Restrictions given by AMOUNT and PERCENTAGE in Examples 8.1 through 8.3 will be transformed into constraints in the optimization model for portfolio decisions described in Chapter 11.

8.3   SOURCES FOR KNOWLEDGE ACQUISITION

It is not difficult to find experts in various aspects of investing from whom to acquire knowledge, but few regularly provide reliable knowledge for public use. One reason is that the computational complexity associated with making investment decisions is such that local heuristics are rarely consistent; thus, human experts' knowledge is generally ad hoc, biased, and localized. Automatic knowledge acquisition from a machine-learning system may be utilized to overcome such human expert limitations. Machine learning, to be discussed in the next chapter, may be used to automate the production of value-based investment rules from inputs such as financial ratios and to produce synergistic sets of short-term trading rules that exploit recurrent short-persistence price anomalies.

Human experts are the only media from which one can collect nonrecurrent knowledge; thus, human expert knowledge will always supplement

Figure 8.3
Mixed-Knowledge Acquisition Strategy

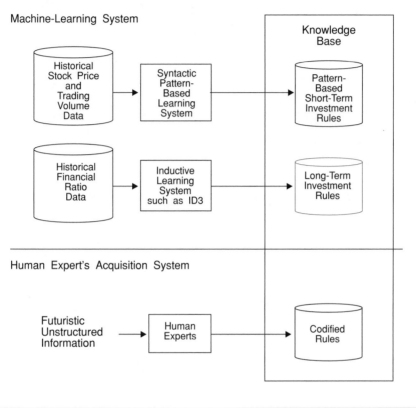

machine-learned knowledge. K-FOLIO employs a mixed-knowledge acquisition strategy (see Figure 8.3).

8.4   KNOWLEDGE STRUCTURE AND MAINTENANCE

8.4.1   Structuring Knowledge

To allow the classification of rules to be visualized, the subjects of rules can
be abstracted in a hierarchical structure (see Figure 8.4). Subjects may be
regarded as attributes in rules; a rule that includes more than one subject
would be indexed by more than one parent subject. This classification

Figure 8.4
Hierarchical Knowledge-Structuring by Subject

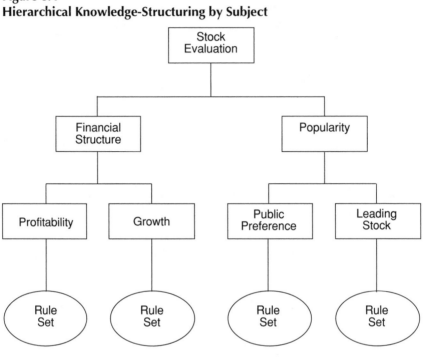

structure is helpful for confirming and modifying the rules for a certain subject. Using frames, the hierarchical structure can be succinctly represented as follows:

{{Stock Evaluation
 FACTORS : Financial Structure, Popularity}}

{{Financial Structure
 FACTORS : Profitability, Growth}}

{{Popularity
 FACTORS : Public Preference, Leading Stock}}

{{Profitability
 RULES :Rule 30, Rule 41, Rule 52, Rule 73}}

{{Growth
>   *RULES : Rule 35, Rule 43, Rule 55}}*

{{Public Preference
>   *RULES : Rule 12, Rule 38}}*

{{Leading Stock
>   *RULES : Rule 27, Rule 49, Rule 78}}*

When a rule is inputted or changed, the subject structure should be displayed to cue the user to enter or possibly revise the classification. To maintain consistency between the rule set and subject indices, the system may conservatively reject the storage of a new rule unless the associated subject is confirmed.

8.4.2   Maintenance Aids

Meta-knowledge (knowledge about knowledge) is useful for maintaining knowledge. Relevant meta-knowledge includes the use of knowledge (whether for evaluation of individual stocks or for general equity buy-sell timing decisions), investment horizon (long, medium, or short-term), author, entry date, and expiration date. Meta-knowledge may be represented by extending the rule syntax in Figure 6.2 to the format shown in Figure 8.5.

Using meta-knowledge, knowledge engineers can retrieve rules that satisfy criteria, such as the following:

1.   What knowledge did George enter during October?

2.   What knowledge expires today?

3.   What knowledge is available for evaluating stocks from a long-term investment perspective?

Through the meta-knowledge facility, inquiries about all possible combinations of USAGE, HORIZON, AUTHOR, ENTRY-DATE, and EXPIRATION-DATE can be retrieved; this will improve knowledge maintenance productivity.

Figure 8.5
Extended Syntax of Rules That Include Meta-Knowledge

{ {Rule rulename
    CREDIBILITY: percentage
    IF: statement A
      (AND statement B)
      (OR   statement C)

      . . .

    THEN: [statement ZZ
              GRADE = grade]
              (BECAUSE statement)
              (EXCEPT statement)
    USAGE : [evaluation   buy/sell]
    HORIZON : [long   medium   short]
    AUTHOR : name
    ENTRY-DATE : date
    EXPIRATION-DATE : date} }

Legend

    Capital letter : reserved words
    ( ) : optional statement
    [ ] : one of the statements should be chosen

8.5   THE SELECTIVE INTEGRATION OF RELEVANT KNOWLEDGE

Knowledge critical for short-term investment decisions may be relatively unimportant for long-term investment, and vice versa. For example, short-duration excess returns may have little effect on long-holding-period returns; therefore, it is desirable to classify the usage of knowledge (see Section 8.4.2).

Another factor to be considered is the user's set of assumptions about the environment. Different people would probably give different answers to questions such as: *Will the current international crisis last more than a month? Will the economy recover this year? Will the U.S. dollar be stronger or weaker over the next 18 months?* Depending on the answer to a particular question or assumption, the relevant portion of the knowledge base will vary; thus, knowledge must be linked with assumptions. Syntactically speaking, the assumption may be regarded as another type of attribute; nevertheless, differentiating assumptions from other attributes is helpful in dialogue. For example, consider the following two assumptions about a hypothetical Mideast crisis, long- or short-lasting:

{{ASSUMPTION: Mideast Crisis lasts long
  THEN: Oil price hikes}}
{{RULE automobile
  IF: Oil price hikes
  AND: Industry = automobile
  THEN: Grade = C}}

{{ASSUMPTION: Mideast Crisis lasts short
    THEN: Oil price declines}}

{{RULE automobile
  IF: Oil price declines
  AND: Industry = automobile
  THEN: Grade = A}}

If the user assumes the Mideast crisis will be long-lasting, the automobile industry will receive an unfavorable grade; if the user assumes the opposite, the automobile industry will receive a favorable grade. Therefore, environmental assumptions should be elicited at the beginning of a dialogue so that the system can select only the relevant knowledge bases. Some common assumptions would be those associated with the strength of the dollar, continuation of expansion or recession, the labor relations climate, the inflation outlook, and political outcomes. Figure 13.2 shows the typical dialogue associated with various environmental assumptions.

8.6   CONCLUSIONS

Knowledge acquisition is crucial to any expert system, and it becomes a serious problem if human experts cannot effectively provide knowledge. One solution is the use of machine learning, to be discussed in the next chapter. A system generally has multiple knowledge bases developed from several acquisitional sources (human experts, investors, and machine learning); therefore, it is inevitable that, depending on its source, knowledge will be selectively integrated into the system in various ways. Because knowledge maintenance under these conditions is very complex and error prone, the hierarchical structuring of knowledge and the use of meta-knowledge are useful methods to follow.

REFERENCES

Lee, J. K., S. Chu, and H. Kim. "Intelligent Stock Portfolio Management System." *Expert Systems* 6 (April 1989), pp. 74–87.

Gaines, B. R., and J. H. Boose, eds. *Knowledge Acquisition for Knowledge-based Systems*, Vols. 1 and 2. New York: Academic Press, 1988.

Chapter 9

Machine Learning

9.1 Introduction
   9.1.1   Why Machine Learning?
   9.1.2   Machine-Learning Systems
   9.1.3   Learning Strategies
9.2 Implied Distribution Surrogates
9.3 Inductive Learning
   9.3.1   ID3
   9.3.2   The Concept-Learning Algorithm
   9.3.3   Application of Inductive Learning to Investment Decisions
   9.3.4   The Potential of Inductive Learning in Investment
9.4 Syntactic Pattern–based Learning
   9.4.1   The SYNPLE Framework
   9.4.2   Performance
9.5 Genetic Adaptive Algorithms
   9.5.1   The Genetic Algorithm Approach to Learning
   9.5.2   Problem Representation Issues
   9.5.3   A Genetic Algorithm for Trading Rule Generation
9.6 Conclusions

9.1 INTRODUCTION

9.1.1 Why Machine Learning?

Machine learning is a medium for automatic knowledge acquisition that can be used when expert knowledge (1) does not exist, (2) is not sufficiently reliable, (3) is prohibitively expensive, or (4) is not available on a continuous

131

and timely basis. Unfortunately, knowledge in the investment domain is characterized by all of these features to varying degrees. In the experience of the authors, as well as that of others who have built expert systems for this domain, it is extremely difficult to find human investment consultants who are competent, cooperative, and reliable enough to consistently provide superior knowledge for formal public use. Thus, automatic knowledge acquisition through machine learning appears to be an essential element of knowledge-based systems for investment management.

9.1.2   Machine-Learning Systems

Auto-learning systems were briefly described in Chapter 4. *Machine learning* refers to specific mechanisms through which learning may take place in an auto-learning system. Figure 9.1 depicts the machine-learning process. The system generates knowledge from the environment and from critics concerning the gap between real-world results and the system's output. The goal is to transform the environmental and critics' responses into the form of knowledge discussed in Section 6.2. One difficulty in learning from critics is that any existing gap could be the result of the combined effects of deficiencies in the quality of knowledge generated from machine learning and the adequacy of inference. However, if the inference scheme is proven and frozen, fluctuations in the quality of the system's output can be attributed solely to the effectiveness of the machine-learning scheme.

Figure 9.1
Machine-Learning Procedure

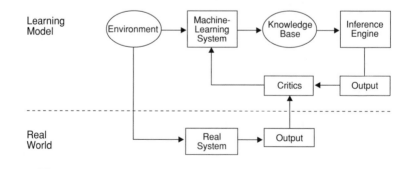

9.1.3   Learning Strategies

Learning strategies that have received significant attention in AI literature include inductive learning, syntactic pattern–based learning, genetic adaptive algorithms, neural networks, case-based learning and reasoning, genetic algorithms, and learning by taking advice. This chapter reviews concepts common to all learning strategies, then evaluates the potential of several approaches and shows how they can be used for investment knowledge generation. At present, the most popular and promising approaches for investment decisions appear to be those of neural networks, inductive learning, syntactic pattern–based learning, and genetic algorithms, so these four will be given special attention. Chapter 10 focuses more intensively on neural networks.

9.2   IMPLIED DISTRIBUTION SURROGATES

As discussed in Section 2.6.2, historical security price and trading volume series contain valuable, though incomplete, information about share acquisition cost distributions. To the extent that the price paid for a security will influence subsequent liquidation price and timing decisions, the security's market supply ought to be affected by the cost-distribution parameters. Much evidence suggests that it is not necessary to have a lengthy history of trading data to generate effective rules based on this concept. As we will see, statistically significant qualitative predictions of short-term price movements have been achieved by using collections of rules derived over relatively short time frames. The reason for this is probably that a substantial portion of the activity on most issues is attributable to regular traders, including specialists, who continually revise their holdings of the security.

Combinations of primitives (features) from two or more time-series charts of price, volume, moving averages, correlations, and so on may be utilized as surrogates for implied price distributions, which (for reasons discussed in Section 2.6.2) cannot be represented quantitatively with any degree of precision. Consider, for example, the following combinations and probable (but not certain) implications for the distribution of share costs over a given time frame:

Price random, high volatility $\Rightarrow$ wide uniform distribution

Price random, low volatility ⇒ narrow uniform distribution

Price trend up, volume constant ⇒ uniform distribution,
    mean below current price

Price trend up, volume decreasing ⇒ trapezoidal distribution,
    mean below current price

Price trend up, volume low—then high—then low ⇒ unimodal
    distribution, mean below current price

Price trend down, volume high—then low—then high ⇒ bimodal
    distribution, mean above current price

Price up—then down, volume constant ⇒ uniform distribution,
    mean above current price

Relationships such as these can be converted to rules by using Bayesian, certainty factor, or fuzzy logic approaches (see Chapter 7). Since the exact mechanisms through which distribution characteristics affect supply–demand equilibrium are unknown and probably dynamic, one may skip directly to price change predictions as the conclusions of such rules. Employment of chart primitives in such a surrogate role is not to be confused with naive conventional chartist methodologies. The advantages of using chart primitives for representation are that they can be rapidly extracted from existing raw data; not suffer from ambiguity; and, when graphically displayed, can aid in the explanation process.

9.3   INDUCTIVE LEARNING

Inductive learning seeks to produce generally applicable rules from the examination of past specific examples. Thus, inductive learning is also called *learning-from-example (LFE)*. Since inductively generated rules are usually used for classification problems, a common concern is the performance relative to other existing models for classification, such as statistical discriminant analysis. Unlike discriminant analysis, inductive learning makes no a priori assumptions about forms of the distribution of data (e.g., a normal distribution) or function forms of relationships (e.g., a linear model). Inductive learning allows both quantitative and qualitative variables and has been shown to be at least as robust as discriminant analysis

(Messier and Hansen, 1988; Shaw and Gentry,1988; Weiss and Kapouleas, 1989; Tam, 1990). A recent concern is the performance of inductive learning versus neural networks. Software tools for inductive learning are widely available. Popular products such as EXPERT-EASE, VP-EXPERT, and UNIK-INDUCE are equipped with inductive learning facilities.

9.3.1   ID3

ID3 was one of the first inductive learning algorithms. According to Quinlan (1979), ID3 generates rules by the procedure shown in Figure 9.2. First, one selects *instances* (i.e., cases, occurrences, or historical examples), which constitute a set called the *window*. The window, in conjunction with the *concept-learning algorithm*, is used to generate rules (see Section 9.3.2). If the rule can cover the entire set of instances, the rule set is perfect; otherwise, exceptional instances are incrementally incorporated into the window to improve the current rule set. This procedure is continued until the formed rule set becomes perfect or at least meets some minimum criterion of satisfaction.

9.3.2   The Concept-Learning Algorithm

The concept-learning algorithm constructs decision trees by using a top-down, divide-and-conquer approach (Michalski, Carbinol, and Michelle, 1983). Assume there are two graphs, referred to as charts 1 and 2, from each of which two kinds of attributes and a scalar measure can be drawn. These graphs can be combined with a price change conclusion column (see Figure 9.3). The attributes of charts 1 and 2 are varying patterns, while numeric percentages are represented in the column numeric 3. The observed price change for each instance is classified into one of three classes: *up, down*, or *sustained*. From these instances, the concept-learning algorithm first selects the attribute that has the highest discriminating power with respect to price change. In this example, chart 1 has the highest discriminating power, so it is placed at the top of the classifying tree. The occurrence of pattern 1B in chart 1 provides sufficient evidence to conclude that the price change is *sustained*; pattern 1A, however, needs additional information from chart 2 to reach a conclusion, and pattern 1C needs information from numeric 3 to reach a conclusion. This process continues until no ambiguous conclusions

Figure 9.2
ID3 Algorithm

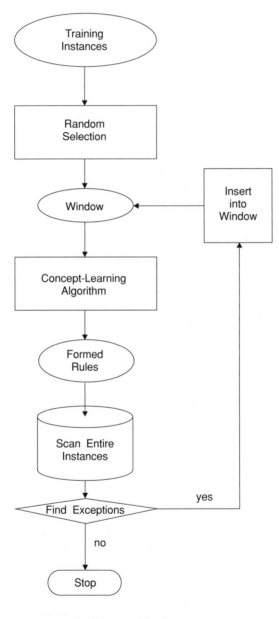

Figure 9.3
Inductive Learning Procedure

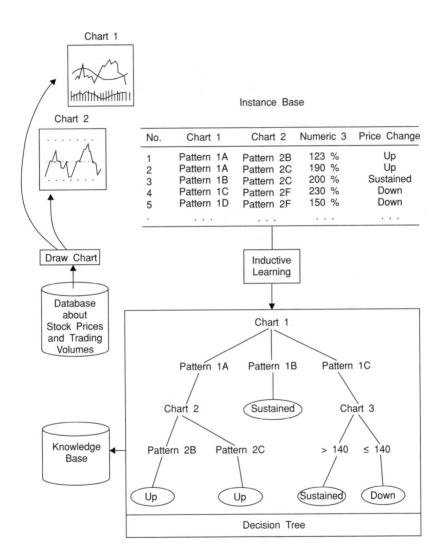

Chart 1

Chart 2

Instance Base

No.	Chart 1	Chart 2	Numeric 3	Price Change
1	Pattern 1A	Pattern 2B	123 %	Up
2	Pattern 1A	Pattern 2C	190 %	Up
3	Pattern 1B	Pattern 2C	200 %	Sustained
4	Pattern 1C	Pattern 2F	230 %	Down
5	Pattern 1D	Pattern 2F	150 %	Down
.	. . .	. . .	. . .	. . .

Draw Chart

Database about Stock Prices and Trading Volumes

Inductive Learning

Knowledge Base

Chart 1

Pattern 1A   Pattern 1B   Pattern 1C

Chart 2   Sustained   Chart 3

Pattern 2B   Pattern 2C   > 140   ≤ 140

Up   Up   Sustained   Down

Decision Tree

are left. To measure discriminating power, Quinlan uses the following *entropy* metric:

$$\text{Entropy} = \sum_{i=1}^{k} [- \frac{n_i}{\sum_i n_i} \log_k (n_i / \sum_i n_i)]$$

where k is the number of classes and n_i is the number of instances in the conclusion class i.

For example, suppose the numbers of patterns in chart 1 for the three classes are $n_{up} = 0$, $n_{down} = 0$, and $n_{sustained} = 30$. Then the entropy for chart 1 becomes zero, because chart 1 can classify these instances with no ambiguity. Another extreme example would be $n_{up} = 10$, $n_{down} = 10$, and $n_{sustained} = 10$. Now chart 1 has no discriminating power at all, so its entropy is 1. When $n_{up} = 20$, $n_{down} = 10$, and $n_{sustained} = 0$, the entropy value is 0.579. Thus, the degree of conformity among the instances in a class can provide a reasonable measure of *credibility* for rules (see Section 6.2).

A decision tree generated by the concept-learning algorithm can be transformed into rules. The decision tree in Figure 9.3, for example, implies the following rules:

IF   Chart 1 = Pattern 1A
AND   Chart 2 = Pattern 2B
THEN   Price Change = Up

IF   Chart 1 = Pattern 1A
AND   Chart 2 = Pattern 2C
THEN   Price Change = Up

IF   Chart 1 = Pattern 1B
THEN   Price Change = Sustained

IF   Chart 1 = Pattern 1C
AND   Numeric 3 > 140%
THEN   Price Change = Sustained

IF   Chart 1 = Pattern 1C
AND   Numeric 3 ≤ 140%
THEN   Price Change = Down

9.3.3   Application of Inductive Learning to Investment Decisions

In their 1987 study, Braun and Chandler adopted the ID3 approach in an attempt to predict stock market movements (see Chapter 4). The authors used 20 attributes out of the potential cues listed in Table 9.1, which generated a set of rules from 108 examples collected weekly at the Friday close of market; these rules predicted correctly 64.4 percent of the time. The three classes employed were bullish (predicting an upward trend), bearish (predicting a downward trend), and neutral (predicting a sideways market). These classifications were prepared to provide moderate-risk and aggressive investors with weekly recommendations. Since a single investment analyst had selected and interpreted the attributes and outcomes for the preparation of the experimental data, the rule set undoubtedly reflected the biases of this particular expert.

In an experiment in pattern-based inductive learning (Kim, 1987; Kim, Chu, and Lee, 1988), the success ratio on two classes of movement (up or down) ranged from 68 percent to 74.15 percent. This study employed eight attributes: 25-, 75-, and 150-day moving averages of stock prices, 6- and 25-day moving averages of trading volumes, a price–trading volume correlation curve, a volume ratio, and a psychological line. The rules used for performance evaluation in Chapter 11 were also generated by the concept-learning algorithm. In this case, 18 attributes were used to classify stocks into five classes.

According to Tam (1991), inductively learned rules could outperform the NYSE composite and S&P 500 indices' risk-adjusted annual returns. To discriminate those NYSE stocks most likely to double in price within a year, the eight variables shown in Table 9.2 were used. The three generated rules are shown in Figure 9.4. Training samples were selected from the period 1980–84 and tested for 1985–88. Annual returns for the test period are summarized in Table 9.3.

9.3.4   The Potential of Inductive Learning in Investment

The inductive learning technique can be used to generate rules that classify stocks and bonds into grades. In using the technique for fundamental analysis, attributes should be selected from the financial data with the longest evaluation time lag. On the other hand, in using inductive learning

Table 9.1
Potential Cues

1   Put-call ratio, Chicago Board of Options Exchange (PCCBOE)[a]

2. Put-call ratio, American Options Exchange (PCAMEX)[a]

3. Granville Cumulative Climax Indicator (GCCI), nonconfirmation cumulative climax[c]

4. GCCI, retrogress (GRANRET)[a]

5. GCCI, trend (GRANTRN)[a]

6. Weinstein Last-Hour Activity, volume NYSE index nonconfirmation[c]

7. Weinstein Last-Hour Activity, volume NYSE index trend[c]

8. Weinstein Last-Hour Activity, price DJI nonconfirmation[c]

9. Weinstein Last-Hour Activity, price DJI trend[c]

10. Dow Jones moving average, 10-day cycle (DJI10)[a]

11. Dow Jones moving average, 30-day cycle (DJI30)[a]

12. Dow Jones moving average, conjointly (when DJI10=DJI30)[b]

13. On-balance volume DJI, trend (OBVDOW)[a]

14. On-balance volume DJI, nonconfirmation

15. Cash of DJI, trend (CASHDOW)[a]

16. Cash of DJI, nonconfirmation (NETCDOW)[a]

17. Specialist short sales, ratio vs. odd-lot sales (SSOLS)[a]

18. Specialist short sales, 4-week moving vs. total shorts (SSTS)[a]

19. Market pressure index, 1-day moving average (MPI)[a]

20. Omtemsotu DJI, trend (expert's trend model)[b]

21. Intensity DJI, nonconfirmation (expert's trend model)[b]

22. Dow theory, compare transportation to industrials[b]

23. Dow theory, overbought oversold oscillator (OBOSOS)[a]

---

[a] Variable used as cue to develop rule.
[b] Variable used primarily for long-term fluctuations.
[c] Unable to use because of insufficient data.
Source: Braun and Chandler (1987)].

Table 9.1
Continued

24. NYSE composite index, trend and field trend (NYSECI)[a]

25. NYSE composite index, nonconfirmation vs. DJI price index[c]

26. Dow Jones Industrial, trend and field trend (DJIFT)[a]

27. Dow Jones Transportation, trends and field trend (DJTT)[a]

28. Dow Jones Transportation, trend breaks (DJTTB)[a]

29. S&P front spread, trend[c]

30. S&P front spread, nonconfirmation[c]

31. Cash of DJI Weekly, trend[b]

32. Cash of DJI Weekly, nonconfirmation[b]

33. Dow Jones figure point objective, 5 points[c]

34. Dow Jones figure point objective, 10 points[c]

35. Optimism-pessimism index, trend[c]

36. Optimism-pessimism index, nonconfirmation[c]

37. Optimism-pessimism index, 10-point figure chart[c]

38. Optimism-pessimism index, 25-point figure chart[c]

39. Wycoff Wave, trend (WWTRN)[a]

40. Wycoff Wave, nonconfirmation (WWREV)[a]

41. Trend barometer, momentum[b]

42. Trend barometer, force[b]

43. Trend barometer, technometer[b]

44. Ratio of ratios, trend of 6-day ratio[b]

45. Ratio of ratios, value of 6-day ratio (RATRAT)[a]

46. Ratio of ratios, trend of 10-day ratio[b]

47. Ratio of ratios, value of 10-day ratio[b]

Figure 9.4
Inductively Generated Rules

Rule 1

IF   relative strength ≤ 0.1734
        THEN the stock is not a high-growth stock
ELSE
        the stock is a high-growth stock

Rule 2

IF   relative strength is ≤ 0.145
        THEN the stock is not a high-growth stock
ELSE
   IF price to book ratio ≤ 2.37
        THEN the stock is a high-growth stock
   ELSE
     IF change in quarterly earnings ≤ –0.018
        THEN
             IF net current asset value ≤ 3.50
                 THEN the stock is a high-growth stock
             ELSE
             the stock is not a high-growth stock
       ELSE
             the stock is a high-growth stock

Rule 3

IF   relative strength ≤ 0.154
        THEN the stock is not a high-growth stock
ELSE
   IF net current asset value > 7.38
        THEN the stock is a high-growth stock
   ELSE
     IF change in quarterly earnings > –0.28
        THEN the stock is a high-growth stock
     ELSE
       IF price to book ratio > 2.34
           THEN the stock is a high-growth stock
       ELSE
             the stock is not a high-growth stock

Source: Tam (1991)

Table 9.2
Variables Used for Classification

Variable name	Definition
Shares outstanding	Number of common shares outstanding
Price ratio	Ratio of the quarter's closing price to the highest price in the previous two years
Return on equity	Net income divided by stockholders' equity
Net current asset value	Net current asset per common share outstanding
Price to book ratio	Ratio of the market value of equity to its book value
Relative-strength	Weighted average of quarterly price changes during the previous year, where the last quarter has a weight of 40% and each of the other three quarters has a weight of 20%
Change in quarterly earnings	Change in quarterly earnings between –2 and –1 quarters
Market capitalization	Number of common shares outstanding multiplied by the stock's closing price at quarter end

Source: Tam (1991).

for stock analysis based on trading data, patterns should be automatically detected from charts and evaluated by using a very short time lag (e.g., see Section 9.4). When used for classification problems, the inductive learning scheme seems to compete well with the syntactic pattern–based learning (to be discussed next) and with neural network approaches.

9.4   SYNTACTIC PATTERN–BASED LEARNING

In the syntactic pattern recognition approach, patterns are viewed as complexes of *primitives* and *compositional operators*, and the structure of legitimate patterns is analogous to the syntactic grammar of language. This approach has been applied to a variety of scientific domains, including the

Table 9.3
Comparison of Annual Returns in Each Holding Period (%)

Holding Period	NYSE Composite	S&P 500	Rule 1	Rule 2	Rule 3	Rules 1, 2	Rules 1, 3	Rules 2, 3	Rules 1,2, 3
3/85 – 3/86	31.2	28.9	40.8	39.0	38.0	37.0	37.0	38.0	37.0
3/86 – 3/87	20.5	22.0	19.3	21.0	22.3	20.7	21.9	21.6	21.5
3/87 – 3/88	–8.5	–8.0	–8.0	–0.4	3.4	–3.9	2.4	3.2	2.0
3/88 – 12/88*	8.8	9.8	13.9	13.5	15.7	13.1	15.1	15.4	12.7

* Annual returns based on nine months period.
Source: Tam (1991).

classification of fingerprints (Rao and Black, 1980) and carotid pulse waves (Stockman, Kanal, and Kyle, 1976). However, little syntactic pattern recognition research has been oriented toward security investment applications. Kandt and Yuenger (1988) describe a system under development that appears to include a syntactic pattern recognition capability, but they offer no details about the mechanism or performance of the system. We will discuss next a price pattern recognition system, SYNPLE, that is based on syntactic pattern learning theory (Lee, Kim, and Trippi, 1992).

9.4.1   The SYNPLE Framework

SYNPLE is a system that recognizes primitives contained in charts and synthesizes legitimate patterns with the highest probability classification power. SYNPLE has four steps.

Selection of Charts

The first step of the syntactic pattern recognition approach is to select appropriate charts. In this example, the charts are stock price trend lines (Figure 9.5), moving-average curves of stock price (Figure 9.6), moving-average curves of trading volume (Figure 9.7), and a price-volume correlation curve (Figure 9.8).

Figure 9.5
Illustrative Stock Price Trend Lines

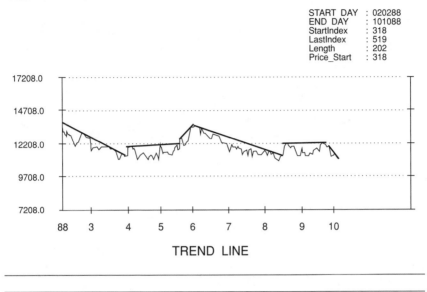

TREND LINE

Figure 9.6
Illustrative Moving-Average Stock Price Curves

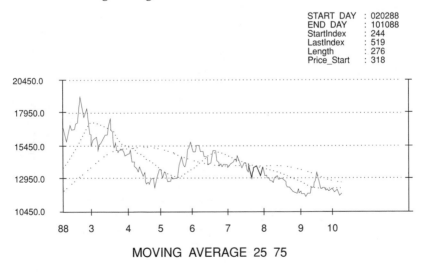

MOVING AVERAGE 25 75

Figure 9.7
Illustrative Moving-Average Trading Volume Curves

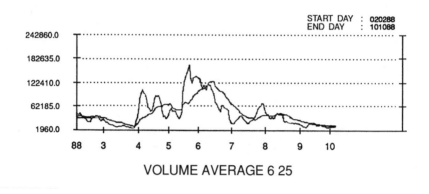

VOLUME AVERAGE 6 25

Figure 9.8
Illustrative Price-Volume Correlation Curve

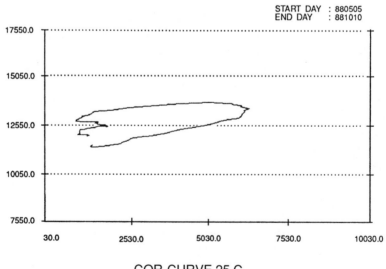

COR-CURVE 25 C

Definition of Elements

From each of the selected charts, users define those elements they would like to detect. (An element is a *preprimitive* that lacks information about the duration of the occurrences.) Elements are specified by the composition of attributes and their corresponding values (see Table 9.4). For instance, an element from the trend line type is

$$\{\{TLP\text{-}1$$
$$LINE\text{-}TYPE : central\text{-}line$$
$$TOLERANCE : 20$$
$$SLOPE : 0\ 15$$
$$SHIFT\text{-}AT\text{-}TAIL : up\}\}. \tag{9.2}$$

The element *TLP-1* means the line type is the central line of stock price with the tolerance of average error 20 (a smaller tolerance indicates a tighter fit to the local trend); the slope of the line belongs to the interval of 0 to 15 degrees; and the beginning point of the succeeding line is shifted upward. One hundred fifty-eight such elements are defined using the reserved attributes and values in Table 9.4.

Definition of Duration

Care must be taken in attaching duration to the elements defined above because the primitive could lead to a different conclusion depending on the length of its duration. This is apparent from an examination of the sensitivity to duration of the lower supporting line with a tolerance of 10 and a slope interval of [45, 90] (see Figure 9.9).

1. If duration $\leq$ 6 days, the mean price moves upward.

2. If 6 < duration $\leq$ 16, the mean price is sustained.

3. If duration > 16, the mean price moves downward.

The primitive is fully defined by attaching duration to the element.

Synthesis of Patterns

The SYNPLE algorithm detects the primitives defined above and selects the conclusion class with the highest probability of occurrence. This process builds primitive-based rules, each of which has a pattern (set of primitives)

Table 9.4
Illustrative Elements Specified by Charts, Attributes, and Values

Chart	Attribute	Values
Trend line of stock price	Line type	central line, upper supporting line
	Tolerance	40, 60, 80 (central line) 10, 15, 20 (upper supporting line, lower supporting line)
	Slope	$(-90, -45)$, $(-45, -20)$, $(-20, 0)$, $(0, 20)$, $(20, 45)$, $(45, 90)$
	Shift direction	shift-up, shift-down
	Gap	wider, narrower (between upper supporting line and lower supporting line)
Moving average of stock price	Slope	increase, decrease
	Rate of slope change	increase, decrease
	Length	1, 6, 25, 75
	Gap	narrower, wider (between 1-day and 6-day, 6-day and 25-day, 1-day and 25-day, 25-day and 75-day moving averages)
	Relative position	above, below (between 1-day and 6-day, 6-day and 25-day, 1-day and 25-day, 25-day and 75-day moving averages)
Moving average of trading volume	Slope	increase, decrease
	Length	6, 25, 75
	Gap	narrower, wider (between 1-day and 6-day, 6-day and 25-day, 1-day and 25-day, 25-day and 75-day moving averages.)
	Relative position	above, below (with 1-day and 6-day, 6-day and 25-day, 1-day and 25-day, 25-day and 75-day moving averages)
Price-volume correlation curve	MAP slope	increase, decrease, sustain
	MAV slope	increase, decrease, sustain
	Length	25, 75

Figure 9.9
Sensitivity of Duration in Lower Support Line to
Stock Price Trend Line

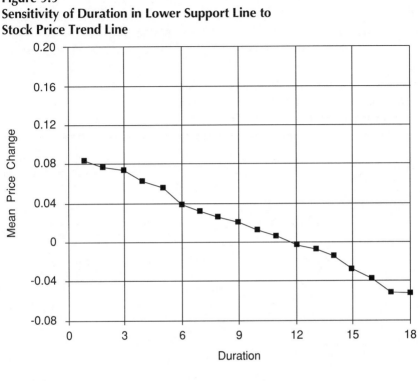

as a condition with a corresponding conclusion class. Probability in this context is essentially the same as the *credibility* of the rule. Primitives are composed into patterns via the operators CONCURRENCE and SEQUEN-TIAL; this process eventually leads to more complex patterns with higher credibility and continues until a sufficient level of credibility is established or until no further improvement occurs.

9.4.2   Performance

In an empirical test of SYNPLE that used Korean stock market data taken from the period April 22, 1987 to October 22, 1987, the number of pattern instances detected and synthesized into the stock price "up" class was 1,857 and the number for the stock price "down" class was 1,187. Three hundred ex ante rules were generated from the composed instances. As summarized in Table 9.5, the normalized mean actual stock price in the up class of 0.2398 was significantly higher than the –0.2015 of the down class. The rules generated from the first-period data were tested on the four succeeding periods.

The mean next-period price of stocks in the up class was significantly higher than prices in the down class, with a p-value of less than 0.0001 for all four subsequent test periods. The results are shown graphically in Figure 9.10. One peculiar feature is the performance of period 2's down class. In this period, even the average down class stock increased in value, most likely because of the 24th Olympic Games, which were held in Seoul. Based

Figure 9.10
Mean Price Change by the Rules Generated from the First Data Set

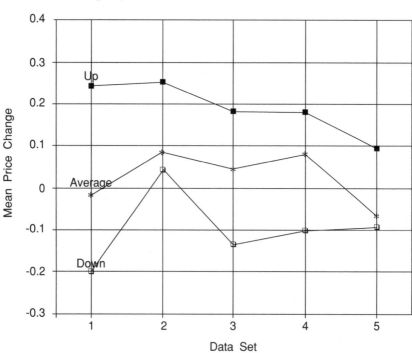

Table 9.5
Performance of Generated Rules

	1 4/22/87– 10/22/87	2 10/23/87– 4/22/88	3 4/23/88– 10/22/88	4 10/23/88– 4/22/89	5 4/22/89– 10/22/89	Average (periods 2–5)
Overall mean	-0.0109	0.0803	0.0347	0.0811	-0.0695	
Class "up"						
Mean	0.2398	0.2515	0.1837	0.1826	0.0942	0.188
Variance	0.01915	0.01708	0.01370	0.01187	0.00416	
Credibility	0.925	0.825	0.830	0.758	0.971	0.823
Instances	1,857	2,583	5,929	3,381	1,189	
Class "down"						
Mean	-0.2015	0.0444	-0.1265	-0.1030	-0.0914	-0.093
Variance	0.00135	0.00106	0.00163	0.00053	0.00001	
Credibility	1.0	0.293	0.973	0.995	0.990	0.921
Instances	1,187	167	445	936	200	
z-value	130.37	57.41	126.76	141.42	98.83	
p-value	<0.0001	<0.0001	<0.0001	<0.0001	<0.0001	

on these preliminary results, the syntactic pattern–based learning approach appears to be a promising one.

9.5   GENETIC ADAPTIVE ALGORITHMS

9.5.1   The Genetic Algorithm Approach to Learning

The genetic algorithm approach to machine learning was proposed and popularized by Holland (1975). Genetic algorithms are a robust and effective approach to limiting search efforts over large, combinatorial search spaces. For example, a genetic algorithm was used to generate the Poker axiom, which was perfectly attained after just 4,200 iterations. The essence of a genetic algorithm for machine learning is the systematic evaluation of the current set of rules and the propagation of new rules (see Figure 9.11). The algorithm starts with an initial rule set, which may be generated randomly. In each iteration, t, every rule R_i is evaluated by a certain measure, U, such as the credibility of the rule or some other measure of performance on a particular data set. Rules with the lower scores on this measure are discarded.

At each iteration of a genetic algorithm, also called a *generation,* there is a predetermined number of surviving "individuals," each of which represents a different solution. Individuals are represented by strings or vectors. In a machine-learning context, the elements of such strings are generally parameters of rules. New rules are generated through the use of genetic operators, including crossover, inversion, and mutation. Crossover operations sever pairs of surviving individuals at a randomly selected point, and interchange the two tails (Figure 9.12). *Inversion* replaces one portion of a string with its complement. *Mutation* refers to the random inversion of one or more elements of the string of one or more surviving individuals. Although the appearance of perfect or "optimal" individuals is not guaranteed, populations of surviving individuals will, on average, display better and better "fitness" scores in each successive generation.

The Holland genetic operators can be applied indirectly through the syntactic pattern–based learning methodology discussed earlier. New rules may be generated by systematically modifying values such as those in Table 9.4 with the use of a genetic algorithm that seeks improvements. Currently commercially available off-the-shelf packages for implementing genetic algorithms include BEAGLE, Evolver, Genitor, GA-Tool, and Genesis/OOGA (Colin, 1994).

Figure 9.11
Genetic Adaptive Algorithm

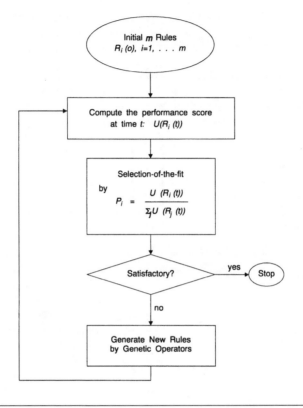

9.5.2   Problem Representation Issues

One major issue in the application of genetic algorithms is how to represent the individuals, or prospective solutions. In this aspect of genetic algorithm design, there is as much room for creativity as in the specification of the genetic operators to be applied at each step of the algorithm. For example, consider applying a genetic algorithm to solve the "Traveling Salesman Problem," which seeks to find the shortest path connecting n points and returning to the starting point. A natural way to represent a possible solution is by the order in which each numbered point (integers from 1 through n) appears in a string whose ends are implicitly connected, forming a cyclical permutation (Ambati, Ambati, and Mokhtar, 1991).

Figure 9.12
Genetic Crossover Operation

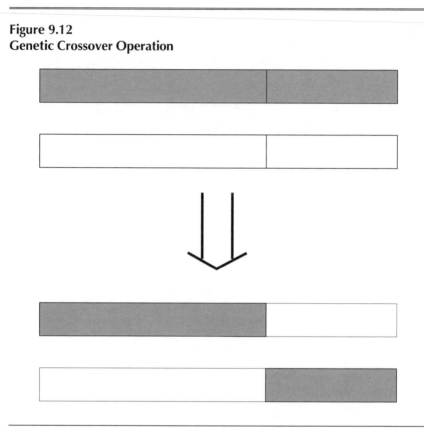

In many genetic algorithm applications, solutions are represented by strings of binary variables, each element of which can only take on the value of 0 or 1. The position of each element in such a *bit string* corresponds in some fashion to a particular rule parameter. Even if the parameters can take on continuous values, it may be possible to discretize them to a sufficient level of accuracy and represent the resultant discrete values as binary substrings. This approach to representation is illustrated in the next section.

9.5.3   A Genetic Algorithm for Trading Rule Generation

Bauer and Liepins (1992) applied a genetic algorithm to search for macro-economics-based rules for stock market timing over the period January 1961 through December 1988 that would maximize average return per trade.

There is ample empirical evidence that excess returns may be generated through the intelligent use of lagged macroeconomic data (e.g., see Fama and French, 1988, 1989) and that the effectiveness of an optimal macroeconomic specification for the forecasting of returns persists (Pesaran and Timmerman, 1994). Therefore, successful automated methods for generating such rules would be applicable to the tactical management of asset class portfolios.

With a few additional restrictions, Bauer and Liepins applied rules of the following form to each month:

> *If the year-to-year percentage change in series* S *is* greater/less than P *percent, then* L *months later* buy/sell *the S&P 500 index, and hold for one month.*

The number of macroeconomic time series examined (from *Business Conditions Digest*) was 361; the lag *L* ranged from one to three months; *P* was discretized into 128 possible values; and there were two *greater/less than* settings and two *buy/sell* settings. Thus, the solution space comprises $361 \times 3 \times 128 \times 2 \times 2$, or 554,496 possible combinations. Buy and sell rules were represented by 20-element bit strings, organized as follows:

Position in Bit String	Rule Parameter
1	*Greater/less than* setting (0 or 1)
2–4	Lag *L* (values above 3 not considered)
5–13	Leading macroeconomic economic series *S* (values above 361 not considered)
14–20	Percentage parameter *P* (discretized to values of 0 through 127)

The fitness score for any newly generated string that violates one of the preceding range limits is set to $-\infty$, effectively precluding its being a candidate for survival into the next generation.

The algorithm was run using a crossover rate of 0.6 and a mutation rate of 0.002. In 10 experiments of 10 trials each using different starting strings, the average monthly returns of the best rule parameters ranged from 6.04 to 7.52 percent, ignoring transaction costs. Although these results were converged on rapidly by the genetic algorithm, they do not differ much from those of the optimal rules obtained through a time-consuming, exhaustive search, which ranged from 6.44 to 7.52 percent. Optimal rules triggered only six to eight trades. The genetic algorithm found 1 of the top 10 rules identified by the exhaustive search in 5 out of the 10 experiments. This procedure can be easily extended to compound rules constructed as conditional statements involving two or more economic series simultaneously.

For more information on genetic algorithm theory and design, see Goldberg (1989) and Schwefel (1995). For a comprehensive treatment of genetic algorithms in investing, see Bauer (1995).

9.6   CONCLUSIONS

Because of both the difficulty of acquiring superior knowledge from humans in a timely manner and the proprietary problems associated with human expert knowledge sources, adopting machine-learning mechanisms for rule generation is the key to success for systems used for investment decision making. Machine learning is especially applicable to the generation of synergistic sets of rules that exploit subtle or highly convoled price anomalies.

REFERENCES

Ambati, B., J. Ambati, and M. Mokhtar. "Heuristic Combinatorial Optimization by Simulated Darwinian Evolution: A Polynomial Time Algorithm for the Traveling Salesman Problem." *Biological Cybernetics* 65 (1991), pp. 31–35.

Bauer, R. J. *Genetic Algorithms and Investment Strategies.* New York: John Wiley & Sons, 1995.

Bauer, R. J., and G. Liepins. "Genetic Algorithms and Stock Market Timing Trading Rules." Working paper, St. Mary's University, 1991. Appears also in *Expert Systems in Finance,* edited by D. E. O'Leary and P. R. Watkins. Amsterdam: Elsevier Science Publishers, 1992.

Braun, H., and J. S. Chandler. "Predicting Stock Market Behavior Through Rule Induction: An Application of the Learning-from-Example Approach." *Decision Sciences* 18 (1987), pp. 415–29.

Colin, A. C. "Genetic Algorithms for Financial Modeling." In *Trading on the Edge: Neural, Genetic, and Fuzzy Systems for Chaotic Financial Markets,* edited by G. J. Deboeck. New York: John Wiley & Sons, 1994.

Fama, E. F., and K. R. French. "Permanent and Temporary Components of Stock Prices." *Journal of Political Economy* 96 (1988), pp. 246–73.

Fama, E. F., and K. R. French. "Business Conditions and Expected Returns on Stocks and Bonds." *Journal of Financial Economics* 25 (1989), pp. 23–49.

Goldberg, D. E. *Genetic Algorithms in Search, Optimization, and Machine Learning*. Reading, MA: Addison-Wesley, 1989.

Holland, J. H. *Adaptation in Natural and Artificial Systems*. Ann Arbor: University of Michigan Press, 1975.

Kandt, K. and P. Yuenger. "A Financial Investment Assistant." *Proceedings of the 24th Annual Hawaii International Conference on Systems Sciences*, 1988, pp. 510–17.

Kim, H. S. "Generating Rules by Inductive Machine Learning: Exploratory Application to Stock Investment." Unpublished master's thesis, Korea Advanced Institute of Science and Technology, Department of Management Science, Seoul, 1987.

Kim, H. S., S. C. Chu, and J. K. Lee. "Stock Investment Rule Generation by Inductive Learning: Korean Stock Market Case." KAIST working paper, 1988.

Lee, J. K., H. S. Kim, and R. R. Trippi. "Security Trading Rule Synthesis: A Syntactic Pattern-Based Learning Approach." *Heuristics: The Journal of Knowledge Engineering* 5, no. 4 (Winter 1992), pp. 47–61.

Messier, W. F., and J. V. Hansen. "Inducing Rules for Expert System Development: An Example Using Default and Bankruptcy Data." *Management Science* 34, no. 12 (1988), pp. 1403–15.

Michalski, R. S., J. G. Carbinol, and T. M. Michelle. *Machine Learning: An Artificial Intelligence Approach*. Palo Alto, CA: Toga Publishing, 1983.

Pesaran, M. H., and A. Timmerman. "Forecasting Stock Returns: An Examination of Stock Market Trading in the Presence of Transaction Costs." *Journal of Forecasting* 13 (1994), pp. 335–67.

Quinlan, J. R. "Discovering Rules by Induction from Large Collections of Examples." In *Expert Systems in the Micro Electronic Age*, edited by D. Mitchie. Edinburgh: Edinburgh University Press, 1979.

Rao, K., and K. Black. "Type Classification of Fingerprints: A Syntactic Approach." *IEEE Transactions on Pattern Analysis and Machine Intelligence* 2, no. 3 (1980), pp. 223–31.

Schwefel, H. *Evolution and Optimum Seeking.* New York: John Wiley & Sons, 1995.

Shaw, M. J., and J. Gentry. "Using an Expert System with Inductive Learning to Evaluate Business Loans." *Financial Management* 17, no. 3 (1988), pp.45–56.

Stockman, G., L. Kanal, and M.C. Kyle. "Structural Pattern Recognition of Carotid Pulse Waves Using a General Waveform Parsing System." *Communications of the ACM* 19, no. 12 (1976), pp. 688–95.

Tam, K. Y. "Automated Construction of Knowledge Bases from Examples." *Information Systems Research* 1, no. 2 (1990), pp. 144–67.

Tam, K. Y. "Applying Rule Induction to Stock Screening." *Proceedings of the First International Conference on Artificial Intelligence Applications on Wall Street.* New York: IEEE Computer Society Press, 1991.

Weiss, S., and I. Kapouleas. "An Empirical Comparison of Pattern Recognition, Neural Nets, and Machine Learning Classification Methods." *Proceedings of the 11th International Joint Conference on Artificial Intelligence,* Detroit, 1989, pp.781–87.

Chapter 10

Neural Networks

10.1 Introduction
10.2 Architecture of Neural Networks
10.3 Learning in Neural Networks
10.4 Strengths and Weaknesses
10.5 Neural Network Applications
    10.5.1   Neural Networks for Stock Price Prediction
    10.5.2   Other Neural Network Applications
10.6 Example of Integrating Neural Networks and Rules
10.7 Conclusions

10.1 INTRODUCTION

The study of artificial neural networks (in short, neural networks) originally stemmed from efforts to simulate the functioning of the human brain. Neural networks differ radically from the algorithmic model used by conventional systems. Neural computation is massively parallel, typically employing from several hundred to millions of individual simple processors, arranged in a communicative network. Thus, some view the architecture of a neural network as being similar to that of the human brain. Neural networks are especially suited to simulating intelligence in pattern detection, association, and classification activities. Financial organizations are second only to the U.S. Department of Defense in sponsoring research in neural networks. The Department of Defense, which in 1989 embarked on a five-year, multimillion-dollar program for neural network research, plans to spend an additional $15 million in neural network research over the period 1995 to 2000.

159

In addition, the Japanese have embarked on a 10-year, $15 million program to further develop neural network technology.

In this chapter, we will first review architectures, learning processes, and modeling processes of neural networks. Then we will discuss the generic strengths and weaknesses of neural networks in comparison with statistical models. We will also consider typical applications to investment problems in such areas as stock price prediction, bond rating, business failure, debt risk, time series forecasting, credit approval, and foreign exchange rate prediction.

10.2   ARCHITECTURE OF NEURAL NETWORKS

Neural networks consist of many simple processors, all of which are programmed to perform the same elementary task for which each uses a small local memory area. An individual processor is referred to as a *processing element (PE)* or *node*. Each has one output but more than one input (see Figure 10.1). Outputs of one PE become inputs to other PEs or outputs of the network. An output may be fed back as an input to the same PE. The model depicted in Figure 10.2 is called a *feedforward network* because it contains no feedback connections. A variety of feedback topologies are in common use. The one most commonly used for time series forecasting in investment decision making is the recurrent network shown in Figure 10.3.

Figure 10.1
A Neural Processing Element

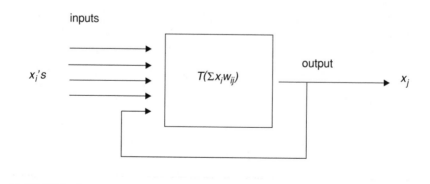

Figure 10.2
Typical Neural Network Architecture

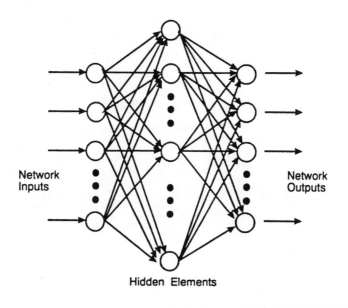

In most neural network paradigms, the actual processing that takes place is relatively simple: taking a weighted sum of the inputs and calculating an output value that is a function of that sum. The process is represented as

$$x_j = T\left(\sum_i w_{ij} x_i\right),$$

where x_j is the output of processing element j, w_{ij} is the weighting coefficient of the interconnect link between processing elements i and j, and T is a *transfer* or *activation function*. The most commonly used transfer functions are variations of the S-shaped sigmoid,

$$T(y) = (1 - e^{-y})^{-1}.$$

However, other functions, including Z-shaped (hard limiting) and threshold detector (flip-flop), are also used in some applications. The PE's local memory stores interconnect weights and parameters used by its

Figure 10.3
Architecture of a Recurrent Neural Network

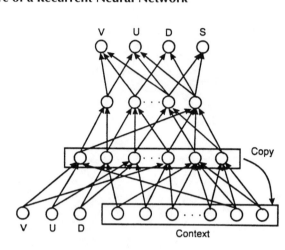

transfer function. When many processors are linked, a neural network is created.

What mainly distinguishes one neural network from another is the pattern of interconnections among the PEs. Some 20 different network configurations exist, about a dozen of which are commonly employed. In most of these configurations, individual networks are combined in layers that operate in synchrony with one another. Normally there are an input layer, an output layer, and one or more intermediate or "hidden" layers. Theoretically, one hidden layer is sufficient to express the nonlinear relationship between the input and output PEs (Hecht-Nielson, 1990). Therefore, most neural networks used for investment decisions have the multi-layered feedforward network topology shown in Figure 10.2.

10.3   LEARNING IN NEURAL NETWORKS

Learning takes place through incremental changes in interconnect weight coefficients according to a learning rule. For example, under the *delta rule* for learning, the change in interconnect weight w_{ij} is made proportional to the error between the desired output o_j and the actual output x_j:

$$w_{ij} = ke_j x_i,$$

where x_i is the level of the input to PE j from PE i, e_j is the error $o_j - x_j$, and k is a constant that determines the learning rate. The delta rule is somewhat analogous to gradient descent in that changes made lead to local improvement only. About a half-dozen different learning rules are in common use.

In a multilayered feedforward network, the errors are detected by the output PEs. These errors are propagated back to the PEs in the previous layer, and the process is repeated until the input layer is reached. An effective algorithm that learns in this fashion (adjusting the weights incrementally toward reducing the errors to within some threshold) is the backpropagation algorithm (Rumelhart, Hinton, and Williams, 1986). The discovery of this algorithm was largely responsible for the renewal of interest in neural networks in the mid-1980s, after a decade of dormancy.

During the learning process, as each data instance is applied to the neural network, network output values are computed using the current weights. Then the weights are readjusted to reduce some error measure, and another data instance is applied. When all data instances have been applied, the entire process is repeated again as long as some significant degree of error reduction continues to be achieved. Each pass of the entire data set through the network is called an *epoch*. For practical problems, it may take thousands or tens of thousands of epochs to achieve a stable solution. Therefore, a critical issue in the use of neural networks is the time needed to learn or become *trained*.

Once an acceptably stable set of weight parameters has been achieved, the network is run in a feedforward mode to classify new cases, make predictions, and so on. Actually using the trained neural network on a new instance, called *recalling* the network, is much faster because it requires only a single, one-way feedforward computation. Therefore, although learning may be slow, the trained model can easily be used on a real-time basis.

A sometimes troubling property of neural networks is that during the learning process the error measure may not always decrease monotonically. Therefore, it is not always easy to decide when to terminate the learning phase. Another important neural network issue is the overfitting problem. Although an "overfed" neural network model will have its error minimized during the learning phase, this does not necessarily result in the lowest error level in testing against out-of-sample instances. Therefore, if test data are available, the amount of training should also consider performance on the test data.

In summary, building a neural network involves several steps. We will assume the default topology is a fully connected, multilayered (one or two hidden layers) feedforward network, because most neural networks applied in investment decisions adopt this architecture. The model builder has to select the appropriate pairs of input variables (in statistical terms, independent variables) and the output variables (in statistical terms, dependent variables). The number of hidden nodes is often determined by trial and error. As a guideline, Kolmogorov's mapping neural network existence theorem states that $2n + 1$ hidden nodes are sufficient to approximate any real function (Hecht-Nielson, 1990). Then a learning algorithm (such as the backpropagation algorithm) is selected, along with parameters that affect the learning rate. Finally, some rule for termination of training must be provided.

10.4   STRENGTHS AND WEAKNESSES

Neural network technology has some advantages over conventional ES approaches in some applications. For one, since neural networks do not require that knowledge be formalized, they are appropriate for domains in which knowledge is scanty. In this sense, a neural network may replace a rule-based system. However, other options are the inductive learning methods described in Section 9.3. Many comparative studies have shown that neural networks can perform at least as well as inductive learning systems (Han, 1993). Unfortunately, the neural network model inherently lacks explanatory capability. The output of a neural network investment model will rarely contribute to theory and reasoning. The network is judged to be successful or unsuccessful strictly on its economic performance.

Since many of the most important neural network applications involve classification, it is worth comparing the merits of neural networks against those of regression and other competing statistical models. Recall that the earliest neural network configuration, the Perceptron (Rosenblatt, 1958, 1962), lacked hidden layers. The weights were derived from applying an incremental learning scheme for estimation in place of the ordinary least-squares method that is used for linear models. Whatever the learning (or estimation) process was, the resulting model was linear and therefore could not perform the "XOR"-type nonlinear discrimination (Minsky and Papert, 1969). Because of this limitation, neural network research became stalled for nearly a decade until the topology of multilayered networks and an efficient algorithm, the backpropagation algorithm, was devised. Multilayered neural networks can develop input-output map boundaries that are highly nonlinear (see Figure 4.2c). Some types of problems benefit greatly from this capability.

Another advantage of neural networks is that they can comprehend qualitative as well as quantitative factors. In addition, the data points do not have to follow a certain distribution; the sample size effect is not as critical as in regression analysis (although a larger sample size is still beneficial), and multicollinearity is a lesser problem (although elimination of highly correlated input variables can make the model more robust). These issues are examined in depth in Lee and Kim (1994), who show, for example, how input variables selected by a stepwise regression analysis can often outperform the entire candidate input variable set. In time-series forecasting, it has been demonstrated that the (recurrent) neural network will generally outperform the Box-Jenkins ARIMA (auto-regressive integrated moving average) forecasting model (Lee and Jhee, 1994).

In certain topological configurations, neural networks can act as "universal function approximators." Indeed, because of this capability, overfitting to individual cases is often a problem in the training of neural nets. This capability can be exploited, however, in the pricing of novel derivative assets whose value is related in a complex and imperfectly understood way to any arbitrary set of observable variables, such as the price and volatility of an underlying asset, contract specifications, and prices and volatilities of other assets. For example, a neural network has been able to "learn" a price-time-rate-volatility-moneyness relationship for options that is very close to that of the Black-Scholes model for pricing options (Hutchinson, Lo, and Poggio, 1994). With the rapid introduction of new and more complex financial products and commonly occurring divergences between prices given by analytic models and prices observed in the market, this approach, given its generality, appears to have a great deal of potential.

Neural networks also have their weaknesses. One is that they may identify certain factors as being important for decision making when those factors are actually irrelevant or conflict with traditional theories in the knowledge domain. This can occur because, as discussed earlier, the method is purely data bounded. Since the scope of training is always limited to some extent by economics and time, networks that contradict accepted theory run the risk of lacking generality or of functioning well only on data with a structure similar to that of the training set. Another potential problem is that most neural networks cannot guarantee an optimal or completely certain solution to a problem or, sometimes, even repeatability with the same input data. Nevertheless, as we will see in later examples, properly configured and trained neural networks often make consistently good classifications, generalizations, or decisions in a statistical sense.

10.5 NEURAL NETWORK APPLICATIONS

Neural networks can be useful in automating both routine and ad hoc financial analysis tasks (Chithelin, 1989). Production neural network–based decision aids have been built for the following applications:

- Credit-authorization screening

- Mortgage-risk assessment

- Project management and bidding strategy

- Economic predictions

- Risk rating of exchange-traded, fixed-income investments

- Detection of irregularities in security price movements

- Portfolio selection and diversification

Prototype neural network–based systems that are still mainly in the research, development, and evaluation stages include the following applications::

- Simulation of market behavior

- Index construction

- Identification of explanatory economic factors

- "Mining" of financial and economic databases

In the area of securities selection, for example, LBS Capital Management employs neural networks for the selection of individual stocks in the management of more than $300 million in assets. Fidelity's Growth America Fund (Canada) uses neural network technology for stock selection as well. Other major investment concerns, including Swiss Bank Corporation, utilize neural networks mainly for market timing decisions. Most such commercial fund management systems are highly proprietary, and thus performance data strictly attributable to the neural network component of the investment program are difficult to come by. However, some idea of the potential of neural networks in stock selection and timing may be gleaned from the studies described in the next section.

10.5.1   Neural Networks for Stock Price Prediction

Yoon and Swales (NYSE)

Yoon and Swales (1991) adopted a four-layered network (see Figure 10.4) with nine input parameters: confidence, economic factors outside the firm's control, growth, strategic plans, new products, anticipated loss, anticipated gain, long-term optimism, and short-term optimism. These factors were selected from studies of Fortune 500 and *Business Week*'s top 1,000 firms. Output parameters have two nodes: well-performing and poorly performing

Figure 10.4
Four-Layered Network

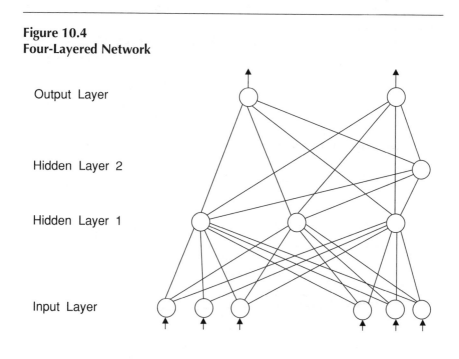

Output Layer

Hidden Layer 2

Hidden Layer 1

Input Layer

firms. Fifty-eight cases were used for training, and the trained network was applied to 40 cases. Eighteen out of 20 (90 percent) well-performing firms and 13 out of 20 (65 percent) poorly performing firms were correctly classified. On the average, 77.5 percent of test cases were correctly classified. This result outperformed the classifying power of multiple discriminant analysis, which correctly classified only 65 percent.

NEC Network

Kamijo and Tanigawa (1990) developed a recurrent neural network model to predict a price pattern, called the "triangle" pattern, from a candlestick chart (see Figure 10.5). The candlestick is a symbol that shows opening, closing, high, and low prices for the week. For a white (black) candlestick, the opening (closing) price is lower than the closing (opening) price, and the top and bottom of the candlestick represent the closing (opening) and the opening (closing) prices. The vertical lines on the top and beneath the bottom that run through the candlestick depict high and low prices during the period. The two oblique lines in the triangle pattern are also called *resistance lines,* which to a traditional chartist implies the beginning of a sudden stock-price rise.

The normalized high, low, and average prices from this chart were inputted to the neural network, and the output was recurrently used as input

---

Figure 10.5
Candlestick Chart and Triangle Pattern

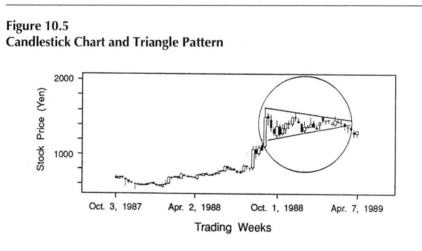

for the next time period; the eventual output was the confirmation of the occurrence of triangles. After the network was trained for 15 triangle patterns by iterating 2,000 times, it correctly classified 15 out of 16 test cases.

TOPIX

Kimoto, Asakawa, Yoda, and Takeoka (1990), under the sponsorship of Fujitsu Laboratories and Nikko securities, developed a network to determine optimal buy-and-sell timing for the TOPIX (Tokyo Stock Exchange Price Index). The network's input parameters include a vector curve, turnover, interest rate, foreign exchange rate, Dow Jones average, and several others. A single output node signals whether to buy or sell; an output value equal to or greater than 0.5 indicates "buy," while a value of less than 0.5 indicates "sell." The network was trained and tested by using monthly data from the period January 1987 to September 1989. The performance of the network's buy-and-sell strategy is compared with that of a buy-and-hold strategy (see Figure 10.6). The terminal investment value of 3,129 at September 1989, which would have resulted from following the neural network model recommendations, exceeded the 2,642 TOPIX value at that date by 487 points—a significant difference.

There have also been inclusive results with the TOPIX. Yoda (1994) reported an experiment in which one neural network outperformed the index, but another, based on a mechanical trend following model, did not. Thus, with neural networks, one has to be careful in assessing the reason

Figure 10.6
Performance of the Prediction System

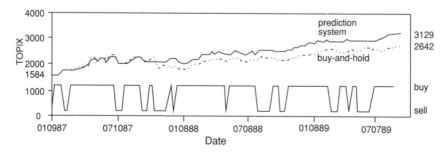

for poor performance: Was it the architecture and learning algorithm or the wrong inputs?

Taiwan Stock Market

In a study by Jang and Lai (1994) using Taiwan stock data, the annual rates of return generated by a neural network–driven buy-and-sell strategy were considerably higher than those of a competing buy-and-hold strategy. In fact, the returns, assuming 1 percent transaction costs, were superior to those of all the Taiwan closed-end funds that were managed under different disciplines by human experts. For their study, Jang and Lai devised a unique dual adaptive neural network. The training data covered the period 1987 through mid-1990, and the test period was from late 1990 through 1991.

Quebec Stock Market

Kryzanowski, Galler, and Wright (1993) used a type of neural network referred to as a *Boltzman machine* to predict the direction of movement of 120 publicly traded Canadian companies' stock prices in the subsequent year. Data from three overlapping four-year periods were used for training, covering the period 1984 to 1989. Eighty-eight inputs were used, including macroeconomic, company-specific fundamental, and industry ratio data. The forecasts of direction were correct in more than two-thirds of the cases.

10.5.2   Other Neural Network Applications

The ability of neural networks to classify data with attributes that are highly correlated makes them quite useful for risk assessment applications. The Nestor Company has used neural networks in the area of mortgage underwriting to make risk classification decisions based on historical data (Collins, Ghosh, and Scofield, 1988). Nestor's network is designed to produce predictive risk assessments of mortgage insurance policies. After being trained on previous underwriter judgments, the system produced more consistent classifications than did the company's human underwriters.

The AVCO Corporation was one of the first to apply a neural network to consumer credit scoring. The trained network reportedly was able to increase lending volume by more than 25 percent over that produced by conventional statistical scoring procedures, without increasing the default rate. Also, the company discovered in field trials that of the 96 individual score items normally used, only 46 were actually needed for making satisfactory assessments of risk. Today most major consumer credit-rating agencies and several credit card companies routinely use neural networks in place of or as a supplement to traditional statistical procedures.

In risk assessment, which is a generalization problem, a network is expected to correctly predict an output from an input that is not contained in the set of examples with which the network was trained. Dutta and Shekhar (1988) have successfully applied neural network technology to the generalization problem of rating bonds. Their network was able to categorize bonds with a total squared error an order of magnitude less than the most competitive conventional approach (multiple regression). Standard ES approaches (e.g., rule-based systems) are difficult to apply successfully to this particular problem, because the domain lacks a well-defined model or theory.

Other applications of neural networks of potential interest to investment managers include economic forecasting, index construction, portfolio selection, and financial market simulation. Certain types of neural networks are designed to recognize regularities in time series even when the functions are highly nonlinear. Demonstrations for neural network products often include the predicting of stock prices from historical data.

White (1988) employed a neural network approach to search for regularities in returns on IBM stock. The training sample covered a 1,000-day period from late 1974 to early 1978. The evaluation periods were the 500 days immediately preceding and following the training period. Although White was unable to reject the efficient market hypothesis using this approach, other researchers have reported favorable results from uncovering subtle price anomalies via neural networks.

Theoretically, neural networks could also construct indexes by using individual time series as building blocks, thereby reducing massive data sets to a manageable number of utilitarian figures. The components of the index and their weights would be generated to effectuate the index's intended use. For example, a neural network–generated leading index of interest rates would incorporate weights for individual rates and other components that maximize its predictive power. These weights could be found by training the network with historical data. Analogously to statistical smoothing, network-generated weights would be adaptive, with values that drift over time. Periodically some components could drop out entirely, to be replaced by others.

This computational approach would be especially useful in cases where it is not certain which economic variables are affecting the phenomenon in question. For example, according to arbitrage pricing theory (APT), stock returns are generated by some sort of factor model. However, there may be hundreds or even thousands of factors to choose from. Neural networks could determine, possibly with a much greater degree of accuracy than conventional statistical techniques, which of these factors are most pervasive for particular stocks.

Another potentially fruitful area for the employment of neural networks is in "database mining" (Hecht-Nielson, 1987). Here the object is to discover anomalous trends and correlations among seemingly unrelated data. Given the tremendous amount of private and public financial and economic information available, conventional technology would quickly be overwhelmed by such a task.

In a pioneering paper, Hopfield and Tank (1985) reported that they solved a particularly difficult type of optimization problem, known as the "traveling salesman problem," by using a two-layer neural network. They and other researchers have subsequently experimented with neural networks in solving a variety of optimization problems. Of particular relevance to investment is a neural network methodology developed by Zhao and Mendel (1988) for solving a quadratic programming problem closely related to that of the Markowitz portfolio diversification model (see Chapter 3). Because neural networks potentially have a computational speed many times faster than that of conventional computers, these networks may eventually be used to do dynamic adjustment of portfolio mixes that use thousands of available assets, and to keep the huge covariance matrix updated in real time.

On a somewhat different track, advances in hardware implementation of neural computer technology has great potential for revolutionizing the design and execution of detailed simulation experiments involving models of economic (and physical) systems composed of numerous, highly diffused elements. The behavior of commodity and security markets may be simulated with far more realistic detail and complexity than is possible using conventional sequential-processing computer technology. As a result, more definitive research on the institutional factors and policies affecting market stability could be accomplished with great efficiency through exploiting parallel-processing properties of hardware-implemented neural architectures.

10.6   EXAMPLE OF INTEGRATING NEURAL NETWORKS AND RULES

To compensate for the poor explanatory capability and neglect of domain theory characteristic of neural network–based systems, a great deal of interest has developed in developing architectures that can integrate neural networks with rule-based systems (e.g., Barker, 1993; Lyons and Persek, 1991; Hiemstra, 1994). Such integration can be realized in a variety of ways.

Trippi and DeSieno (1992) describe a simple way to use rules to refine the output of multiple neural networks. It is common for backpropagation networks to be sensitive to initial conditions. In addition, the user may want to incorporate into the decision-making process networks that vary with respect to input variables, number of hidden nodes, or learning rule. Trippi and DeSieno employed feedforward networks trained over the period from 1986 to 1990, to make long or short recommendations for the day trading of S&P 500 futures contracts in 1991. Inputs included open, high, low, and close price information, plus several statistics derived from past price data, including recent volatility. The only real-time information used from the current trading day were the opening price and the price 15 minutes after the market opening.

To exploit possible synergism among networks, six differently configured networks, labeled Net1 through Net6, were trained using the same historical data. Their performance is shown in Table 10.1. An ID3-like composite rule generation procedure was developed that examined the results of all possible combinations of networks on trading days on which no rule yet applies. If the expected value of trades resulting from applying one or more of these newly synthesized rules is greater than that of the best individual network (in this case, Net2), the best rule is added to the current rule set. This process continues until no more days are left unexamined or the rules become very complex (exceeding five logical operations).

Table 10.2 shows the first rule set that was developed, *Composite1*, which includes Net1 through Net5 and is designed to be scanned sequentially. Table 10.3 shows the performance of the individual rules on the days on which they applied or "fired." The performance of a composite trading system using these rules in combination exceeded that of the best single network (Net2) by 21 percent. The combined system traded 84 out of 106 days, or 79 percent of the time.

Table 10.1
Performance of Individual Networks

Network	Number of Gains	Number of Losses	Percent Gains	Average Gain	Average Loss	Number of Stops	Maximum Drawdown	Total Gain	Expected Value	Percent ROI
Net1	49	57	46.2	1,320.10	786.31	67	8,195.00	19,865.00	187.41	150.5
Net2	56	50	52.8	1,261.43	803.00	64	8,620.00	30,490.00	287.64	223.9
Net3	51	55	48.1	1,303.24	786.82	62	4,985.00	23,190.00	218.77	232.2
Net4	54	52	50.9	1,241.85	836.92	61	7,830.00	23,540.00	222.08	183.5
Net5	54	52	50.9	1,221.48	804.23	63	9,880.00	24,140.00	227.74	162.2
Net6	48	58	45.3	1,194.17	851.81	69	14,485.00	7,915.00	74.67	40.6

Table 10.2
Rules for Combining Outputs of Networks

Composite1

Rule 1:   If all nets agree, make the indicated trade.

Rule 2:   If Net1 and Net2 agree and one of Net3, Net4, or Net5 disagrees, then follow Net1.

Rule 3:   If Net1 and Net2 agree and two out of Net3, Net4, or Net5 disagree, then follow Net1.

Rule 4:   If Net1 and Net2 agree and the others disagree, then follow Net3.

Rule 5:   If Net2 and Net3 agree and the others disagree, then do not trade.

Rule 6:   If Net1 and Net2 disagree and the others have the same decision, then do not trade.

Rule 7:   If Rules 1 through 6 do not apply, then follow Net2.

Composite2

Rule 1:   If all nets agree, make the indicated trade.

Rule 2:   If Net1 and Net2 agree and one of Net3, Net4, or Net5 disagrees, then follow Net1.

Rule 3:   If Net1 and Net2 agree and two out of Net3, Net4, or Net5 disagree, then follow Net1.

Rule 4:   If Net1 and Net2 agree and the others disagree, then follow Net3.

Rule 5a: If Net2 and Net3 agree and the others disagree, then do the opposite of Net6.

Rule 6a: If Rules 1 through 5 do not apply, then follow Net6.

Table 10.3
Performance of Rules 1–7

Rule	No. Days Fired	Expected Value	Gain	Cumulative Gain
1	30	549.00	16,470.00	16,470.00
2	20	388.75	7,775.00	24,245.00
3	12	606.67	7280.00	31,525.00
4	7	665.00	4,655.00	36,180.00
5	8	—	—	36,180.00
6	12	—	—	36,180.00
7	17	41.17	700.00	36,880.00

Again using the rule synthesis procedure, the investigators examined whether the incorporation of Net6, a deliberately overtrained net, could in any way improve the composite system performance. This resulted in the rule set *Composite2*, also shown in Table 10.2, in which rules 5, 6, and 7 are replaced with the new rules 5a and 6a. This rule set traded every day and had a per-trade expected value of $460 and a cumulated gain of $48,750 over the initial test period.

Figure 10.7 shows a typical daily decision map for one of the networks, and Figure 10.8 shows a typical daily decision map for a composite trading decision rule set that combines the outputs of several networks. Both figures, with short recommendations represented by darker regions, show complex nonlinearity of decision map partitions.

Figure 10.9 shows regression lines for the S&P 500 and Composite2 (labeled "system value"), the latter with its 99 percent confidence limits on either side. The expected gain per contract was $317.06 per day, which is significantly different at the 99 percent confidence level from the $139.06-per-day index trend over this time period. Using the Composite2 rule set, both actual and simulated trades of the September S&P 500 contract were made over the period from June 24 through August 16, 1991, showing a cumulative gain of $14,247. For the 39 days on which trading took place, there were gains on 24 days, or 61.5 percent of the time. The average gain was $961.23, and the average loss was $588.15. An $81.49 average actual

Figure 10.7
Typical Net2 Decision Map

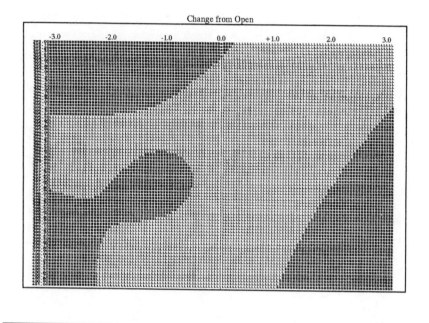

commission per contract was deducted in evaluating the Composite2 rule set. The probability of a random trading strategy meeting or exceeding the Composite2 rule set's performance was only 0.01.

10.7   CONCLUSIONS

It is widely accepted that the capability of neural networks to deal with nonlinearities enables them to outperform regression and discriminant models in many types of classification tasks of relevance to investment. There is also strong empirical evidence that neural networks can outperform conventional statistical models for time-series forecasting, such as ARIMA and regression. A number of recent studies suggest that neural nets do exhibit predictive power at least as good as, and often superior to, competing conventional statistical forecasting techniques on a wide range of financial variables, including commodity and currency prices and stock excess

Figure 10.8
Typical Neural Network Composite Rule Set Decision Map

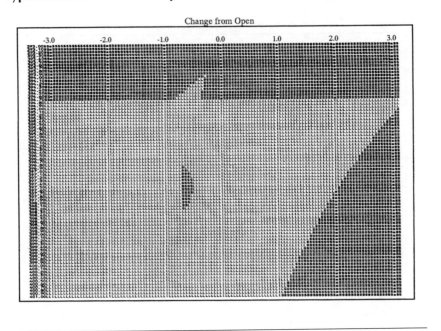

Figure 10.9
S&P 500 Index versus Composite2 System Performance

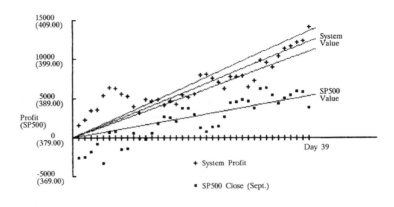

returns (e.g., see Lee, White, and Granger, 1993; Refenes, 1993; Hiemstra, 1994; and Hiemstra and Haefke, 1995).

As a result, there has been tremendous interest in using neural network components in investment decision support systems. Both research and applications along the lines discussed in this chapter are likely to become more widespread in the future. For a comprehensive survey of neural network applications in investing, see Trippi and Turban (1993).

REFERENCES

Barker, D. "Analyzing Financial Health: Integrating Neural Networks and Expert Systems." In *Neural Networks in Finance and Investing,* edited by R.R. Trippi and E. Turban. Chicago: Probus Publishing, 1993, pp. 85–102.

Chithelin, I. "New Technology Learns Wall Street's Mindset." *Wall Street Computer Review,* June 1989, pp. 19–21.

Collins, E., G. Ghosh, and C. Scofield. "An Application of a Multiple Neural Network Learning System to Emulation of Mortgage Underwriting Judgment." *Proceedings of the IEEE International Conference on Neural Networks,* July 1988, pp. II–459–66.

Dutta, S., and S. Shekhar. "Bond Rating: A Non-Conservative Application of Neural Networks." *Proceedings of the IEEE International Conference on Neural Networks,* July 1988, pp. II–443–50.

Han, Ingoo. "Performance of Artificial Intelligence Models in Business Classification." *Proceedings of the 1993 Korea/Japan Joint Conference on Expert Systems,* 1993, pp. 326–45.

Hecht-Nielson, R. *Neurocomputing.* Reading, MA: Addison-Wesley, 1990.

Hecht-Nielson, R. "Neurocomputer Applications." *National Computer Conference Proceedings,* 1987, pp. 239–44.

Hiemstra, Y. "Linear Regression versus Backpropagation Networks to Predict Quarterly Excess Returns." *Proceedings of the Second International Workshop on Neural Networks in the Capital Markets,* Pasadena, November 1994.

Hiemstra, Y. "The Application of Intelligent Systems to Tactical Asset Allocation." *Workshop on AI in Finance and Business,* 11th European Conference on AI, ECCAI, Amsterdam, 1994, pp. 83–92.

Hiemstra, Y., and C. Haefke. "Predicting Quarterly Excess Returns: Two Multilayer Perceptron Training Strategies." *Proceedings of The Third International Conference on Artificial Intelligence Applications on Wall Street.* Gaithersburg, MD: Software Engineering Press, 1995, pp. 212–17.

Hopfield, J., and D. Tank. "Neural Computation of Decisions in Optimization Problems." *Biological Cybernetics* 52 (1985).

Hutchinson, J., A. Lo, and T. Poggio. "A Nonparametric Approach to Pricing and Hedging Derivative Securities Via Learning Networks." *Journal of Finance* 49, no. 3 (July 1994), pp. 851–89.

Jang, G., and F. Lai. "Intelligent Trading of an Emerging Market." In *Trading on the Edge: Neural, Genetic, and Fuzzy Systems for Chaotic Financial Markets,* edited by G. Deboeck. New York: John Wiley & Sons, 1994.

Jhee, W., and J. Lee. "Performance of Neural Networks in Managerial Forecasting." *Intelligent Systems in Accounting, Finance & Management* 2, no. 1 (1993).

Kamijo, K., and T. Tanigawa. "Stock Price Pattern Recognition: A Recurrent Neural Network Approach." *Proceedings of the International Joint Conference on Neural Networks,* San Diego, IEEE Network Council, Vol. 1, 1990, pp. 215–21.

Kimoto, T., K. Asakawa, M. Yoda, and M. Takeoka. "Stock Market Prediction System with Modular Neural Networks." *Proceedings of the International Joint Conference on Neural Networks,* San Diego, IEEE Network Council, Vol. 1, 1990, pp. 1–6.

Kryzanowski, L., M. Galler, and D. W. Wright. "Using Artificial Neural Networks to Pick Stocks." *Financial Analysts Journal,* July–August 1993, pp. 21–27.

Lee, J., and W. Jhee. "A Two Stage Neural Network Approach for ARMA Model Identification with ESACF." *Decision Support Systems* 11 (1994), pp. 461–79.

Lee, J., and H. Kim. "Man-hours Requirement Estimation for Assemblies Using Neural Networks." *Proceedings of the Japan/Korea Joint Conference on Expert Systems,* Tokyo, March 22–24, 1994.

Lee, T. H., H. White, and C. W. J. Granger. "Testing for Neglected Nonlinearity in Time Series Models—A Comparison of Neural Network Methods and Alternative Tests." *Journal of Econometrics* 56, no. 3 (April 1993), pp. 269–90.

Lyons, P. J., and S. C. Persek. "Integrating Networks and Expert Systems for Merger and Acquisition Analysis." *Proceedings of the First International Conference on Artificial Intelligence Applications on Wall Street,* New York, 1991, pp.200–5.

Minsky, M. L., and S. A. Papert. *Perceptrons.* Cambridge, MA: MIT Press, 1969.

Refenes, A. N. "Constructive Learning and Its Application to Currency Exchange Rate Forecasting." In *Neural Networks in Finance and Investing,* edited by R. Trippi and E. Turban. Chicago: Probus Publishing Co., 1993.

Rosenblatt, F. "The Perceptron: A Probabilistic Model for Information Storage and Organization in the Brain." *Psychological Review* 65 (1958).

Rosenblatt, F. *Principles of Neurodynamics.* Washington, DC: Spartan Books, 1962.

Rumelhart, D. E., G. E. Hinton, and R. J. Williams. "Learning Internal Representations by Error Propagation." In *Parallel Distributed Processing, Vol. 1: Foundations,* edited by D. E. Rumelhart, J. L. McLennand, and the PDP Research Group. Cambridge, MA: The MIT Press, 1986.

Trippi, R., and D. DeSieno. "Trading Equity Index Futures with a Neural Network." *Journal of Portfolio Management* 18, no. 5 (Fall 1992), pp. 27–33.

Trippi, R., and E. Turban, eds. *Neural Networks in Finance and Investing.* Chicago: Probus Publishing, 1993.

Utans, J., and J. Moody. "Selecting Neural Network Architectures via the Prediction Risk: Application to Corporate Bond Rating Prediction." *Proceedings of the First International Conference on Artificial Intelligence Applications on Wall Street,* New York, 1991, pp. 35–41.

White, H. "Economic Prediction Using Neural Networks: The Case of IBM Daily Stock Prices." *Proceedings of the IEEE International Conference on Neural Networks,* July 1988, pp. II–451–58. Reprinted in *Neural Networks in Finance and Investing,* edited by R. Trippi and E. Turban. Chicago: Probus Publishing Co., 1993.

Yoda, M. "Predicting the Tokyo Stock Market." In *Trading on the Edge: Neural, Genetic, and Fuzzy Systems for Chaotic Financial Markets,* edited by G. Deboeck. New York: John Wiley & Sons, 1994.

Yoon, Y., and G. Swales. "Predicting Stock Price Performance: A Neural Network Approach." *Proceedings of the 24th Annual Hawaii International Conference on Systems Sciences,* Hawaii, IEEE Computer Society Press, Vol. 4, 1991, pp. 156–62.

Zhao, X., and J. Mendel. "An Artificial Neural Minimum-Variance Estimator." *Proceedings of the IEEE International Conference on Neural Networks,* July 1988, pp. II–499–506.

CHAPTER 11

Integrating Knowledge with Portfolio Optimization

11.1 Introduction
11.2 An Unenhanced Markowitz Model Example
11.3 The Interpretation of Knowledge
11.4 Quadratic Programming with Prioritized Decision Variables
11.5 Performance Evaluation
11.6 Conclusions

11.1 INTRODUCTION

The Markowitz mean-variance optimization model (1952) is currently the most popular quantitative approach to building portfolios. As discussed in Chapter 3, in this approach the objective is to minimize the portfolio risk involved in realizing a given return. The coefficients in the model, which are usually estimates computed from historical data, may not be effectively adaptive to day-to-day changes in the securities markets; for this and other reasons (see Chapter 3), it is desirable to have a mechanism for incorporating various types of up-to-date knowledge into the Markowitz model. This chapter examines how knowledge is interpreted by the K-FOLIO system for integration with the Markowitz model and illustrates the potential effects of such integration with an empirical example.

11.2   AN UNENHANCED MARKOWITZ MODEL EXAMPLE

As discussed in Chapter 3, the Markowitz model is a quadratic program (QP) that requires as input a vector of expected security returns $(R_1, \ldots R_n)$ and a matrix of return covariances $\| \sigma_{ij} \|$. A single or multi-index model may be used to facilitate the computation of return and covariance coefficients (Sharpe, 1963). The output solution is a vector $(x_1, \ldots x_n)$ of fractions (interpreted as percentages) that represent the relative amounts of each security to be included in the portfolio. The QP model may also be modified to a quadratic version of the goal programming model, if both the return and the risk levels are pretargeted (Ignizio 1976).

Example 11.1

Suppose $50,000 is invested in 30 candidate stocks, and the target weekly return, R_p, for the portfolio is 0.0015. Using data collected for 30 major stocks in Korea from 1981 to 1986, the minimum risk value obtained from the basic Markowitz model is a weekly variance of 2.52×10^{-4}. The optimal portfolio percentages are

X_1	= 0.00	X_2	= 0.00	X_3	= 2.13
X_4	= 0.00	X_5	= 4.89	X_6	= 0.00
X_7	= 0.00	X_8	= 3.11	X_9	= 7.78
X_{10}	= 3.45	X_{11}	= 0.00	X_{12}	= 1.71
X_{13}	= 0.00	X_{14}	= 0.00	X_{15}	= 12.80
X_{16}	= 2.37	X_{17}	= 0.00	X_{18}	= 0.00
X_{19}	= 0.57	X_{20}	= 0.00	X_{21}	= 8.62
X_{22}	= 7.57	X_{23}	= 0.43	X_{24}	= 38.02
X_{25}	= 0.00	X_{26}	= 0.00	X_{27}	= 0.80
X_{28}	= 0.00	X_{29}	= 0.00	X_{30}	= 5.65

11.3   THE INTERPRETATION OF KNOWLEDGE

If knowledge and preference factors are to be integrated with the QP model, they must be interpreted such that they are compatible with the structure of that model. The process of integration is graphically depicted in Figure 11.1.

The role of the interpreter is to translate the knowledge and preference system output to feed smoothly into the QP model. In general, knowledge can be incorporated into the basic model by modifying coefficients and augmenting the model with additional constraints. In the K-FOLIO ES, the typical statements used by the interpreter are **AMOUNT, PERCENTAGE,** company name, industry name, **EXCEPT**, and composite **GRADE**s of companies. The company name, industry name, and **EXCEPT** statements determine the decision variables; **GRADE** determines priority on decision variables; and **AMOUNT** and **PERCENTAGE** determine the right-hand-side values of auxiliary constraints.

The following examples show how knowledge can be transformed into rules.

Example 11.2

RULE   Rule 81
CR =   0.7
IF   Company $= C_1$
OR   Company $= C_2$
THEN   GRADE $=$ AA
          AMOUNT $\leq 100{,}000$
AND   PERCENTAGE $= 10\%$

The constraints derived from Rule 81 are

$$M(x_1 + x_2) \leq 100{,}000 \qquad (11.1)$$
$$x_1 + x_2 = 0.1, \qquad (11.2)$$

where x_1 and x_2 are the fractions of a portfolio held in stocks C_1 and C_2, respectively, and M is the amount of total investment.

Figure 11.1
Integration of Knowledge and Preference Systems with the Quadratic-Programming Model

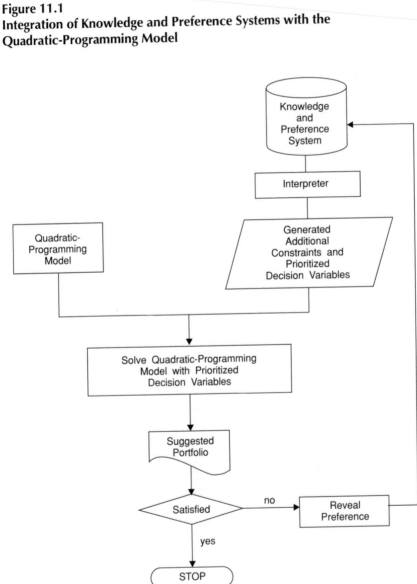

Example 11.3

RULE Rule 82
CR = 0.8
IF   Industry $= I_1$
THEN AMOUNT $\leq 500{,}000$
OR   PERCENTAGE $\leq 20\%$
          EXCEPT C_3, C_4

The constraints derived from Rule 82 are in the following mixed 0-1 integer programming form:

$$M \cdot \sum_{\substack{i \in I_1 \\ i \neq C_3, C_4}} x_i - By_1 \leq 500{,}000 \tag{11.3}$$

$$\sum_{\substack{i \in I_1 \\ i \neq C_3, C_4}} x_i - By_2 \leq 20\% \tag{11.4}$$

$$y_1 + y_2 \leq 1 \tag{11.5}$$

$$y_1, y_2 = 0, 1 \tag{11.6}$$

where B stands for a very big number.

Example 11.4

RULE Rule 83
CR = 0.9
IF   P/E Ratio ≤ 7
AND   Annual Sales Growth Rate $\geq 30\%$
THEN AMOUNT $= 400{,}000$

To interpret Rule 83, it is necessary to identify the companies that satisfy the condition. The derived constraint is

$$M \cdot \sum_{i \in D} x_i = 400{,}000, \tag{11.7}$$

where D is the company set that satisfies the condition of Rule 83.

11.4   QUADRATIC PROGRAMMING WITH PRIORITIZED DECISION VARIABLES

Thus far, these example rules have not mentioned GRADE or credibility. As discussed, information about GRADE and credibility is incorporated into the composite grade for each company in the *composite-grade base*. Since each company has its own unique grade, the notion of grade can be interpreted as being a priority of the decision variables. For instance, the grade AAA has top priority, the grade AA has the next highest priority, and so on. The modified QP solution process with prioritized decision variables is as follows:

1. Formulate the original QP model given by formulas (3.1), (3.2), (3.3), and (3.4) in Chapter 3. The additional types of constraints described in that chapter could be included as well. Except for the return on portfolio R_p, which is provided by the investor, all coefficients are retrieved from the database.

2. Add the appropriate *derived constraints,* such as those in (11.1) through (11.7), to the QP model.

3. Group the decision variables by their priority level:

Grade	Priority Group
AAA	P_1
AA	P_2
A	P_3
. . .	. . .

4. Set P_1 as the active candidate decision variable group; that is, P_k = P_1 and r_k = 1 for equation 11.9 (below).

5. Solve the QP model by using the modified objective function (11.8) below, subject to the original Markowitz model con-

straints (3.2) and (3.4), plus the constraints (11.9), (11.10), and (11.11):

$$\underset{X, s_k \,/\, i,\, j \in P_k}{\text{minimize}} \quad \sum_{i=1}^{n} \sum_{j=1}^{n} \sigma_{ij} x_i x_j + s_k \qquad (11.8)$$

subject to

$$\sum_{i=1}^{n} R_i x_i = R_p \qquad \{(3.2)\}$$

$$x_i \geq 0, \quad i = 1, \dots n, \qquad \{(3.4)\}$$

$$\sum_{i \in P_k} x_i + s_k = r_k \qquad (11.9)$$

$$s_k \geq 0 \qquad (11.10)$$

plus the set of *derived constraints*. (11.11)

6. The s_k can be viewed as a slack variable. If $s_k = 0$, the current priority group (including the higher-priority groups) can absorb the entire available capital; thus, the solution has been found, so stop.

7. If $s_k > 0$, the current priority group cannot absorb the available capital. Therefore, set $r_{k+1} = s_k$, and select P_{k+1} as the new active candidate decision variable group. Go to step 5.

Example 11.5

From Example 11.1, suppose the expert's knowledge has rated companies C_1, C_9 as AAA, C_{12}, C_{27} as AA, and so on. In addition, suppose the investor has revealed a preference by the following rules:

RULE Rule 88

CR = 0.8

IF   Company = C_1

OR   Company = C_3

OR   Company = C_{27}

THEN GRADE = A

      $0.35 \leq$ PERCENTAGE ≤ 0.5

      BECAUSE . . .

RULE Rule 89

IF   P/E Ratio ≤ 10

AND   Annual Sales Growth Rate ≥ 50

THEN $10,000 \leq$ AMOUNT $\leq 20,000$

      (C_9 and C_{27} satisfy Rule 89)

RULE Rule 90

IF   Company = C_5

OR   Company = C_9

OR   Company = C_{12}

THEN $0.3 \leq$ PERCENTAGE ≤ 0.7

      BECAUSE . . .

Step 1: Constraint Derivation: The constraints derived from the preference rules are

$$0.35 \leq X_1 + X_3 + X_{27} \leq 0.5$$
$$10,000 \leq 50,000 \ (X_9 + X_{27}) \leq 20,000$$
$$0.3 \leq X_5 + X_9 + X_{12} \leq 0.7.$$

Step 2: The priority levels classified by composite grade are

AAA :	C_1, C_9
AA :	C_{12}, C_{27}
A :	$C_2, C_5, C_{11}, C_{17}, C_{20}, C_{21}$
BBB :	$C_4, C_6, C_7, C_{13}, C_{24}$
BB :	$C_8, C_{10}, C_{22}, C_{28}, C_{29}$

$$B: \qquad C_{14}, C_{23}$$
$$CCC: \qquad C_{15}, C_{25}$$
$$CC: \qquad C_3, C_{16}, C_{19}, C_{26}$$
$$C: \qquad C_{18}$$
$$D: \qquad C_{30}.$$

Step 3: Initially focus on priority level AAA.

Step 4: The modified constraints for level AAA are

$$0.35 \leq X_1 \leq 0.5$$
$$10,000 \leq 50,000 \, X_9 \leq 20,000$$
$$0.3 \leq X_9 \leq 0.7.$$

Solve the QP with the above additional constraints, which gives the solution
$X_1 = 35.00\%$ $\qquad$ $X_9 = 35.60\%$.

The slack s_1 is 0.294, which means that 29.4 percent of total investment is remaining for further investment in stocks having priority level AA or lower.

Step 5: Set $r_2 = s_1 = 0.293$, and now focusing on priority level AA, repeat step 4. Keeping in mind that priority AA variables X_{27} and X_{12} must be nonnegative, the additional constraints are

$$0.35 - 0.35 \leq X_{27} \leq 0.5 - 0.35$$
$$\max (0, 10,000 - 50,000 \bullet 0.356) \leq 50,000 \, X_{27} \leq 20,000 - 50,000 \bullet 0.356$$
$$\max (0, 0.3 - 0.356) \leq X_{12} \leq 0.7 - 0.356.$$

The new solution is

$$X_{12} = 29.35\% \qquad X_{27} = 0.05\%,$$

and the final portfolio is

$$X_1 \ = 35.00\% \qquad X_9 \ = 35.60\%$$
$$X_{12} = 29.35\% \qquad X_{27} = 0.05\%.$$

Note that this portfolio differs considerably from the one obtained using the unenhanced Markowitz model in Example 11.1.

11.5   PERFORMANCE EVALUATION

To illustrate the potential effects of considering knowledge in portfolio selection, the results of an empirical study using K-FOLIO are summarized in Tables 11.1, 11.2, and 11.3 (Lee, Trippi, Chu, and Kim, 1990). For the first working day of each month from January through December 1987, Table 11.1 shows actual average market returns (in real time, on a percentage basis); Table 11.2 shows the realized returns of the unenhanced Markowitz model; and Table 11.3 shows the realized returns of K-FOLIO's portfolios. Tables 11.2 and 11.3 show actual portfolio returns for expected or target annual returns ranging from 10 to 20 percent. The rules were induced from weekly data for 1986.

For this static rule set, the incorporation of knowledge by K-FOLIO enables its portfolios to beat the average market return and the unenhanced Markowitz model for the first two months of use. From March 1987 on,

---

Table 11.1
Monthly Market Returns

Last Working Day of	Average Return on Market (%)
January	22.538
February	13.147
March	25.474
April	−11.835
May	6.917
June	2.537
July	5.805
August	−6.411
September	−1.445
October	0.809
November	−1.595
December	13.179

Table 11.2
Realized Returns of Markowitz Portfolios

Last Working Day of	Annual Expected Return Target (%)					
	10	12	14	16	18	20
January	19.128	21.442	23.636	25.280	26.329	30.948
February	33.101	33.044	33.403	33.601	33.720	29.742
March	47.769	39.947	31.859	23.706	19.210	18.572
April	−9.327	−9.549	−9.695	−9.891	−10.163	−9.337
May	6.659	7.601	8.530	9.396	9.499	7.995
June	4.970	4.819	4.733	4.851	4.832	3.356
July	1.972	1.163	0.421	0.021	−0.578	−0.892
August	−4.310	−3.885	−3.524	−3.529	−2.256	1.805
September	−1.752	−1.330	−0.942	−0.852	−0.737	−0.775
October	2.654	3.088	3.495	3.857	3.916	3.447
November	1.829	3.024	4.258	5.341	6.601	6.407
December	9.725	7.768	5.694	3.709	2.127	1.449

Table 11.3
Realized Returns of K-FOLIO Portfolios

Last Working Day of	Annual Expected Return Target (%)					
	10	12	14	16	18	20
January	28.027	31.339	34.652	37.964	37.532	41.626
February	39.386	38.668	37.950	37.232	34.711	19.897
March	56.886	46.045	35.203	24.361	15.608	14.210
April	−11.080	−12.031	−12.982	−13.933	−13.942	−13.505
May	3.479	5.337	7.195	9.054	8.129	3.789
June	6.019	6.837	7.655	8.473	8.718	6.786
July	−0.350	−1.122	−1.893	−2.665	−3.887	−4.555
August	−2.329	−3.875	−5.421	−6.967	−7.115	−5.218
September	−0.508	−0.867	−1.226	−1.585	−2.440	−3.980
October	3.861	4.363	4.865	5.367	5.120	4.271
November	0.425	1.394	2.364	3.333	3.602	1.019
December	9.879	8.512	7.145	5.779	5.572	8.395

however, K-FOLIO's returns are no longer consistently superior to those of the unenhanced Markowitz model. As the anomalies that generated superior returns appear to have a persistence measured in, at most, months, it is important to update the knowledge base fairly frequently.

It is interesting that even without updating, K-FOLIO returns exceed average market returns and unenhanced Markowitz model returns 9 and 8 months out of 12 for the target portfolio return of 10 percent. K-FOLIO returns exceed average market returns only 6 times out of 12 when the target returns are 16 percent, 18 percent, and 20 percent, but the accumulated K-FOLIO returns exceed average market return over the entire year.

It is apparent that the realized return is very sensitive to the target return R_p; thus, the choice of this parameter is important to the performance of the system. Figures 11.2 and 11.3 plot the realized returns versus time for targets of 12 percent and 18 percent, respectively.

11.6 CONCLUSIONS

Knowledge can be interpreted as priorities and constraints in the Markowitz model. In an illustrative empirical study, it was shown that integrating knowledge with the Markowitz model can significantly improve the

Figure 11.2
Realized Returns; 12% Target

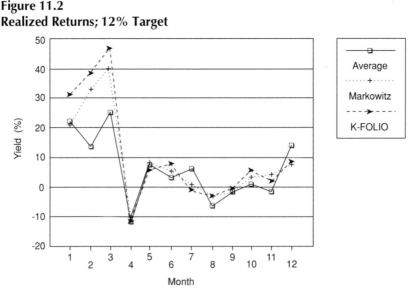

Figure 11.3
Realized Returns; 18% Target

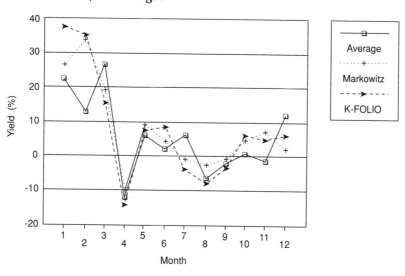

model's performance. Thus, knowledge can be beneficially used in making portfolio selection decisions as well as in evaluating and explaining individual stocks.

REFERENCES

Ignizio, J. P. *Programming and Extensions*. Lexington, MA: Lexington Books, 1976.

Lee, J. K., R. R. Trippi, S. C. Chu, and H. S. Kim. "K-FOLIO: Integrating the Markowitz Model with a Knowledge-based System." *Journal of Portfolio Management* 17 (Fall 1990), pp. 89–93.

Markowitz, H. "Portfolio Selection." *Journal of Finance* 7 (March 1952), pp. 77–91.

Sharpe, W. F. "A Simplified Model for Portfolio Analysis." *Management Science* 9 (January 1963), pp. 277–93.

CHAPTER 12

Integrating Knowledge with Databases

12.1 Introduction
12.2 Database Evolution
    12.2.1 Relational Databases
    12.2.2 The Advent of Knowledge Bases
    12.2.3 Object-Oriented Databases
12.3 The Management of Financial Data
    12.3.1 The Organization of Financial Data
    12.3.2 The Use of Financial Data
12.4 The Management of Price and Trading Volume Data
    12.4.1 The Organization of Price and Volume Data
    12.4.2 The Uses of Price and Volume Data
12.5 Management of the Function Base
    12.5.1 Functions
    12.5.2 Reserved Words
12.6 Conclusions

12.1   INTRODUCTION

Section 6.3 introduced the role of databases in portfolio decision making. This chapter reviews in more detail the components of databases that support investment decisions; identifies the distinguishing characteristics of relational, object-oriented, and knowledge bases; discusses the management of financial data and price and trading volume data; and examines the methods by which the capabilities of databases can be extended through the use of predefined functions.

12.2   DATABASE EVOLUTION

As database technology has evolved, so has its terminology. This chapter examines the databases popularly referred to as *relational databases, object-oriented databases,* and *knowledge bases.*

12.2.1   Relational Databases

The terms *database* and *knowledge base* are both widely used in the information systems field. Although the two terms have arisen independently, the software systems they refer to are basically similar.

In the 1970s, products were developed that supported the storage of information in tablelike *databases,* or *relational databases* that had formats such as that shown in Figure 12.1. Earlier storage structure had been mainly of the hierarchical and network types. Database administrators' major concerns at that time were to remove redundancy in corporate databases; determine the efficiency of *relational algebras* for retrieving, updating, and joining data having multiple relations; and find a type of *relational calculus* that could represent information for retrieval without ambiguity (see Date, 1986).

In the early days of computer information systems, databases were used to facilitate corporate-level data sharing and consisted of large-scale mainframes attached to a number of terminals. The first databases to handle stock price and trading volume data were generally of this type. As a result of the widespread availability of microcomputers and electronic data sources during the 1980s, investment databases began to include personal computer DBMSs (database management systems); thus, downloading of

Figure 12.1
Example of Relational Format

Stock Name	Price	Trading Volume	Date	
Slick Oil Co	99 1/2	22,500	3/10/95	
Junk Food Co	15 1/4	9,200	3/10/95	
MBT Electric	28	65,000	3/10/95	
Bank East	12 3/8	7,500	3/10/95	
Go Motor Corp	52	88,300	3/10/95	
Fast Computer	12 5/8	25,000	3/10/95	
Slick Oil Co	98 3/4	18,000	3/11/95	
Junk Food Co	15 1/2	11,700	3/11/95	
•	•	•	•	
•	•	•	•	
•	•	•	•	

a local or remote mainframe's database to the PC database and the management of distributed databases have become important concerns for users of investment databases and online data services. Some popular DBMSs are DB2, INGRES, ORACLE, dBASE, SYBASE, and FoxBase.

12.2.2   The Advent of Knowledge Bases

In the 1980s, many expert system community members referred to their databases as *knowledge bases.* In the earliest versions of rule-based shells, the knowledge base was divided into a rule base and a fact base (sometimes called *working memory*). In most systems, the role of a fact base is exactly the same as that of a traditional database. Because of this, in the ES world the fact base is sometimes called a database.

In early ESs, fact bases were simply lists and were very inefficient for the retrieval and modification of data. Today it is possible to interface a relational database with an ES's fact base or to replace the fact base entirely with a relational database (or with something else). Most of the commercially successful ES shells interface with popular databases such as dBASE and with spreadsheets rather than using these products for primary data storage.

Workstation-level tools such as Prokappa, ART*Enterprise, UNIK, and Nexpert Object support frame-based knowledge representation as well as rule-based representation. In these hybrid tools, the fact base can take the form of a frame base such as that described in Section 5.3. Also, in most of these products, the relational database is not absorbed into the expert system; it is merely interfaced. In the 1990s, such frame-based ES tools as Kappa PC, ART-IM, UNIK, and Nexpert Object migrated from workstations to personal computers.

12.2.3   Object-Oriented Databases

To most knowledge engineers, a relational database is just another means of storing knowledge. To database developers, a knowledge base is nothing more than a sophisticated database. As a result, terms such as *deductive database* and *object-oriented database* have emerged. As illustrated in the Prolog language example (see Figure 12.2), a deductive database adds rules on top of an existing database. Any rule-based system can be considered a deductive database if one focuses on its database. Which function is viewed as major and which is viewed as supplementary is a matter of perspective. Currently, it is common for the term *object-oriented database* to be used interchangeably with the term *frame-based knowledge base*. To be consis-

---

Figure 12.2
Illustrative Facts and Rules in Prolog

```
horizon (short_term)
risk_attitude (adverse)
dollar (strong)
labor_relations (bad)
inflation (high)
gulf_crisis (last_short)

use (machine_learned_knowledge) if horizon (short_term)
recession (end) if gulf_crisis (last_short)
```

---

tent with popular usage, these will also be referred to as *object-oriented databases*.

12.3   THE MANAGEMENT OF FINANCIAL DATA

This section examines the data management issues that arise among investors. Naturally, one data type of universal interest to this group is financial (including ratio) data.

12.3.1   The Organization of Financial Data

Accounting and other publicly available financial data are usually updated quarterly or annually. Since both expert systems and other reporting systems make use of financial data on individual stocks, companies, and industries, it is necessary to maintain these data in both object-oriented and relational databases. For stocks, data on average price, average trading volume, price-earnings ratio, and beta will be needed. For companies, data must be kept on sales, sales growth rate, amount of exports, debt ratio, fixed ratio, major products, assets, and profits as a percentage of sales, equity, and so on. For industries, data on average price index, total trading volume, total sales, sales growth rate, amount of exports, profitability, tax advantages, and stage in life cycle must be maintained.

Inheritance from higher to lower level and average-up or sum-up from lower to higher level are effective ways to handle the class-instance relationships of stocks, companies, and industries. For example, industry-level tax benefits can be inherited by companies in the industry, while the sum of sales, sales growth, and amount of exports can be summed up from companies to industries. The price and trading volume of stocks can also be averaged up to both company and industry levels.

As illustrated in Figure 12.3, which shows direct input, sum-up, and average-up mechanisms, the object-oriented database can be highly effective for representing such relationships. Since such data are also necessary for other reports, a relational database normally must be maintained in parallel for the same data (see Figure 12.4). Since data are usually received first into the relational database, a facility is required to make the transformation into the object-oriented database. The inheritance and average-up/sum-up facility will probably not exist in the relational database, so specific programs will have to be written in the host language to derive the necessary data items.

Figure 12.3
Object-Oriented Database

{{Industry
  AVERAGE PRICE INDEX: *average-up from stocks*
  TOTAL TRADING VOLUME: *sum-up from stocks*
  TOTAL SALES: *sum-up from company*
  SALES GROWTH RATE: *average-up from company*
  AMOUNT OF EXPORTS: *sum-up from company*
  PROFIT (%): *average-up from company*
  TAX BENEFIT: *direct input*
  STAGE IN LIFE CYCLE: *direct input*}}

{{Company
  SALES: *direct input*
  SALES GROWTH RATE: *direct input*
  AMOUNT OF EXPORT: *direct input*
  DEBT RATIO: *direct input*
  FIXED RATIO: *direct input*
  MAJOR PRODUCTS: *direct input*
  ASSETS: *direct input*
  PROFITS (%): *direct input*
  TAX BENEFIT: *inherit from industry*
  AVERAGE PRICE: *average-up from stocks*
  AVERAGE TRADING VOLUME: *average-up from stocks*
  PRICE-EARNINGS RATIO: *average-up from stocks*
  BETA: *average-up from stocks*}}

{{Stock
  AVERAGE PRICE: *direct input*
  AVERAGE TRADING VOLUME: *direct input*
  PRICE-EARNINGS RATIO: *direct input*
  BETA: *direct input*
  SALES: *inherit from company*
  SALES GROWTH RATE: *inherit from company*
  AMOUNT OF EXPORT: *inherit from company*
  DEBT RATIO: *inherit from company*
  FIXED RATIO: *inherit from company*
  MAJOR PRODUCTS: *inherit from company*
  ASSETS: *inherit from company*
  PROFITS (%): *inherit from company*
  TAX BENEFIT: *inherit from company*}}

FIGURE 12.4

Industry

Industry	Tax Benefit	Stage in Life Cycle

Company

Company	Sales	Sales Growth Rate	Amount of Export	Debt Ratio	Fixed Ratio	Major Product	Assets	Profit

Stock

Stock	Average Price	Average Trading Volume

Relational Database

12.3.2   The Use of Financial Data

Currently available financial data can be sent through either interactive retrieval or matching with rules. In K-FOLIO, financial data may be retrieved during stock evaluation dialogues (see Section 6.5). Financial data may also be matched with the rule set to identify relevant rules for each stock. (See the inference procedure described in Section 6.4.)

Through the use of inductive learning mechanisms (see Chapter 9), historical financial series can be used to generate rules for long-term fundamental analysis. Since these data are usually updated quarterly or annually, a machine-learned rule may last for three or six months; thus, it is not necessary to update or match such rules over fairly long time intervals.

12.4   THE MANAGEMENT OF PRICE AND TRADING VOLUME DATA

12.4.1   The Organization of Price and Volume Data

Price and trading volume data should be updated at least daily; these data are frequently displayed in graphs showing stock price trend lines, moving-average curves of stock prices, moving-average curves of trading volume, and price-volume correlation curves (see Figures 9.5 through 9.8). One reason for displaying current price and trading volume dynamically in graphical form is to make it easier to interpret suspected price anomalies. For example, Section 9.4 showed how the SYNPLE algorithm can generate credible pattern-based rules from such data. The quantity of data to be saved varies; if moving averages are rule inputs, quantity will be determined by the interval of the longest moving average. As new data enter, old data can be dropped.

To uncover any anomalies that may involve both trading and fundamental data and generate corresponding rules, it is desirable to keep historical daily data for years. Since pattern-based inductive learning takes a significant amount of computing time, one would probably want to use a dedicated personal computer or workstation for this purpose. Once rules are generated, the rule file can be transferred to the operating computer.

If charts showing daily price and trading volume are to be displayed, recently daily data must be kept in the object-oriented database. Since price and volume data are usually obtained from the mainframes of security companies or from independent online data services, at least one download daily to the expert system–serving workstation will be needed. It is common for data to be downloaded continuously, with a signal given when a desired action is triggered.

12.4.2   The Uses of Price and Volume Data

Daily price and trading volume–based rules are usually used for short-term trading, but if the interval of data collection is expanded for weekly and monthly averaging, these data can also be used for investment strategies that employ long-term data.

12.5   MANAGEMENT OF THE FUNCTION BASE

If only the data items in the database are to be utilized, the attributes of rules should be limited to such items. This is a fairly strict restriction, so the scope of rule statements could be severely limited. To overcome such a limitation, one can utilize *functions* incorporating *reserved words.*

12.5.1   Functions

Suppose the database includes *net profit growth rate* and *sales growth rate* and that the attribute to be included in a rule is the ratio of net profit growth to sales growth. This can be accomplished by defining the following function:

Ratio of net profit growth to sales growth

= Net profit growth rate / Sales growth rate.

The function base includes a collection of such functions that can operate on the data items in the database. This approach extends the boundary of data items greatly, without adding significantly to the storage burden.

To facilitate the creation of required functions, the inference engine needs to identify attributes that do not currently exist in either the database attributes list or the function base. The user can then define additional functions, assuming the necessary attributes can be derived from the existing data items. If the derivation is not possible, that attribute in the rule base should either be avoided or added to the database items.

12.5.2   Reserved Words

In addition to functions, and to allow compact expressions in rule specifications, K-FOLIO supports the following reserved words associated with stock price and trading volume: SIGMA, MAX, MIN, WHENMAX, WHENMIN, and SELECT. Following are some examples of how these reserved words may be used for a certain stock:

SIGMA(VOLUME, 040195, –30): Sum of trading volumes for 30 days previous to April 1, 1995

MAX(PRICE, 040195, 10): Maximum stock price for 10 days after April 1, 1995

MIN(PRICE, 040195, –10): Minimum stock price for 10 days previous to April 1, 1995

WHENMAX(VOLUME, 040195, 20): The date with the highest trading volume among the 20 days following April 1, 1995

WHENMIN(PRICE, 040195, –20): The date with the minimum stock price among the 20 days previous to April 1, 1995

SELECT(PRICE, 040195): The stock price on April 1, 1995

By combining functions with reserved words, more complex functions can be defined, as in the following examples:

SIGMA(PRICE, today, –30)/30: 30 days moving average of stock price

SELECT(PRICE, WHENMAX(VOLUME, 040195, 10)): The stock price on the day with the maximum trading volume during the 10 days following April 1, 1995

The values derivable by functions and reserved words can also be retrieved as though they were items defined in the database.

12.6   CONCLUSIONS

It is important to incorporate the knowledge base with security, company, and industry databases. Relational databases, object-oriented databases, and knowledge bases can all be used for portfolio decision support in ESs. The theoretical distinction between data and knowledge is vague and sometimes arbitrary, and the conventional relational databases that store financial data, stock prices, and trading volumes are used not only by the ES but also by other reporting systems. Generally, then, it is best to loosely couple the relational database with the object-oriented database (Jarke and Vassiliou, 1983). Maintaining consistency between a corporate- and/or investor-level relational database and a localized object-oriented database should be a key part of investment data management.

REFERENCES

Date, C. J. *An Introduction to Database Systems,* 4th ed. Reading, MA: Addison-Wesley, 1986.

Jarke, J., and Y. Vassiliou. "Coupling Expert Systems with Database Management." In *Artificial Intelligence Applications for Business,* edited by W. Reitman. Proceedings of the NYU Symposium, 1983, pp. 65–86.

CHAPTER 13

An Illustrative Session with K-FOLIO

13.1 Introduction
13.2 Selecting Investment Characteristics, Environmental
     Assumptions, and Knowledge Sources
13.3 Individual Stock Evaluation
13.4 Industry Evaluation
13.5 Criteria-Based Dialogue
13.6 Grade-Based Listing
13.7 Portfolio Selection
13.8 Conclusions

13.1 INTRODUCTION

By describing a typical dialogue session with K-FOLIO, this chapter illustrates many of the concepts discussed in this book. The dialogues are arranged as follows: selection of investment characteristics, environmental assumptions, and knowledge sources; individual stock or industry evaluation; criteria-based evaluation; grade-based listing; and portfolio selection. The version of K-FOLIO used for the dialogue examples was implemented at the Seoul-based Lucky Securities Company. The system, called BRAINS, runs on a client's IBM-compatible personal computer and on a SUN workstation server.

13.2   SELECTING INVESTMENT CHARACTERISTICS, ENVIRONMENTAL ASSUMPTIONS, AND KNOWLEDGE SOURCES

Since investment characteristics and environmental assumptions determine the selection of relevant knowledge, the dialogue begins with the selection of characteristics and assumptions. As shown in Figure 13.1, investment characteristics may be defined by selecting an investment horizon and a risk attitude. The investment horizon is to call up relevant knowledge and determine the evaluation time lag in the machine-learning scheme (see Section 9.3). The risk attitude query is used to select the target return for the Markowitz model.

Figure 13.1
Selection of Investment Characteristics

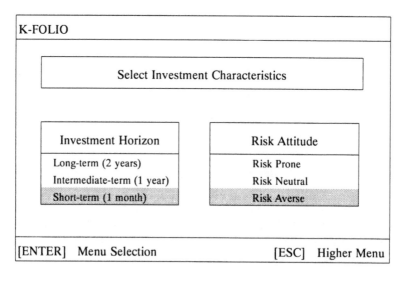

Figure 13.2
Selection of Assumptions

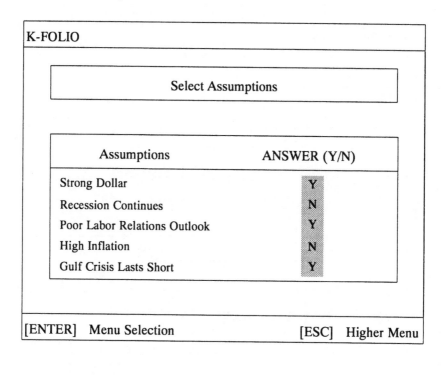

A binary selection of assumptions (Y or N) is illustrated in Figure 13.2. In this example, the environmental factors are the strength of the dollar, the recession, labor relations, inflation, and the duration of a Persian Gulf political crisis. Because binary selection of assumptions is a relatively crude facility, fuzzy membership values can be assigned to factors for which binary selections are difficult to make.

As shown in Figure 13.3, the last preliminary step is to select a knowledge base. In this example, the expert knowledge base (see Section 6.2) and machine-learned knowledge base (see Chapter 9) are selected. After completing the dialogues shown in Figures 13.1 through 13.3, the user is ready to select the options shown in Figure 13.4.

Figure 13.3
Selection of Knowledge Bases

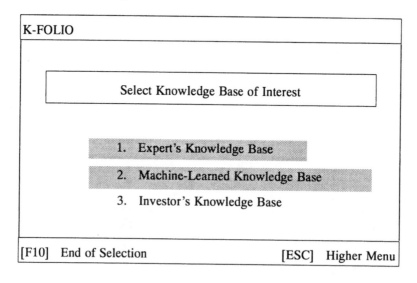

13.3   INDIVIDUAL STOCK EVALUATION

To initiate stock evaluation, the user can select option 1 from those given
in Figure 13.4. The display will then show candidate stocks and enable the
user to select an individual stock (see Figure 13.5). In this case, stock ABC
has been selected, and the screen shown in Figure 13.6 appears. This screen
shows a composite grade BBB and ordered reasons by the grade level. If
the user cannot agree with the elementary grades and credibilities in the
Reasons section, he or she can modify them interactively. As shown in
Figure 13.7, the grade and credibility of reason 3 are modified to the values
A and 1.0, and the composite grade is recomputed to the value A (see Figure
13.8). Note that the order of reasons is also rearranged.

13.4   INDUSTRY EVALUATION

To initiate industry evaluation, the user selects option 2 in Figure 13.4,
which brings up the screen shown in Figure 13.9. If, for example, industry
"An_Industry" is selected, the industry evaluation screen shown in Figure

Figure 13.4
Dialogue Menu

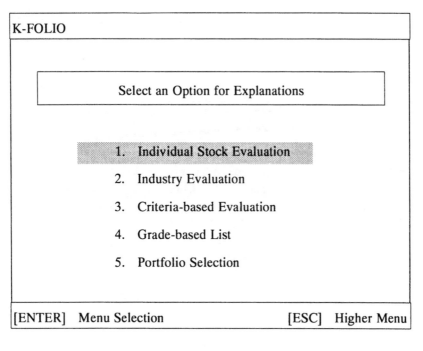

13.10 will be displayed. Interactive dialogue is supported for both industry and individual stock evaluation (see Figures 13.7 and 13.8).

13.5   CRITERIA-BASED DIALOGUE

To evaluate the stocks that satisfy a certain set of criteria (see Section 6.5.3), the user can select the desired criteria from the menu shown in Figure 13.11. In this case, debt ratio is selected as the first criterion. If the user selects operator "<" and types in *300*, the statement *debt ratio < 300* will be generated (see Figure 13.12). If a criterion (e.g., industry) has predefined multiple choices, the candidate values will be displayed (see Figure 13.13). The user is then shown the average grade of the stocks that satisfy the criteria, along with a list of the stocks (see Figure 13.14).

Figure 13.5
Selection of Individual Stocks

K-FOLIO	Individual Stock: Short-term

> ### Select a Stock

ABC	Aetna Life & Casualty	Alcan Aluminum Ltd.
Amax. Inc.	Amerada Hess Corp.	American Home Products
AT&T	Anheuser-Busch, Inc.	Atlantic Richfield
Campbell Soup Co.	Carnation Co.	CBS, Inc.
Chase Manhattan Co.	Coca-Cola Co.	Conoco, Inc.
Digital Equipment Co.	Dow Chemical Co.	Emerson Electric
Exxon Corp.	Federated Dept. Store	Florida Power & Light
Foster Wheeler Co.	Gannett, Inc.	General Electric
General Motors	Georgia-Pacific	Gulf Oil Corp.
INA Corp.	Ingersoll Rand	IBM
Johnson & Johnson	Koppers, Inc.	Kroger Co.
Lone Star Industries	R. H. Macy & Co., Inc.	Maytag Co.
McDonald's Corp.	Medtronic, Inc.	Melville Corp.
Merck & Co., Inc.	Midland Ross Corp.	Minnesota M & M
Monsanto Co.	Motorola, Inc.	NCNB Corp.

[ENTER] Menu Selection	[ESC] Higher Menu

13.6   GRADE-BASED LISTING

The grade-based list of stocks is obtained by selecting menu item 4 from the screen shown in Figure 13.4. The new screen is shown in Figure 13.15.

Figure 13.6
Grade and Reasons for Individual Stock

```
┌────────────────────────────────────────────────────────────────┐
│ K-FOLIO                              Individual Stock:  Short-term│
├────────────────────────────────────────────────────────────────┤
│                                                                  │
│    Grade of ABC = BBB                                            │
│                                                                  │
│    Reasons:                                                      │
│                                                                  │
│    (1)  Grade = AA with CR = 0.8                                 │
│         The electronic industry that the company ABC belongs to │
│         is a high-growth industry.                              │
│                                                                  │
│    (2)  Grade = BBB with CR = 0.8                                │
│         Reserved Ratio > 200                                     │
│                                                                  │
│    (3)  Grade = BB with CR = 0.9                                 │
│         Sales Growth Rate ≥ 20%                                  │
│                                                                  │
│                                                                  │
├────────────────────────────────────────────────────────────────┤
│ [F4 Graph]    [F5 Timing]    [ENTER Continue]    [ESC Higher Menu]│
└────────────────────────────────────────────────────────────────┘
```

13.7   PORTFOLIO SELECTION

To construct a portfolio by using the knowledge-augmented Markowitz optimization model, the user selects menu item 5 from the display (see Figure 13.4). The interpreter (see Section 11.3) is then invoked. In formulating the optimization models, the investment amount and average annual expected return are inputted (see Figure 13.16). The user then chooses one of two possible strategies for applying the knowledge: *composite-grade-*based order or *degree-of-underestimation*-based order (see Figure 13.17). The composite-grade-based order strategy applies grades as the preemptive priority; thus, stocks with AAA will be selected first; stocks with AA will be selected second; and so on. The degree-of-underestimation ordering strategy categorizes stocks according to the magnitude of the difference between the realized stock-price level and the computed grade. If a stock is highly undergraded, it is considered to have good appreciation potential.

Figure 13.7
On-Screen Edit

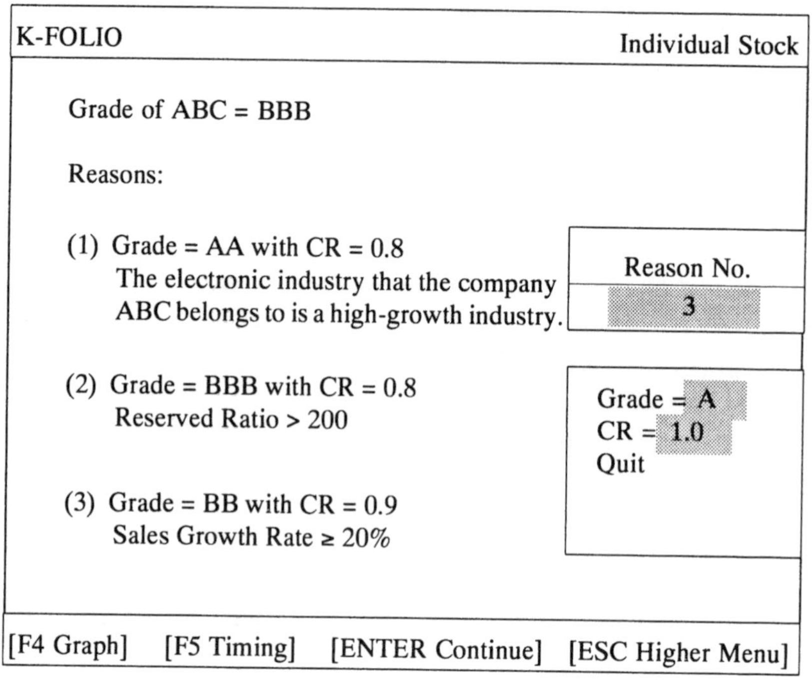

```
┌─────────────────────────────────────────────────────────────┐
│ K-FOLIO                                     Individual Stock  │
├─────────────────────────────────────────────────────────────┤
│                                                               │
│    Grade of ABC = BBB                                         │
│                                                               │
│    Reasons:                                                   │
│                                          ┌─────────────────┐  │
│    (1)  Grade = AA with CR = 0.8         │   Reason No.    │  │
│         The electronic industry that the company ├──────────┤  │
│         ABC belongs to is a high-growth industry.│    3     │  │
│                                          └─────────────────┘  │
│    (2)  Grade = BBB with CR = 0.8        ┌─────────────────┐  │
│         Reserved Ratio > 200             │  Grade = A      │  │
│                                          │  CR = 1.0       │  │
│                                          │  Quit           │  │
│    (3)  Grade = BB with CR = 0.9         │                 │  │
│         Sales Growth Rate ≥ 20%          │                 │  │
│                                          └─────────────────┘  │
│                                                               │
├─────────────────────────────────────────────────────────────┤
│ [F4 Graph]   [F5 Timing]   [ENTER Continue]  [ESC Higher Menu]│
└─────────────────────────────────────────────────────────────┘
```

If the composite-grade-based strategy is selected, a trial portfolio is returned (see Figure 13.18). The difference between the current portfolio and suggested trial portfolio defines the trades that should be executed. If the user has no objection, the dialogue can be terminated; if the user wishes to modify the suggested portfolio, some stocks can be eliminated and others can be added on. Stocks to be eliminated are selected from the list in Figure 13.19. The grade of such stocks is treated as ZZZ in the investor preference base (see Chapter 8), which implies a grade of D irrespective of the grades of the other factors (see Section 6.4.2). On the other hand, the newly added stocks are treated as "***", which implies a grade of AAA irrespective of the grades of other factors. With the internal revision of these grades, the

Figure 13.8
Modified Screen after Revision

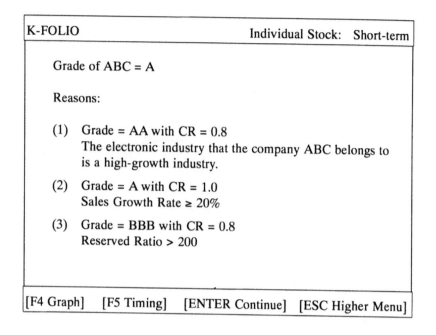

```
K-FOLIO                                Individual Stock:   Short-term

    Grade of ABC = A

    Reasons:

    (1)   Grade = AA with CR = 0.8
          The electronic industry that the company ABC belongs to
          is a high-growth industry.

    (2)   Grade = A with CR = 1.0
          Sales Growth Rate ≥ 20%

    (3)   Grade = BBB with CR = 0.8
          Reserved Ratio > 200



[F4 Graph]     [F5 Timing]     [ENTER Continue]    [ESC Higher Menu]
```

modified optimization model is rerun to generate a new portfolio. The user can then again initiate the evaluation of individual stocks (see section 13.3).

13.8 CONCLUSIONS

The example session described in this chapter shows how the K-FOLIO system can implement the concepts described in earlier chapters. At the beginning of the dialogue, K-FOLIO requests investment characteristics (time horizon and risk attitude), environmental assumptions, and knowledge sources (expert, machine-learned, or investor); relevant knowledge bases are then selected. At this point, a user can acquire evaluations of industries and individual stocks and generate a set of criteria-satisfying stocks. After the knowledge base is merged with the optimization model, a portfolio can be generated.

Figure 13.9
Selection of Industry

K-FOLIO	Industry: Long-term

Select an Industry

Aerospace	Agriculture and food
Air transport	Apparel
Banks	Business machines
Business services	Chemicals
Construction	Consumer durables
Containers	Domestic oil
Drugs and medicine	Electronics
Energy raw materials	Energy utilities
Forest products and paper	Gold mining and securities
Insurance	International oil
Liquor	Media
Miscellaneous and conglomerates	Miscellaneous finance
Motor vehicles	Nondurables and entertainment
Nonferrous metals	Photographic and optical
Producer goods	Railroads and shipping

[F4 Graph]   [F5 Timing]   [ENTER Continue]   [ESC Higher Menu]

Figure 13.10
Grade and Reason for an Industry

K-FOLIO	Industry

Grade of An_Industry = AA

Reasons:

(1) Grade = A with CR = 0.9
High-Growth Industry

(2) Grade = AAA with CR = 0.8
Technologically Competitive Against Japanese Companies

[F4 Graph]   [F5 Timing]   [ENTER Continue]   [ESC Higher Menu]

Figure 13.11
Selection of Criteria

K-FOLIO	Criteria

Select Criteria

Accum. Debt to Fixed Assets	Assets Turnover
Borrowing & Bonds Payable Ratio	Current Ratio
Debt Ratio	Depreciation Ratio
Equity Growth	Equity Ratio
Equity Turnover	Financial Exp. to Borrowings
Financial Exp. to Sales	Fixed Assets Growth
Fixed Assets to Equity & Liabil.	Fixed Assets Turnover
Gross Margin on Sales	Gross Value Added Growth
Industry	Net FX Gains to Sales
Net Income Growth	Ordinary Income on Sales
Ordinary Income on Total Assets	R&D to Sales
Receivables Turnover	Return on Capital Stock
Return on Equity	Return on Sales

[ESC Quit]

Figure 13.12
Numeric-Type Criteria Specification

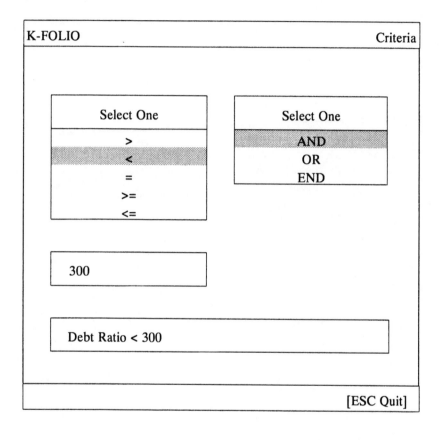

Figure 13.13
Value-Type Criteria Specification

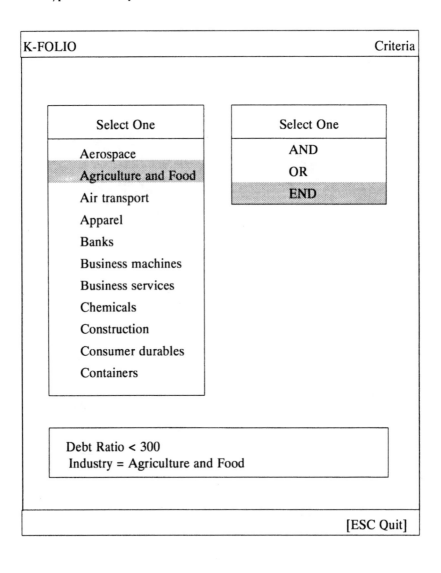

Figure 13.14
Output from Criteria-Based Dialogue

K-FOLIO		Criteria
Stock	Debt Ratio	Industry
AF1	153.99	Agriculture and Food
AF2	161.20	Agriculture and Food
AF3	186.05	Agriculture and Food
		[ESC Quit]

Figure 13.15
Grade-Based List

K-FOLIO		Grade
(1) AAA :	AAA1 AAA2 AAA3 AAA4 AAA5 AAA6 AAA7 AAA8 AAA9 AAA10	
(2) AA :	AA1 AA2 AA3 AA4 AA5 AA6 AA7 AA8 AA9 AA10 AA11 AA12	
[F4 Previous]	[F5 Next]	[F6 Enter]

Figure 13.16
Input of Investment Amount and Expected Return Target

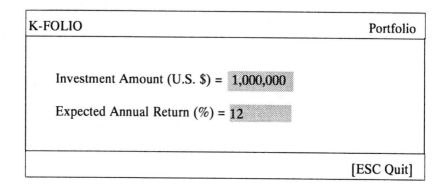

Figure 13.17
Selection of Knowledge Application Strategy

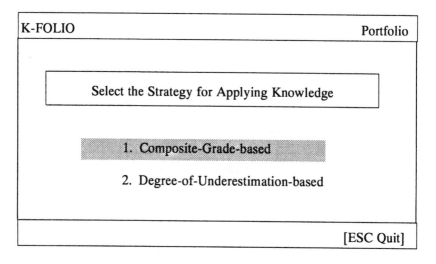

Figure 13.18
Trial Portfolio

K-FOLIO			Portfolio

Investment Amount (U.s. $) = 1,000,000
Expected Annual Return (%) = 12
Risk of Portfolio = Low (Standard Deviation = 0.8884)

Portfolio

Stock	Percentage	Amount	Volume
ABM	3.83	38,300	1,201
MLC	29.18	291,800	2,212
PNZ	3.91	39,100	1,597
ASQ	7.80	78,000	23
UGE	3.86	38,600	100
LRS	22.86	228,600	113
GLG	18.23	182,300	219
RAT	10.33	103,300	841
	100.00%	$1,000,000	

[F1 DOS]   [F3 Modify Portfolio]   [ESC Higher Menu]

Figure 13.19
Elimination of Unfavorable Stocks

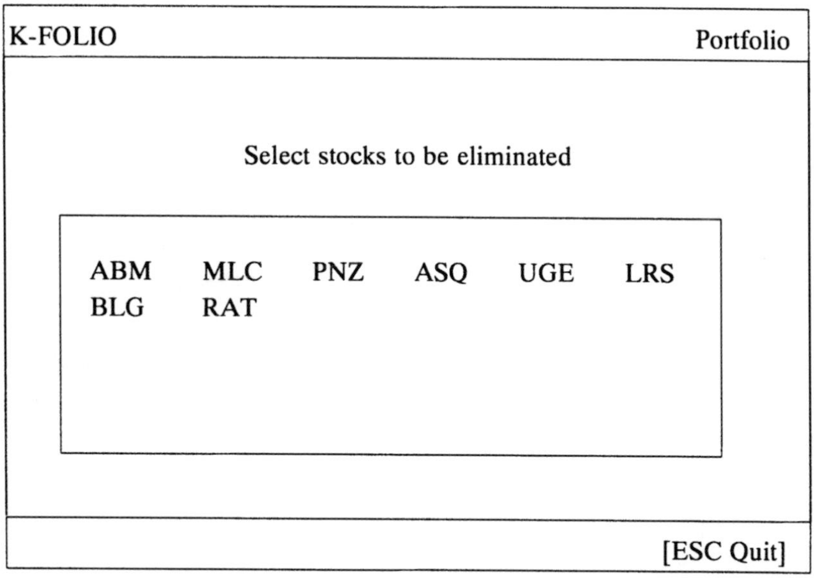

K-FOLIO	Portfolio

Select stocks to be eliminated

| ABM | MLC | PNZ | ASQ | UGE | LRS |
| BLG | RAT | | | | |

[ESC Quit]

REFERENCES

K-FOLIO User's Manual. KAIST, 1990, 1995.

CHAPTER 14

Concluding Remarks

14.1 System Design Criteria: A Summary
14.2 Directions for Future Research

14.1 SYSTEM DESIGN CRITERIA: A SUMMARY

This book has covered many aspects of building and using artificial intelligence–based systems for investment decision making. The key system design issues can be summarized as follows:

1. Rules provide an effective way to represent knowledge in the security-investment domain. The rule-based paradigm can efficiently generate evaluations of securities and industries as well as the reasons leading to those evaluations. Each rule should incorporate a credibility measure and such meta-knowledge as usage, investment horizon, author, entry date, and expiration date. Meta-knowledge facilitates knowledge acquisition and maintenance tasks.

2. For portfolio decisions, a frame-based system is an ideal form of object-oriented database; it provides inheritance, average-up, and sum-up facilities, which are useful for linking securities, industries, and asset classes. To extend the scope of usable data items, virtual data items can be defined by using a function definition

language that specifies new items derived from extant data attributes. A loosely coupled relational database will, however, be necessary to support other reports and online queries for information irrelevant to the expert system.

3. Inference for investment decisions requires a structured organization of the information acquired from diverse sources for individual securities or industries, plus a means of resolving possibly conflicting evidence into simple composite grades. The organized information can be used to explain the reasons for particular conclusions. If the end user does not agree with the reasons, he or she should be able to modify them and observe the impact of the modification without corrupting the common shared-knowledge base.

4. Representation schemes should be selected by considering the availability of data as well as the performance of associated approximate reasoning mechanisms. The Bayesian, certainty factor, and fuzzy logic approaches are all useful for handling investment uncertainties. Nonmonotonic reasoning can also be used to reflect a user's assumptions about the investment environment.

5. If possible, machine learning techniques should be applied to overcome the bottleneck of knowledge acquisition. For knowledge relevant to long-term investment, ID3 or other inductive means can be used to derive rules based on financial data. For knowledge relevant to short-term trading, pattern-based syntactic learning schemes can be used to generate credible rules automatically from price and trading volume data. Such schemes can also be used for long-term investment decisions if the relevant rules involve weekly or monthly data points. Genetic algorithms could also be useful for generating synergistic rule sets, and neural networks are a promising medium for detecting pockets of market inefficiency. Nevertheless, since all machine-learning schemes are based on extrapolation, human knowledge is still necessary to assess the likely impact of nonrecurrent events.

6. Optimization models such as the modified Markowitz model (see Chapter 11) can be used to apply reasoning capability to portfolio-mix decisions. The main issues are those associated with accommodating up-to-date knowledge and preferences within the

selected model. This book has shown how grades of stocks can be treated as priorities on decision variables and how investor-provided restrictions can be treated as additional constraints. In experiments, the knowledge-enhanced optimization model has outperformed both a market index and the unenhanced Markowitz model.

14.2   DIRECTIONS FOR FUTURE RESEARCH

The following issues related to the effectiveness and economy of artificial intelligence–based systems for portfolio management merit further study:

1. The performance of knowledge-based systems can be improved by generating more reliable knowledge via machine learning; thus, more attention should be given to developing learning techniques that will be effective in this particular domain. It would also be helpful to have a framework for synergistically combining such approaches as neural networks, syntactic pattern–based learning, genetic adaptive algorithms, and case-based learning and reasoning schemes. Intensive comparative experiments should accompany the development of any new techniques.

2. More effective synthesis of predictive capability with explanation capability is highly desirable. For example, although clear and concise explanation of reasons is usually essential to investors, neural network–based models often do not provide theoretically acceptable reasons for their recommendations. It is possible, however, that simple probabilities of success will suffice for some types of users, regardless of the reasoning.

3. Incorporating the entire spectrum of concepts and techniques discussed in this book into a single system may be inappropriate, impractical, or too costly for many prospective users. An economical solution to this problem would be to develop a system generator capable of generating specific portfolio investment systems that satisfy a set of specifications given by the prospective user.

Name Index

A

Akgiray, V., 46, 51
Ambati, B., 153
Ambati, J., 153
Asakawa, K., 169
Athena Group, 57
Avera, W.E., 8

B

Baker, D., 173
Barletta, R., 60
Bauer, R.J., 154-156
Berg-Cross, G., 60
Bestor, J., 51
Black, K., 144
Boose, J.H., 120
Booth, James R., 40
Braun, H., 56, 139, 140
Buta, P., 60

C

Carbinol, J.G., 135
Chandler, J., 56
Chandler, J.S., 139, 140
Chandra, M., 54
Chen, K., 54
Chen, M., 60
Chen, P., 61
Chi, R., 60
Chithelin, I., 166
Chu, S., 57, 82, 120
Chu, S.C., 139, 192
Clarkson, G.P., 24, 52, 53
Claudio, L., 60
Cohen, P., 26

Colin, A.C., 156
Collins, E., 170
Cooper, S.K., 8
Cootner, P., 11
Cryer, C., 56

D

Date, C.J., 198
Deboeck, G.J., 60, 61
DeBondt, W., 17
Deco, G., 61
DeSieno, D., 173
Dodd, D., 9
Dodd, P., 12
Doyle, J., 116
Dutta, S., 171

E–F

Elton, E.J., 33, 39
Faaland, B., 31
Fama, E., 12
Fama, E.F., 155
Forsyth, R., 67
Franks, E., 32
French, K.R., 155
Friedland, J., 51

G

Gaines, B.R., 120
Galler, M., 170
Gentry, J., 135
Gerkey, P., 54
Ghosh, G., 170
Goldberg, D.E., 156
Graham, B., 9

Granger, C.W.J., 178
Groth, J.C., 8
Gruber, M.J., 33, 39
Guy, J., 33

H

Haefke, C., 178
Han, Ingoo, 164
Hansen, J.V., 135
Harriff, R.B., 16, 19, 41
Haugen, R.A., 39
Hecht-Nielson, R., 162, 164, 172
Heuer, S., 56
Hiemstra, Y., 173, 178
Hinton, G.E., 163
Holland, J.H., 152
Holsapple, C., 49
Hopfield, J., 172
Hsieh, D.A., 61
Hutchinson, J., 165

I–J

Ignizio, J.P, 25, 184
Jacobs, B., 10, 11, 13
Jang, G., 170
Jarke, J., 207
Jhee, W., 165

K

Kamijo, K., 168
Kanal, L., 144
Kanal, L.N., 102
Kandt, K., 53, 144
Kapouleas, I., 135
Keane, S., 14
Kiang, M.Y., 60
Kim, H., 165
Kim, H.S., 57, 59, 82, 120, 139, 144, 192
Kimoto, T., 169
Kimpton, M., 12
King, B., 13
King, D., 56
Koch, U., 56
Konno, H., 37, 38
Kraus, A., 40

Kryzanowski, L., 170
Kyle, M.C., 144

L

Lai, F., 170
Landerholm, K., 54
Larrain, M., 61
LeBaron, B., 61
Lee, C.F., 12
Lee, J., 57, 165
Lee, J.K., 57, 59, 82, 120, 139, 144, 192
Lee, T.H., 178
Lemmer, J.F., 102
Levy, K., 10, 11, 13
Liang, T., 54
Lieberman, M., 26
Liepins, G., 154, 155
Lintner, J., 37
Litzenberger, R., 40
Lo, A., 165
Lorie, J., 12
Lyons, P.J., 173

M

Malkiel, B., 12
Markowitz, H., 27, 184
Marsh, T., 8
Mayfield, E.S., 61
Mendel, J., 172
Messier, W.F., 135
Michalski, R.S., 135
Michelle, T.M., 135
Miller, M., 10
Minsky, M.L., 164
Mizrach, B., 61
Modigliani, F., 10
Mokhtar, M., 153
Moody, J., 182
Mossin, J., 37
Mostert, J., 54

N–Q

Naylor, C., 102
Newell, A., 46
Papert, S.A., 164

Perold, A.F., 16
Persek, S.C., 173
Pesaran, M.H., 155
Peters, E.E., 61
Poggio, T., 165
Puelz, A., 26
Puelz, R., 26
Quinlan, J.R., 135, 138

R

Rahman, S., 12
Rao, K., 144
Rao, S., 54
Rau, L, 54
Refenes, A.N., 178
Reilly, F.K., 39
Rissland, E.L., 60
Rock, K., 8
Rosenberg, B., 33
Rosenblatt, F., 164
Ross, S.A., 38
Rubinstein, J., 40
Rumelhart, D.E., 163

S

Scheinkman, J.A., 61
Schmalensee, R., 15
Schuermann, B., 61
Schwefel, H., 156
Scofield, C., 170
Shannon, S., 51
Sharpe, W.F., 16, 32, 37, 39, 184
Shaw, M.J., 135
Shekhar, S., 171
Shortliffe, E., 114
Simon, H.A., 46
Skalak, D.B., 60
Slade, S., 60

Stockman, G., 144
Stohr, E., 57
Sviokla, J., 51
Swales, G., 167

T–V

Takeoka, M., 169
Talluru, L.R., 46, 51
Tam, K.Y., 49, 135, 139, 144
Tanigawa, T., 168
Tank, D., 172
Tehranian, Hassan, 40
Thaler, R., 17
Timmerman, A., 155
Trennepohl, Gary L., 40
Trippi, Robert R., 16, 19, 40, 41, 57, 59,
    61, 62, 144, 173, 178, 192
Turban, E., 62, 178
Urich, T., 33
Utans, J., 182
Vassiliou, Y., 207

W–Z

Waterman, D.A., 67
Weiss, S., 135
Whinston, A., 49
White, H., 171, 178
Willey, T., 61
Williams, John Burr, 9, 10
Williams, R.J., 163
Wolfe, P., 41
Wright, D.W., 170
Yamazaki, H., 37, 38
Yoda, M., 169
Yoon, Y., 167
Yuenger, P., 53, 144
Zadeh, C.V., 112
Zhao, X., 172

Subject Index

A

Abstraction, 46
Acquisition, 53. *See also* Knowledge
  acquisition
  prices, 18
Activation function, 161
Agency effects, 15-16
AI. *See* Artificial intelligence
Anomalies, exploitation, 17-20
Applied Expert Systems, 56
Approximate reasoning, 60
APT. *See* Arbitrage pricing theory
Arbitrage pricing theory (APT), 38, 172
ARIMA. *See* Auto-regressive integrated
  moving average; Box-Jenkins
  ARIMA
Artificial intelligence (AI), 1-3, 69. *See
  also* Investment management
  concluding remarks, 229-231
  future research, directions, 231
  introduction, 1-5
  technologies, 57-61
Artificial intelligence-based decision
  support systems, 46
Artificial neural networks, 46
Artificial neural systems, 46
Asset allocation, 51
Asset class portfolios, 155
Asset classes, 3, 229
Asset types, 31
Assets. *See* Financial assets; Investment
  assets; Riskless assets; Risky assets
Asymmetrical portfolio return
  distributions, 40
Attenuation. *See* Rules
Attribute-based rules, 82, 84

Auto-learning systems, 45-46, 48, 132
Auto-regressive integrated moving
  average (ARIMA), 165, 177. *See
  also* Box-Jenkins ARIMA
Average-up, 85-87, 96, 201

B

Backpropagation algorithm, 163
Backward-chaining strategy, 73, 77
Bayesian approach, 102-108, 134
  definitions, 102-103
  formulas, 102-103
  inference strategy, 108-111
    discussion, 111
    illustration, 104-106
Beta, 34-37
Beta coefficient, 10, 32
Beta estimates, 33
Beta models, 31-35
Bidding strategy, 166
Bit string, 154
Black box expert systems, 61
Black box investing, 19-20
Black Monday market crash, 15
Black-Scholes model, 165
Boltzman machine, 170
Bond rating, 160
Bottom-up strategy, 73
Box-Jenkins ARIMA, 165
BRAINS, 209
Business failure, 160
Buy-and-hold strategy, 12, 16, 169
Buy-and-sell strategy, 169, 170
Buy-and-sell timing, 169
Buy-sell timing decisions, 52. *See* Equity
  buy-sell timing decisions

C

Capital goods, 32
Capital market line (CML), 37, 42
Capital market surface, 41
Capital-asset pricing model (CAPM), 3,
    11, 14, 37, 38
    extensions, 40-41
    limitations, 38-40
CAPM. *See* Capital-asset pricing model
Case-based learning, 133, 231
Case-based reasoning (CBR), 46, 60, 97,
    133, 231
    process, 77
Cash flow, 14
CBR. *See* Case-based reasoning
Certainty factor (CF) approach, 111-112,
    134
CF. *See* Certainty factor
Chaos theory, 46, 60, 61
Character, 46
Characteristic line, 32
Charting, 12
Circuit breakers, 16
Class-instance relationships, 73
Closed-end funds, 170
CML. *See* Capital market line
Cognitive error, 14-15
Commission savings, 17
Commissions, 8
Common stock, 52
Company classification. *See* Industry
    classification
Company database, 85
Company-based dialogue, 95-96
Company-based relational database, 84
Company-based rules, 82, 84
Company-specific risk, 32
Compensatory fuzzy logic approach, 114
Complex systems, 10
Composite grade, 96, 124, 188, 212
    computation, 97
Composite patterns, 59
Composite-grade base, 92, 95, 98, 188
Composite-grade generation, 89-93
Composite-grade-based strategy, 216
Compositional operators, 143
Concept-learning algorithm, 135-138
Condition-action, 48
Conflict set, 82, 96
Conflict-set generation, 89, 90
Conformance-allocation rules, 24

Connectionism, 57
Constant-proportion insurance strategy, 52
Consumer credit scoring, 170
Contrarian, 24
Corporate bond investments, 54
Corporate earnings, 10
Cost-distribution parameters, 133
Covariance, 33, 34
    matrices, 38
CR. *See* Credibility of rule
Credibility. *See* Rules
Credibility of rule (CR), 115, 138, 149
Credit approval, 160
Credit card companies, 171
Credit lines, 51
Credit-authorization screening, 166
Criteria-based dialogue, 97-98, 213-214
Criteria-based evaluation, 77, 209
Criteria-based questions, 97
Crossover, 152
    rate, 155
Cyclical spectral analysis, 12

D

Data acquisition, 31
Database, 84-89. *See* Integration with a
    database
    commonality effects, 15-16
    evolution, 198-201
    examples. *See* Relational databases
Database management systems (DBMSs),
    198, 199
Databases. *See* Object-oriented databases;
    Relational databases
    integration. *See* Knowledge
Data-driven induction, 49
Data-driven inference, 73
DBMSs. *See* Database management
    systems
DDM. *See* Dividend discount model
Debt ratios, 10, 73, 213
Debt risk, 160
Decision makers, 95, 112
Decision rules, 19-20
Decision support systems (DSSs), 1
Decision variables, 188, 189
Decision-making process, 3
    networks, 173
Deductive database, 200
Default topology, 164
Degree-of-estimation-based ordder, 215

Delta rule, 162
Demons, 74
Derived constraints, 188
Dialogues, 93-98. *See* Company-based
    dialogue; Criteria-based dialogue;
    Grade-based dialogue;
    Industry-based dialogue
Digraph, 71
Dimensionality, 59
Discontinuities, 41
Discriminant analysis, 134
Distribution moments, 40
Diversifiable risk, 32
Diversification, 30, 32, 37, 53
    constraints, 55
    models, 31
Dividend discount model (DDM), 10
Dividend income, 26
Dividends, 11
Domain, 2. *See* Investment domain
Domestic-oriented market, 105
Dow Jones average, 169
DSSs. *See* Decision support systems
Duration. *See* SYNPLE framework
Dynamic decision making, 78
Dynamic diversification, 51

E

Economic predictions, 166
Economic sectors, 32
Efficient dynamic allocation strategy,
    30-31
Efficient frontier, 29-30
Efficient market hypothesis (EMH),
    11-14, 171
Efficient portfolios, 28, 39
EMH. *See* Efficient market hypothesis
Endorsement. *See* Theory of endorsement
Entropy, 138
Environmental assumptions, 210-212
Epoch, 163
Equity buy-sell timing decisions, 127
ES. *See* Expert systems
Evidence. *See* Uncertain evidence
    application, sequence, 109
    integration process, 114
    theory, 102
Exchange-listed stocks, 8
Exchange-traded fixed-income
    investments, 166
Expert knowledge, 120-123

Expert systems (ES), 2, 3, 45, 49, 51-52,
    75, 109, 164, 199, 205. *See also*
    Fuzzy logic-based expert system;
    Portfolio selection
    components, 67-70
    contemporary systems, 53-57
    inference engine, 48
    programming languages, 53
    shell, 48, 200
EXPERT-EASE, 135
Explanation generation, 78
Explanation synthesis, 69, 89, 93
Export-oriented market, 105

F

Feedforward network, 160. *See also*
    Multilayered feedforward network
Financial assets, 8
Financial data
    management, 201-204
    organization, 201-203
    use, 204
Financial planning, 51
Financial ratios, 54
Financial services, 51-52
Fitness value, 59
Flat-file databases, 77
FOLIO, 55. *See* K-FOLIO
Foreign exchange rate, 169
    prediction, 160
Foreign financial market, 93
Foreign markets, 106
Forward-chaining strategy, 73, 77
Frame-based knowledge, 200
Frame-based representation, 75, 76
Frame-based systems, 73-75, 229
Frames, 48
Front-load mutual funds, 9
Function bases, management, 205-206
Functions, 205-206
Fundamental analysis, 10, 11, 56
Fund-specific risk, 16
Futures contracts, 8
Fuzzy evidence, 113
Fuzzy expert system, 59
Fuzzy logic, 46, 59, 102, 112-113
    approach, 112-115, 134. *See also*
        Compensatory fuzzy logic
        approach
    discussion, 115
Fuzzy logic-based expert system, 113-114

Fuzzy membership values, 211
Fuzzy set theory, 59

G–H

GA. *See* Genetic algorithm
Generation, 152
Genetic adaptive algorithms, 133,
    152-156, 231
Genetic algorithm (GA), 4, 59, 133, 152,
    153, 155. *See also* Trading rule
    generation
    applications, 154
Genetic-algorithm approach. *See* Learning
Global declaration, 123
Goal/goals, 49, 51
Goal program, 26
Goal programming, 24-26, 184
    algorithm, 55
Grade-based dialogue, 98
Grade-based listing, 209, 214-215
Growth rate, 73

Hardware, 2, 172
Hedging strategies, 51
Hidden layers, 162, 164
Hidden nodes, 164
Hierarchical structure, 125, 126
Historical data, 77
Hypotheses levels, handling, 108

I

ID3, 78, 135, 230
Implied distribution surrogates, 133-134
Implied probability
    distributions, 17-19
    model, 19
Inclusion/exclusion criteria, 52
Index arbitrage, 54
Index construction, 166
Index models, 31-35
Individual stock evaluation, 77, 212
Inductive learning, 133-143. *See also*
    Investment; Investment decisions
Inductive-learning schemes, 58
Industry classification, company
    classification comparison, 76
Industry database, 85
Industry evaluation, 212-213

Industry-based dialogue, 96
Industry-based rules, 82
Industry-level evaluation, 77
Industry-level inference, 96
Industry-level information, 84
Inference, 81-99. *See also* Investment
        support features; Security inference
    conclusions, 98
    efficiency, 120
    engine. *See* Expert systems
    introduction, 82
    references, 99
    strategy. *See* Bayesian approach;
        Rule-based systems
Inference-stopping conditions, 108
Inflation rate, 24, 34
Information, cost/value, 17
Inheritance, 56, 85-87
Insider trading, 11
Instability, 16-17
Institutional investors, 13, 17, 29, 61
Institutional trader, 16
Institutional trading, 15-17
Integration, 119-130. *See* Relevant
        knowledge
    conclusions, 130
    introduction, 119-120
    process. *See* Evidence
    references, 130
Integration with a database, 77
Integration with optimization, 76
Intelligent Stock Portfolio Management
        System (ISPMS), 57
Intelligent systems, 45-46
Interest, 26
Interest rates, 24, 169
Interday heuristic rules, 53
Interday stock price ranges, 12
Intraday price volatility, 16
Intraday stock price ranges, 12
Intraday volatility, 17
Inversion, 152
INVEST, 56
Investing, 1-3. *See also* Black box
        investing; Value-based investing
Investment, inductive learning potential,
        139-143
Investment assets, characteristics, 8-9
Investment characteristics, selection,
        210-212

Investment decision making, 61, 160
Investment decisions, 70, 104, 162, 230.
    See also Short-term investment
    decisions
    inductive learning application, 139
Investment domain, 4, 60
Investment experts, 52
Investment horizon, 127, 210, 229
Investment management, 23, 53, 132
Investment management, artificial
    intelligence use
    conclusions, 61
    endnotes, 62
    overview, 45-65
    references, 62-65
Investment risk, 14
Investment selection, 59
Investment strategies, 8, 78, 205
Investment support features, 75-79
    explanation, 77-78
    inference, 77-78
Investment theories, 9
Investment uncertainties, 101-117
    conclusions, 116
    introduction, 102
    references, 116-117
Investor preference bases, 120
Investor preferences
    representation, 120-124
    integration, 120-124
    interpretation, 123-124
Investor psychology, 15
ISPMS. *See* Intelligent Stock Portfolio
    Management System

K

K-FOLIO, 5, 57, 79, 82, 93, 112, 116,
    122, 125, 184, 192, 194, 204, 206
    architecture, 80
    conclusions, 217-227
    illustration, 209-227
    introduction, 209-210
    reference, 227
Knowledge. *See* Relevant knowledge
    bases, 2, 82, 123, 129, 198-200
    database integration, 197-207
        conclusions, 207
        introduction, 198
    engineering, 48

Knowledge (Con'd).
    entry, 120
    integration. *See* Portfolio optimization
    interpretation, 185-188
    maintenance, 78-79, 125-128, 130
        aids, 127-128
        productivity, 127
    sources, 76, 210-212
    structure, 125-128
    structuring, 125-127
Knowledge acquisition, 119-130, 230
    conclusions, 130
    introduction, 119-120
    references, 130
    sources, 124-125
Knowledge representation, 75-77
    conclusions, 98
    introduction, 46-50, 82
    references, 99
Knowledge-acquisition system, 69
Knowledge-based portfolio selection
    systems, 24
Knowledge-based systems, 2-5, 20, 23,
    45-46, 54, 61, 67, 132
Knowledge-editing aids, 78
Knowledge-editing process, 78
Korean stock market, 149
Kuhn-Tucker equations, 42
Kuhn-Tucker optimality conditions, 41

L

LA-COURTIER, 55, 56
LBOCON ES, 54
Learning, genetic-algorithm approach,
    152-153
Learning strategies, 133
Learning-based subsystem, 2
Learning-from-example (LFE), 46, 134
Level of confidence, 76
Leverage potential, 8, 9
Leveraged buyouts, 54
LFE. *See* Learning-from-example
Likelihood ratio, 103, 105
Linear program, 26
Linear programming problems, 69
Liquidation, 18
    price, 133
Liquidity, 8
Logic-based computer languages, 48

Long-holding-period returns, 128
Long-term investment, 53, 128
Long-term investors, 18
Low-growth stocks, 55

M

Machine learning, 46, 69, 78-79, 130-158
  conclusion, 156
  introduction, 131-133
  reasons, 131-132
  references, 156-158
Machine-learned knowledge, 125
Machine-learning mechanisms, 156
Machine-learning methodologies, 41
Machine-learning process, 78
Machine-learning schemes, 58, 132
Machine-learning systems, 120, 132
Macroeconomics-based rules, 154
MAD. See Mean absolute deviation
Maintenance, 78-79, 119-130. See also
    Knowledge
  introduction, 119-120
Margin requirements, 9
Market behavior, 15-17, 166
Market clearing, 42
Market inefficiency, 14, 17
Market portfolio, 36, 42
Market psychology, 15
Market return, 194
Market risk, 32
Market timing decisions, 166
Market-timing decisions, 51
Markowitz, H., 27
Markowitz mean-variance optimization
    model, 183
Markowitz model, 27-28, 30, 31, 33, 38,
    70. See also Unenhanced
    Markowitz model, 210, 230
  limitations, 38-40
Markowitz objective function, 34
Markowitz optimization model, 215
Markowitz portfolio
  diversification model, 172
  optimization model, 5
Markowitz QP, 41
Markowitz quadratic programming
    model, 3
  optimization model, 57
Matched rules, 89, 97
MB. See Measure of belief
MD. See Measure of disbelief

Mean absolute deviation (MAD)
  optimization, 37-38
  risk measure, 38
Mean-variance optimization, 24, 26-31
  systems, 31
Measure of belief (MB), 111
Measure of disbelief (MD), 111
Membership function, 112
Memory. See Working memory
Meta-knowledge, 120, 127, 229
Meta-knowledge guide, 78
Meta-rules, 48
Mixed zero-one integer program, 31
Model enhancement, 30-31
Model selection, 46
Model-driven induction, 49
Money supply, 34
Mortgage underwriting, 51
Mortgage-backed debt instruments, 8
Mortgage-risk assessment, 166
Moving-average curves, 204
Moving-average trends, 12
Moving indexes, 12
Moving-average curves, 144
Multidimensional screens, 13
Multilayered feedforward network, 162,
    163
Multimodal portfolio return distributions,
    40
Multiple discriminant analysis, 58, 168
Multiple regression, 34
Multiple-layered architecture, 58
Mutation, 152
Mutual funds, 58

N

Natural language processing, 57, 69
Naylor, C., 104
Near-subsitutes, 39, 40
NEC network, 168-170
Networks, 173-176. See Neural network;
    Neural networks
Neural network
  approaches, 143
  paradigms, 161
  theory, 57
Neural network-based systems, 49
Neural networks, 4, 5, 60, 133, 159-182.
    See also Artificial neural networks;
    Stock price prediction
  applications, 166-172

Neural networks (Con'd).
  architecture, 160-162
  conclusion, 177-178
  introduction, 159-160
  learning, 162-164
  references, 178-182
  rules, integration, 173-177
  strengths/weaknesses, 164-166
New York Stock Exchange (NYSE)
  stocks, 139
Node transfer functions, 49
Noise, 15
Noise-trading strategies, 15
Nondiversifiable risk, 32
Nonlinear dynamic systems, 13
Nonmonotonic reasoning, 102, 116
Non-negative variables, 31
Non-negativity constraint, 28

O

Object-oriented databases, 75, 200-201,
  204
Odds, 013
Optimization. *See* Integration with
  optimization; Mean absolute
  deviation optimization;
  Mean-variance optimization
  model, 124, 231
  problem, 29, 70
Ordered systems, 10
Ordering. *See* Random ordering
Ordering by importance, 109
Output parameters, 167

P

Pattern recognition, 57, 61
Pattern selection, 54
Pattern-based learning, 46
Pattern-based rules, 204
Pattern-based syntactic learning schemes,
  230
Patterns. *See* SYNPLE framework
PE. *See* Processing element
P/E. *See* Price to earnings ratio
Perceptron, 164
Performance evaluation, 192-194
PMIDSS. *See* Portfolio Management
  Intelligent Decision Support System
Portfolio appreciation, 26
Portfolio assets, 29

Portfolio decision making, 76
Portfolio decisions, 33
Portfolio diversification, 166
Portfolio management, 51
Portfolio Management Intelligent
  Decision Support System
  (PMIDSS), 57
Portfolio manager, 16
Portfolio optimization, 19
Portfolio optimization, knowledge
  integration, 183-195
  conclusions, 194-195
  introduction, 183-184
Portfolio optimization model. *See*
  Markowitz portfolio optimization
  model
Portfolio return distributions. *See*
  Asymmetrical portfolio return
  distributions; Multimodal portfolio
  return distributions
Portfolio returns, 39
Portfolio risk, 28, 35, 37. *See* Total
  portfolio risk
Portfolio selection, 23, 25, 27, 58, 166,
  209, 215-217
  expert systems, 52-53
Portfolio selection, modern approaches,
  23-44
  endnotes, 41-42
  introduction, 23-24
  references, 43-44
Portfolio theory, 3
Portfolio-mix decisions, 39
Portfolio-selection system issues, 67-80
  references, 79
Possibility theory, 102, 112
Posterior probability, 103, 105, 107, 109
Preference, 120. *See* Investor preferences
Preprimitive, 147
Price
  anomalies, 124
  appreciation, 9
  distributions, 133
  management, 204-205
  motivation, 9
  organization, 204-205
  pattern recognition system, 144
  performance, 12
  uses, 205
  volatility. *See* Intraday price volatility
Price to cash flow, 10
Price to earnings (P/E) ratio, 10, 13

Price-earnings ratio, 84, 123
Price-volume correlation curve, 144
Primitive-based rules, 147
Primitives, 143
Prioritized decision variables, 188-192
Probability, 102-110
Probability distributions. *See* Implied
    probability distributions
Probability theory, 102
Problem representation issues, 153-154
Problem solving, 68
Problem-solving techniques, 68-69
Processing element (PE), 160-163
Production rules, 48
Program trading, 40-41
    systems, 16
Project management, 166
PROLOG, 48
PROTRADER, 54

Q

QP. *See* Quadratic program
Quadratic program (QP), 28, 37, 42, 184
    model, 185
Quadratic programming, 172, 188-192
    model. *See* Markowitz quadratic
        programming model
Quebec stock market, 170
Quinlan, J.R., 137

R

Random ordering, 109
Random systems, 10
Random walk, 11
    theory, 12
Reasoning. *See* Nonmonotonic reasoning
Recommendation levels, 93
Regression analysis, 58
Relational algebras, 198
Relational databases, 77, 198-199, 201.
        See also Company-based relational
        database
    examples, 84-85
Relevant knowledge, selective
    integration, 128-129
Relevant risk, 35
Representation. *See* Knowledge
    representation; Rule-based systems
Reserved words, 206-207

Residual reversals, 13
Resistance lines, 168
Restriction operations, 54
Return covariances, 184
Return distribution, 40, 41
Returns, time pattern, 8
Risk, definition, 14
Risk attitude, 210
Risk classification decisions, 170
Risk issues, 14-15
Risk modeling. *See* Stochastic risk
    modeling
Risk rating, 166
Risk-free rate, 36, 37
Riskiness, 26, 28
Riskless assets, 40
    role, 36-37
Risk-return characteristics, 37
Risk-return combinations, 29, 36
Risk-return optimization problem, 28
Risky assets, 36, 39, 42
Rule base, 70, 82-84
Rule induction, 46
Rule parameter, 154
Rule synergy, 98
Rules, 68, 113-115, 143, 150. *See also*
        Decision rules
    credibility. *See* Credibility of rule
    credibility, attenuation, 115
    examples, 82-84
    stopping, 110
    syntax, 82, 127
Rule-based paradigm, 229
Rule-based shells, 199
Rule-based systems, 70-73, 164, 173
    inference strategies, 71-73
    representation, 70-71
Rule-value approach, 109

S

Sales forecasts, 10
Sales growth rate, 87
Scenario allocation, 24
SCISOR. *See* System for Conceptual
    Information Summarization,
    Organization and Retrieval
Secondary market, 36
Securitization, 8
Security inference, 89-93
Security investment decisions, 75

Security investment domain, nature, 7-22, 229
  conclusions, 20
  endnotes, 20
  references, 21-22
Security market line (SML), 35, 37
Security markets, 3
Security price, 133
Security returns, 34
Security risk, 35
Selection, 23
Semantic networks, 48
Semistrong form, 11
Sensitivity analysis capability, 116
Shareholders, 18
Share-cost probabilities, 19
Sharpe, W.F., 16, 31, 37, 38, 160
Sharpe-type model. *See* Single-index Sharpe-type model
Shell. *See* Expert systems
Shortliffe, E., 117
Short-term investment decisions, 128
Short-term price movements, 133
Short-term trading, 230
  rules, 124
Sideways market, 139
Single-index Sharpe-type model, 38
Single-market index model, 35
SML. *See* Security market line
Software, 2
  tools, 135
Solution methodology, 46
Standard deviation, 10, 14, 35, 37, 40
  risk, 16
Standard & Poor's 500 (S&P 500), 139, 173, 176
Static asset diversification, 51
Stochastic processes, 10
Stochastic risk modeling, 14-15
Stock analysis, 143
Stock evaluation. *See* Individual stock evaluation
Stock market, 24
  movements, 139
  timing, 154
Stock options, 8
Stock price
  determination, theories, 9-14
  prediction, 160
    neural networks usage, 167-170
Stock prices, 77, 149, 150, 171, 204

Stock return covariances, 32
Stock selection, 53
STOCKEXPERT, 61
Stock-price level, 215
Stocks, grade ordering, 77
Structuring, 46
Subgrades, 91
Sum-up, 85-87, 96, 201
SYNPLE framework, 144-149, 204
  duration, definition, 147
  elements, definition, 147
  patterns, synthesis, 147-149
System for Conceptual Information Summarization, Organization and Retrieval (SCISOR), 54
Syntactic pattern recognition, 59
Syntactic-pattern-based learning, 133, 143-152
  performance, 149-152
System architecture, 79
System design criteria, summary, 229-231
Systematic risk, 32, 35, 38

T

Tactical asset allocation, 24
Taiwan stock market, 170
Tax-free bonds, 55
Technical analysis, 12
Theorems, 116
Theory of endorsement, 102
Time series forecasting, 160
Timing, 23
Timing decisions, 52, 58, 133. *See also* Buy-sell timing decisions; Equity buy-sell timing decisions; Market-timing decisions
TOPIX, 169-170
Total portfolio risk, 35
Trading dynamics, 16-17
Trading rule generation, genetic algorithm, 154-156
Trading unit size, 8
Trading volume, 14, 77, 133, 139, 144
Trading volume data
  management, 204-205
  organization, 204-205
  uses, 205
Trading volume-based rules, 205
Transaction costs, 8, 30, 41, 155, 170
  symmetricality, 9

Transfer function, 161
Transient
    overshoot, 15
    undershoot, 15
Treasury bills. *See* U.S. Treasury bills
Trend analysis, 12
Triangle pattern, 168
Truth maintenance, 116
Turning-point indicators, 12
Turnover, 169
Two-dimensional frequency, 104

U

Uncertain evidence, handling, 106-108
Uncertainty handling, 76, 102
Unenhanced Markowitz model, 184
UNIK-INDUCE, 135
Universal function approximators, 165
Unsystematic risk, 32, 33, 35

U.S. Treasury bills, 39
User interface, 1
Utility function, 29
Utility maximization, 14

V–Z

Value-based investing, 10-11
Value-based investment rules, 124
Vector curve, 169
Voice recognition, 57, 69
Volatility, 173
VP-EXPERT, 135
WATCHDOG, 54
Weak form, 11
Window, 135
Working memory, 87-89
XOR-type nonlinear discrimination, 164
Yield, 14, 104-106, 113, 124
Zero-beta portfolio, 42